CATALOG MARKETING

The Complete Guide to Profitability in the Catalog Business

CATALOG MARKETING

The Complete Guide to Profitability in the Catalog Business

Katie Muldoon

R. R. Bowker Company
New York and London, 1984

To Patrick and Jacob

Published by R. R. Bowker Company
205 East Forty-second Street, New York, NY 10017

Printed and bound in the United States of America

Library of Congress Cataloging in Publication Data
Muldoon, Katie.
Catalog marketing.

Bibliography: p.
Includes index.
1. Mail-order business—United States. 2. Direct marketing—United States. 3. Catalogs, Commercial. I. Title.
HF5466.M84 1984 658.8′72 84-14928
ISBN 0-8352-1907-0

CONTENTS

PREFACE

This book is written for every one of you who has ever opened a catalog and said, "I can do this." It doesn't matter if you plan to do it on your own or within the company you work for. The information given here is basic to our industry and gives you the facts you must have to make an informed decision about the viability of entering the consumer catalog business.

This book is also written for those of you who are already in the catalog business. Many of our agency's clients have said, "I've read everything there is on direct marketing and still don't know enough to ask the right questions about catalog marketing." While there are some excellent books on the direct marketing industry as a whole, only brief chapters within these books are devoted to catalog marketing. None offers, as this book does, the step-by-step, practical guidance necessary to operate catalogs as successful business ventures.

For the would-be and established cataloger alike, enticements are strong. There is national visibility, the thrill of recognition that comes with having your name, or your company's name, associated with a beautiful publication. And there is the lure of profit. Returns on investment of up to 46 percent have been achieved in the catalog marketing business.

Although positive in its approach, *Catalog Marketing* is also realistic. Catalogers do not get rich overnight, nor do they achieve success without a lot of hard work and innovative thinking. The environment of catalog marketing is fast-paced and ever-changing. You've got to stay on top of the changes, and there will be times when the advice of a catalog professional will be in order. Professional help, combined with the knowledge to be gained from this book, will help ensure that your operation gets off on the right foot (or gets back on the right track), begins to make money as soon as possible, and stays profitable.

A glance at the table of contents will show you that we have given you what you need to make any catalog profitable, predictable, and visually powerful. Within the chapters, you will find suggestions and techniques that have never before been published.

As you use this book, it is important to remember that there can never be a single "success formula" that will work for every company. The two maxims you are likely to hear most often from established catalogers are "Test, test, test" and "It depends." These phrases are not meant to be evasive, but reflect one of direct marketing's major advantages and distinctions: We don't guess or "sense" results. Through testing, we really can know what works and what doesn't work—and can continuously improve. One of the things this book gives you are testing techniques.

Almost anything can be sold in a catalog, from cars to books, from circus tents to homemade jellies, from high-ticket designer clothes to low-ticket knickknacks. Nieman-Marcus and Sakowitz seem to try to outdo each other every holiday season and have offered such products as $50,000 dirigibles, $15,000 robots, and $220,000 helicampers. One year,

Nieman's even offered a pair of live buffalos for $11,700! Trendsetting catalogers, such as JS&A—through clever, convincing copy—sold thousands of the "Bone Fone," the forerunner of today's portable stereo/headphones. Omaha Steaks continues to sell prime filet mignon steaks at $23.48 a pound. Conversely, Spencer Gifts, year after year, runs pages and pages of items that sell for only 88 cents each. "Choose any 6 or more items . . . only 88 cents each," runs the copy, with products ranging from frosted mugs to mounting tape to fold-away scissors. What it all comes down to is that all kinds of consumers like the convenience of shopping by mail—and especially by catalog.

This book is based on real-life experiences, accumulated over two decades. Yet it could not have been written without the support and assistance of friends and business associates. The following people graciously reviewed sections that dealt with their areas of expertise:

Karen Burns, formerly of the Direct Marketing Association, now a part-time freelance and a full-time mother; Gerry King of Nationwide Fulfillment Systems, Inc.; Bob Latzen of Gould Paper Corporation; Steve Bogner of The Guild Company; Jo-Ann Jensen of Uni-Mail, Inc.; Bob Russell, Joe Lukens, and Del Bishop of R. R. Donnelley & Sons Company; Pat Moore and Lorrie Pitisano of Chargit; Pete Hoke of Hoke Communications, Inc.; David Katz of David Katz Studios; Roger Abelson of MBS/Multimode; John Mathewson of Pier 1 Imports; and Ron Giller. Although their contributions have been invaluable, any failings or errors are my responsibility.

I would also like to express my appreciation to those who have generously allowed reproduction of specific sections of their catalogs, forms, and other related materials. These graphic depictions enrich the book and provide truly helpful information.

Members of my staff also deserve special acknowledgment, because they not only lent their expertise, but gave their time by volunteering the extra hours necessary to ensure that both the normal agency work and the book stayed on schedule. My thanks go to Carmen Acosta, John Lauricella, Barbara Plotkin, and Norman Rich.

In addition, I will be forever grateful to my editor, Julie Moore, who is responsible for molding my rough manuscript into its present form—and was always there for advice and encouragement.

But it is to my husband, Jacob (Jack) Baer, that I owe the most thanks. He kept me company through the midnight hours it took to write this book and offered constant encouragement and support. And, quite literally, many of the chapters would not have been written except for his knowledge.

Katie Muldoon
Muldoon Direct, Inc.
New York City

Part I
WHAT IS CATALOG MARKETING?

THE MAIL ORDER BOOM

Mail order business is growing at an almost astronomical rate—five times that of retail. New consumer catalogs—really boutiques by mail—are born every day. Names that were unknown a few years ago are fast becoming household words and impressive profit centers. And established companies are discovering the lucrative benefits of diversifying their sales efforts through cataloging.

According to the Direct Marketing Association's *Fact Book on Direct Marketing, 1984 Edition, total goods and services* sold in the United States as a result of direct marketing amounted to $137.9 billion in 1982 and $150.3 billion in 1983. (These figures are based on the estimate that direct marketing costs equal approximately one-fifth of gross sales.) The Direct Marketing Association (DMA) expects sales of *consumer merchandise* to be $44 billion in 1983, up from 1982's figure of $40 billion.

Although the average household receives approximately 40 catalogs a year, a frequent mail order customer can receive that many in a week. And American consumers seem to love it! Some time ago, an A. C. Nielsen survey revealed that six out of ten people like receiving catalogs and an impressive 77 percent have nothing against it. More than three out of four consumers read each one thoroughly or at least thumb through those they receive. And consumers aren't just "looking at the pretty pictures" either. They're buying—a whopping 66 percent of those who receive catalogs say they now buy.

Contributing factors

According to the Census Bureau, 16 percent of the U.S. population (or nearly 12.9 million families) has a minimum household income of $35,000 a year.

The new affluent woman

Recent census data and demographic research indicate that at least 75 percent of America's upscale, affluent women (ages 25 to 65) are in the work force and that affluent single women, those earning $20,000 or more a year, number 3.6 million.

The earning potential for women in general is still far from its peak, and women are entering the work force in unparalleled numbers. This trend does not appear to be changing. A recent poll conducted by the *New York Times* asked 1,309 adults the following question: "If you were free to do either, would you prefer to have a job outside the home, or would you prefer to stay home and take care of your house and family?" Table 1-1 shows the results of the poll.

According to a 1980 Roper/Virginia Slims poll, reported in *ZIP*'s May 1983 issue, single women are aware that they may not marry and, therefore, are giving priority to their own lives and possessions. Credit cards and a discretionary income allow them to buy the items they want for themselves, from stereos to jewelry. And, should they marry, they retain the kind of financial independence that allows them to continue to satisfy these needs.

As these women, who are the traditional shoppers, find their time split between caring for a family and working at a job that is either outside the home or operated from it, they have come to understand that their time is valuable, whether they choose to spend it working, enjoying

TABLE 1-1
Results of *New York Times* poll, "Working or Staying at Home: A Comparison," conducted November 11–20, 1983*

Respondent	Response (%) Job	Response (%) Stay Home
TOTAL	58%	35%
All men	72	21
All women	45	47
Working women	58	33
Working men	72	21
Nonworking women	31	62
Nonworking men	73	21
Working women with children	50	40
Working men with children	70	23
Working women without children	69	24
Working men without children	74	19
Women by age		
18–29	56	37
30–44	47	44
45–64	39	51
65 and over	32	63
White women	42	50
Black women	61	30
Liberal women	55	39
Moderate women	52	41
Conservative women	35	58
Women who are professionals and managers	63	27
Men who are professionals and managers	70	22
Blue-collar women	43	49
Blue-collar men	70	22
Women who are teachers or nurses	60	32
Other white-collar women	65	26
Women making below $10,000	53	36
Women making $10,000–$20,000	62	32
Men making below $20,000	68	24
Women making over $20,000	62	28
Men making over $20,000	77	17

*Source: *New York Times*, December 4, 1983, section 1, p. 1.

their families, or treating themselves to leisure—an area of increasing importance to Americans in general. Hence, women have come to rely on and trust an increasingly popular and convenient method of shopping—the mail order catalog. Not only are they able to shop from the comfort of their homes at any time of the day or night, but the fact that merchandise has been preselected seems to make their lives even easier.

In a properly merchandised catalog, products have been carefully chosen from thousands of possibilities, saving the customer from the hassle of physically searching through store after store and department after department. For the woman whose day often consists of endless decision making, whether in an executive position or answering her child's constant questions, preselected merchandise is a welcome change.

Catalogs also allow the customer to see merchandise as it would appear in her home, or as it would look on women that fit her self-image, or as her husband or child might use it. Catalog copy often suggests ways in which she could use a product to better her life—ways that she may have never had the time to discover.

Because either she or one of her friends has ordered from a catalog before, she knows that merchandise is guaranteed and that, more often than not, customer service is surprisingly caring and prompt. Because she is an experienced shopper, she knows that bargains can be found in catalogs and that most prices are competitive with retail. Most important, she knows that catalogers attempt to maintain a level of quality that will encourage customers to continue to purchase from their catalogs.

Double-income households

With more women in the work force, naturally there are more double-income households, often resulting in larger discretionary income. The current trend indicates that many of these families consider themselves relatively prosperous, but still financially constrained. Such major purchases as homes may be beyond their reach. Yet such symbols of success as designer clothes, electronics, and leisure time activities/products are affordable. This, in part, explains why so many catalogs are directed to serving these needs.

The computer

The computer has had a dramatic influence on direct marketing in so many areas and should be acknowledged for its effectiveness. Because of the computer, catalogers are able to decipher the desires of their customers quickly and accurately. Promptly meeting customers' needs can result in superior merchandising and increased customer loyalty through better customer service. Computerization also allows more cost-effective mailings through timely analysis, improved cash flow due to fast and accurate determination of real inventory needs, and much more. Even for the smallest startup venture, the computer offers such advantages as more comprehensive, essential decision-making and better employee productivity. Used properly, it can make the difference between success and failure.

The energy supply

During the time when consumers waited in line to purchase gasoline at astronomical prices, many discovered the advantages of shopping by mail. Although the urgency of the energy crisis has faded for the present, consumers who benefited from catalog shopping ten years ago have remained loyal. Even today, no one knows whether another energy crisis will develop. A distinct advantage direct marketers have over retail establishments is their ability to prepare for the possibility of curtailed oil supplies and adapt to meet the needs this situation may create.

The population shift

A new analysis of the 1980 U.S. Census shows that rural regions are growing faster than metropolitan areas. According to a December 5, 1983, issue of *Advertising Age,* a study released by the Rand Corporation in 1983 spotlights the nation's desire for country living. The Rand study shows the rate of growth of the rural areas of New Hampshire and a large portion of the Ozarks at twice the national average, with the rate for many metropolitan areas in the same regions below the national average.

Common sense indicates that fewer products are readily available in rural areas, and that selection among these products is limited. If the trend toward country living continues, many new mail order customers will come into the market.

The maturing of an industry

Even though the first mail order advertising circulars appeared in the 1860s, mail order as an industry is still in its infancy.

In 1897, the granddaddy of catalogers, Sears, Roebuck and Company, had a 700-page catalog with 6,000 products. By 1906, this fledgling company had developed sales in excess of $50 million. During 1983, Sears Merchandise Group sales were $2,092,000,000.

Another old-timer in the industry, and one of the first to target a specific market, began with $400 in 1912. L. L. Bean started his company to sell the rubber boot he had invented, adding outdoor clothing and equipment to the line over the years. Today Bean is over the $200 million mark annually.

Spiegel Inc., also an early starter, has made impressive maneuvers lately with its customer base (of names), catalog diversification (13 specialty catalogs have evolved so far, with plans to expand to 20 by the end of 1984), and merchandising. Spiegel predicts $1 billion in sales by 1988, with sales for 1983 reported at $512 million, up from $395 million in 1982.

Hanover House, currently the catalog marketer with the greatest number of different catalogs under one roof (21 at last count), had 1983 sales of $215 million, up from $140 million in 1982.

If mail order and retail sales maintain their current estimated growth rates, mail order merchandise sales will account for $1 out of every $3 spent by the year 2000!

Then and now

Using untested methods, early catalogers directed sales efforts into relatively uncharted territory. Catalogs were few and far between, so there was little competition. The cost of printing, postage, and paper (the three most expensive items for a cataloger) was low compared with today's prices. It wasn't easy even then, but it was easier.

Newcomers appeared on the scene, saw what successful innovators like Roger Horchow were doing, adapted his techniques to a slightly different market, and without changing the basic strategy one iota, succeeded as well. Soon there were catalogs to supply everyone's needs, from electronics to lingerie, from computer software to tools. There was competition and lots of it. And the amazing part is that most catalogers were mailing to the same mail order–responsive customers.

Clouds in a blue sky

As shown in Table 1-2, the 1982–1983 estimated sales volume of leading direct marketers is bullish for the most part. (For some of the 40 direct marketers listed, cataloging is a minor part of their business. However, since many corporations have expanded or added to this area in recent years, the list has been left intact.) Lillian Vernon's sales of $40 million in 1981 rose to $65 million in 1982 and $100 million in 1983. Avon Direct Products has gone from $100 million in 1981 to $121 million in 1982 and onward to $144 million in 1983. Now, however, two troubling questions are being asked: (1) Is there a catalog "glut"? and (2) Are post office inefficiencies causing decreased sales?

Is there a catalog glut?

You would have to have been living in a cave not to have noticed that there are indeed a great many more catalogs now than several years ago. Because most catalogs are privately owned, and some seem to appear and disappear overnight, no one knows for sure how many there are, but estimates range from 6,000 to 10,000 different titles.

Still, consumers continue to respond most favorably. Proof of this is the response to a series of Direct Marketing Association ads designed to allow consumers to have their names deleted from mailing lists. For every person asking to be taken off a mailing list, two to five are requesting to be added! American consumers have discovered shopping by mail and eagerly await the opportunity to purchase even more of the desirable goods they've come to expect.

Additionally, vigorous efforts are under way by established direct marketers and the Direct Marketing Association to make it even easier for the consumer to discover the great variety of new catalogs. An extensive publicity campaign now being planned should be in evidence by 1985.

Instead of lamenting the competition, direct marketers must look at the positive effects. Most catalogs, properly serving the consumers they solicit, will bring even more credibility to the industry as a whole and

TABLE 1-2
Sales volume of 40 leading direct marketers

Company	Sales Volume (in thousands) 1982	1983
Sears Merchandise Group	1,886,600	2,092,000
J C Penney Co. Inc.	1,537,000	1,652,000
Montgomery Ward (Mobil Corp.)*	1,145,000	1,190,000
Colonial Penn Group Inc.	548,000	615,000
Spiegel Inc.	395,000	512,000
Fingerhut & Figi's (American Can Co.)	400,000	512,000
Time Inc. (magazines only)	320,000	385,000
Franklin Mint (Warner Communications Inc.)	410,000	378,000
New Process Co.	235,000	268,000
McGraw-Hill Inc.	215,000	254,000
Columbia House (CBS)	200,000	220,000
Hanover House Industries Inc. (Horn & Hardart Co.)	140,000	215,000
L. L. Bean Inc.	192,000	205,000
American Express (TRS Co./merchandise sales only)	150,000	180,000
Herrschners, Brookstone, Jos. A. Bank Clothiers (Quaker Oats Co.)	120,000	152,000
Avon Direct Products	121,000	144,000
Grolier Inc.	147,000	135,000
AT&T Communications	100,000	120,000
Jackson & Perkins, Harry & David's, Bear Creek (Bear Creek Corp.)	110,400	111,000
Wausau Insurance Co.	—	110,000
RCA Direct Marketing Inc.	100,000	110,000
World Book Encyclopedia Inc. (Scott & Fetzer Co.)	100,000	105,000
New England Business Service Inc.	91,600	103,000
Spencer Gifts (MCA Inc.)	85,000	101,500
Amba Marketing Systems (The MacDonalds Co. Inc.)	70,000	100,000
Lillian Vernon Corp.	65,000	100,000
G-R-I Corp.	78,500	99,000
Allstate Insurance Co. (Sears, Roebuck & Co.)	77,200	97,000
The Bradford Exchange Ltd.	70,100	81,000
Rodale Press Inc.	68,900	77,878
Current Inc. (Looart Press)	75,000	74,000
Physicians Mutual Insurance Co.	56,900	70,200
Cabela's Inc.	43,000	70,000
The Sharper Image	48,000	69,000
Meredith Corp. (books only)	49,800	67,200
Miles Kimball Co.	40,000	51,800
Old American Insurance Co.	40,000	42,000
Exxon Travel Club Inc.	40,800	40,600
Horchow Co.	40,000	40,000
Michigan Bulb Co.	—	35,000

Source: DMA Research Department. Based on figures provided by participating companies, surveyed December 1983–February 1984. Reprinted, by permission, from *Fact Book on Direct Marketing, 1984 Edition*, p. 43. ©1984 by Direct Marketing Association Inc.

*Includes Signature Financial/Marketing Services direct marketing sales.

satisfaction to the public. The "seat of the pants" marketing approach some catalogers have used will no longer be adequate. Catalogers must streamline their operations and learn to interpret what the increasingly time-limited American consumer really wants.

Is the post office a problem?

An organization the size of the post office is not perfect. In 1983, the post office literally handled 119.38 billion pieces of mail—a gargantuan task! But, to the surprise of many direct marketers, the post office does listen. Recent efforts by the Direct Marketing Association have resulted in a better understanding of the value of third-class mail to the postal system. During fiscal years 1981 and 1982, total mail volume in the United States grew by 7.7 billion pieces. Third-class mail accounted for 6.3 billion pieces of the total growth.

In response to delivery problems discovered in a joint 1981 DMA/Doubleday Inc. study, a significant improvement resulted. Nondelivery rates for a typical third-class mailing piece dropped from 8.4 percent in 1981 to 5.4 percent in 1983, and for a similar piece marked "Forwarding and Return Postage Guaranteed," nondelivery dropped from 6.6 percent to 3.1 percent. Problems still exist, but U.S. Postal Service officials have promised to continue to stress the importance of bulk mail to postal workers, who, frankly, are beginning to understand that their very paychecks may depend on the efficient delivery of catalogs. Secret, regional tests are being conducted on an ongoing basis and audits of undeliverable addressed mail are designed to reduce this problem. New procedures, which subject undeliverable mail to supervisory review, continue to show positive results.

Although it may seem minor, the post office has also changed the name of its service to catalogers. Previously called "nonpreferential" mail, it is now bulk business mail. The new attitude is backed by a variety of programs to promote direct marketing to both postal employees and consumers—for example, bumper stickers proclaiming "Shop by Mail," plus brochures and campaign headlined "Go on a Shopping Spree from Your Living Room." New automation, Zip + 4, and E-COM are just a few of the revolutionary operations designed to make mail delivery much more efficient.

Now more than ever, the U.S. Postal Service is hearing demands and doing something about them. Many of the tests and procedures just described were unsolicited and indicate the U.S. Postal Service's appreciation of direct marketing dollars. Certainly, problems still exist and others will develop, but the improved attitude now being shown by both sides will only make problem-solving easier for everyone.

A maturing industry in the process of change is an industry open to the kind of innovative marketing that created it in the first place. Through a combination of real understanding of consumer needs, only recently available technology, and freshly adapted but time-honored techniques, direct marketing to the consumer has no limits.

THE MAIL ORDER MARKET

As with all other industries in the United States, the catalog business depends on the overall economy. However, one big advantage direct marketers have over almost everyone else is the ability to segment their market by geographic region and adapt mailing quantities. If one part of the country shows signs of ailing, mailings can be increased to another part of the country that shows signs of vitality, and decreased to the one in trouble. The result is a relatively recession-proof business.

Market conditions

Still, no business is immune from fluctuations in the economy. The wise direct marketer closely monitors economic events and predictions. According to *Fortune* magazine (January 9, 1984, pp. 43–44)

> Consumers will occupy center stage during the second year of expansion too. With the continued growth of employment, real disposable income will climb at a 4.6% pace in the next 18 months. Though consumers should be saving at a 6% to 6.5% rate by mid-1985, spending should grow at a 3.7% rate over the forecast period. . . . Sales of consumer goods will rise at a 4.3% clip through 1984, before settling down to a still strong 3.8% rate in early 1985.

In the near run, it is a most positive picture.

Savvy direct marketers also look closely at such studies as SRI International's Values and Lifestyles, or VALS as it is commonly called, to learn more about how Americans think and act and to enhance list and merchandise testing. VALS divides consumers into four major categories with a total of nine life-styles (see Figure 1-1). The target audience is defined in terms of attitudes, activities, demographics, needs, and hopes. The information contained in this study might well influence a direct marketer's copy style, choice of models, and more. Such sophisticated techniques as VALS can be invaluable in helping smart catalogers move ahead of their competitors. For more information on VALS, read *The Nine American Lifestyles* by Arnold Mitchell (Macmillan, 1982).

Evaluating potential markets

To identify potential markets, you must be aware of what is happening around you. Do the obvious. Read newspapers and periodicals that clearly state how consumers' needs are changing. The clues are all there; the hard part is interpreting them.

Trends

One of the important trends you may unearth is that marriage is not only "in" again, but people seem to be having more babies. As you can see in Figure 1-2, births started to increase in the late 1970s, and the trend indicates that this "baby boom" will continue. Team this with the fact that mothers are older (see Figure 1-3) and that the percentage of working women is on the increase (see Figure 1-4). The logical conclusion is that there will be an increase in the number of women with a high discretionary income and little shopping time who will need maternity clothes, plus children's clothes and accessories. What's more, the large majority of births will be first children, who require more products than do second

FIGURE 1-1
SRI's VALS categories of American life-styles

THE NEED-DRIVEN GROUPS

Survivors—Old, intensely poor, fearful, far removed from the cultural mainstream. 4% of the U.S. adult population.

Sustainers—Angry, resentful, street-wise, living on the edge of poverty, involved in the underground economy. 7% of the U.S. adult population.

THE OUTER-DIRECTED GROUPS

Belongers—Aging, conventional, content, intensely patriotic, traditional middle Americans. 35% of the U.S. adult population.

Emulators—Young, ambitious, flashy, trying to break into the system. 9% of the U.S. adult population.

Achievers—Middle-aged, prosperous, self-assured; the leaders and builders of the American dream. 22% of the U.S. adult population.

THE INNER-DIRECTED GROUPS

I-Am-Me—Very young, narcissistic, impulsive, exhibitionist; a transitional state to inner-direction. 5% of the U.S. adult population.

Experiential—Youthful, seeking direct experience, artistic, intensely oriented toward inner growth. 7% of the U.S. adult population.

Societally Conscious—Mission-oriented, mature, successful, out to change the world. 8% of the U.S. adult population.

THE COMBINED OUTER- AND INNER-DIRECTED GROUP

Integrated—Psychologically mature, tolerant, understanding, flexible, able to see "the big picture." 2% of the U.S. adult population.

Source: *Fact Book on Direct Marketing, 1984 Edition,* p. 15. Used with permission of the Direct Marketing Association Inc.

and third children (see Figure 1-5). Mail order shopping would be a convenient means to obtain these products.

You may not, however, be the only one to have made these observations. So the next step is to check the competition. Read publications that highlight catalog collections or have special mail order sections (generally at the back of the magazines) to see if a catalog aimed at your intended market is now being offered. If it is, get on the mailing list. Maybe the cataloger's idea of how to serve this market is entirely different from yours. Call such associations as the Direct Marketing Association, or visit their offices to sort through their extensive collections of catalogs. Go to conferences and seminars, not just to learn about the industry but also to get a "feel" from the attendees as to who is entering the industry and in what capacity.

If you decide your first idea of a potential market may not be the best one, keep looking for other niches. Another trend is the increase in the size of the older adult population. A quick look at Table 1-3 shows that,

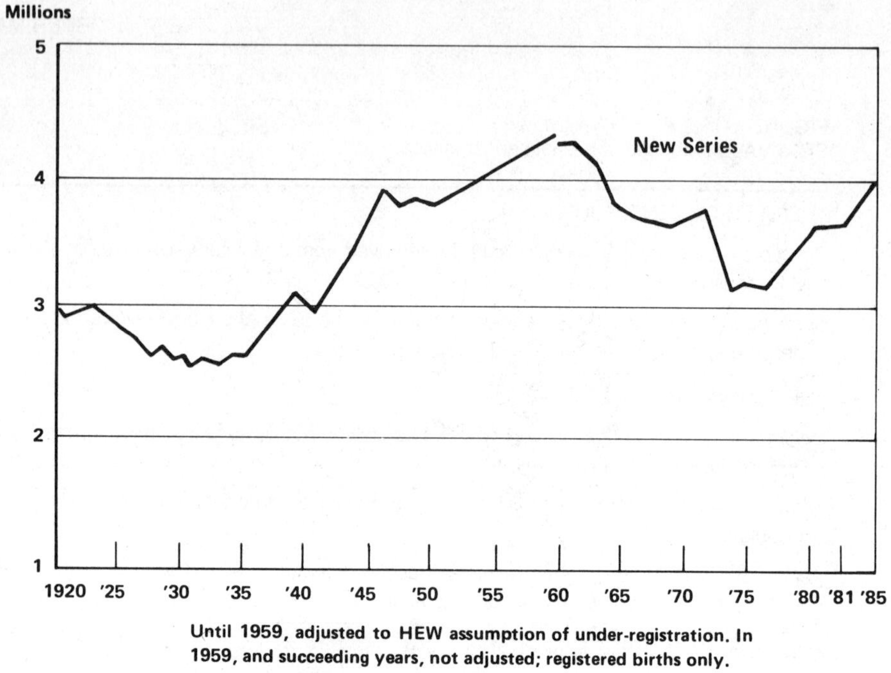

Source: U.S. Dept. of Health & Human Services

FIGURE 1-2
Birthrate in the United States, 1920–1985. Reprinted, by permission, from *Fact Book on Direct Marketing, 1984 Edition,* p. 75. © 1984 by Direct Marketing Association Inc.

FIGURE 1-3
Average number of births by female age groups: 1960, 1976, 1981. Reprinted, by permission, from *Fact Book on Direct Marketing, 1984 Edition,* p. 75. © 1984 by Direct Marketing Association Inc.

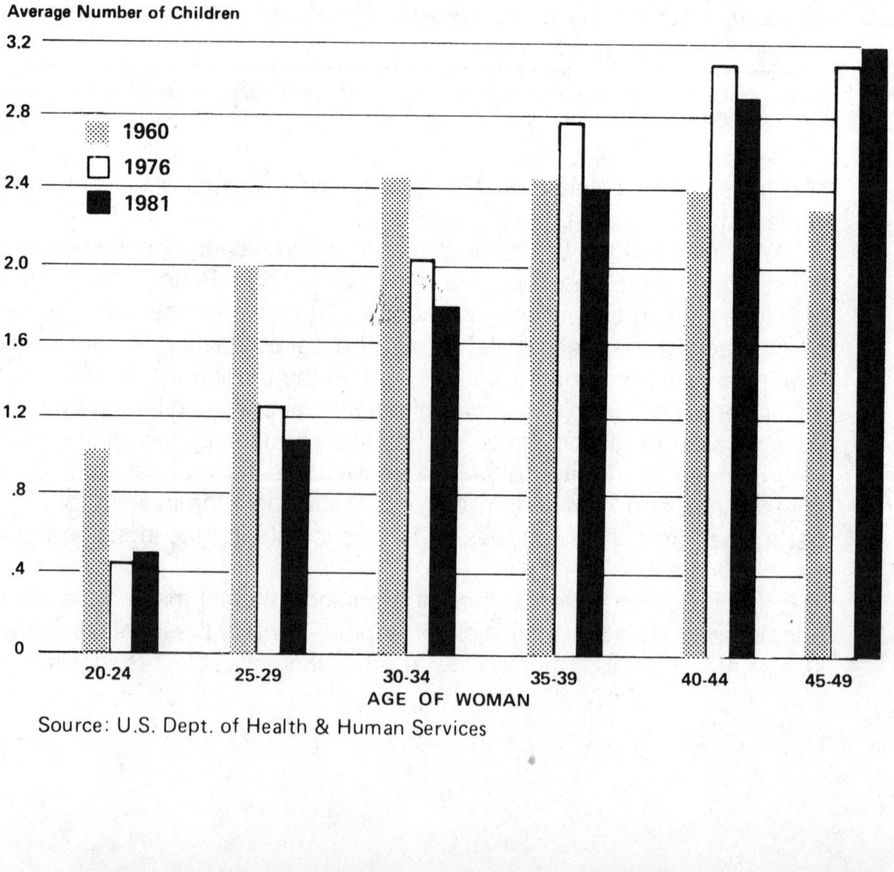

Source: U.S. Dept. of Health & Human Services

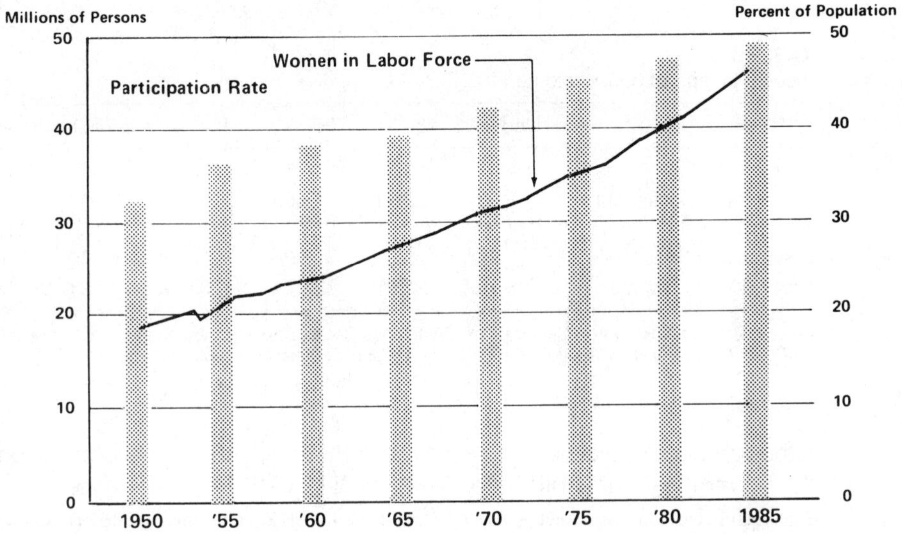

Source: U.S. Bureau of Labor Statistics

FIGURE 1-4
Women in the labor force, 1950–1985. Reprinted, by permission, from *Fact Book on Direct Marketing, 1984 Edition,* p. 75. © 1984 by Direct Marketing Association Inc.

FIGURE 1-5
Birth order in the United States: 1945–1980. Reprinted, by permission, from *Fact Book on Direct Marketing, 1984 Edition,* p. 76. © 1984 by Direct Marketing Association Inc.

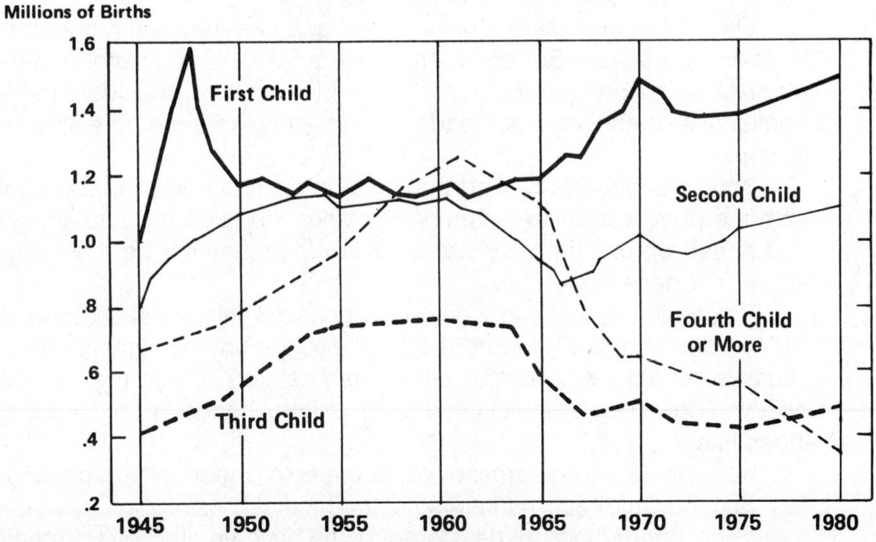

Source: U.S. Dept. of Health & Human Services

TABLE 1-3
Income by age of household head

	Under 25	25–34	35–44	45–54	55–64	Over 64
Households (in millions)	6.4	19.2	14.5	12.7	12.7	16.9
Persons per household	2.23	2.94	3.66	3.26	2.32	1.72
Avg. household income	$14,227	$20,713	$26,052	$28,169	$23,504	$12,628
Distribution of households	7.8%	23.3%	17.6%	15.4%	15.4%	20.5%
Distribution of income	5.3%	22.9%	21.7%	20.6%	17.2%	12.3%

Source: Consumer Research Center of the Conference Board. Reprinted, by permission, from *Fact Book on Direct Marketing, 1984 Edition,* p. 68. ©1984 by Direct Marketing Association Inc.

although household heads over 64 are 25.5 percent of the population, their average household income is only $12,628. But before you immediately discount them because of the low income, consider that many are housebound and would not only enjoy receiving catalogs, but may be excellent prospects for an unusually high response.

Consumer spending patterns

In addition to looking at general trends, investigate growth patterns in consumer spending (see Figure 1-6). The first product line that will undoubtedly catch your eye is televisions, radios, and records, a good indication of why such catalogs as The Sharper Image and JS&A have done so well in recent years. The next most promising line is durable sporting goods and toys. Toys fit right in with the baby boom and may well give you an added reason to investigate this area.

On the negative side, cooking food at home may seem one of the least exciting areas. But don't forget that time is of the essence to most Americans, so before you discount this idea entirely, consider time-saving appliances or convenience foods that would make at-home eating popular again.

You've undoubtedly read that automobile purchases are up again. With the purchase of an automobile comes the need for auto accessories and parts—an unglamorous area, but one that may not be receiving the attention it deserves.

Before deciding on any category, consider this question: How long will the demand last? If the price of oil and the unemployment rate should escalate, would this adversely affect your catalog? Could the merchandise you now plan be quickly adapted to any change in consumer attitudes later?

No formula can determine where the next opportunity in cataloging lies. Successful direct marketers have built their businesses by correctly assessing trends and needs. Corporations have entered direct marketing partly because of their ability to do this well. Success depends on the right combination of research and good instincts—and having the courage to act before the competition does!

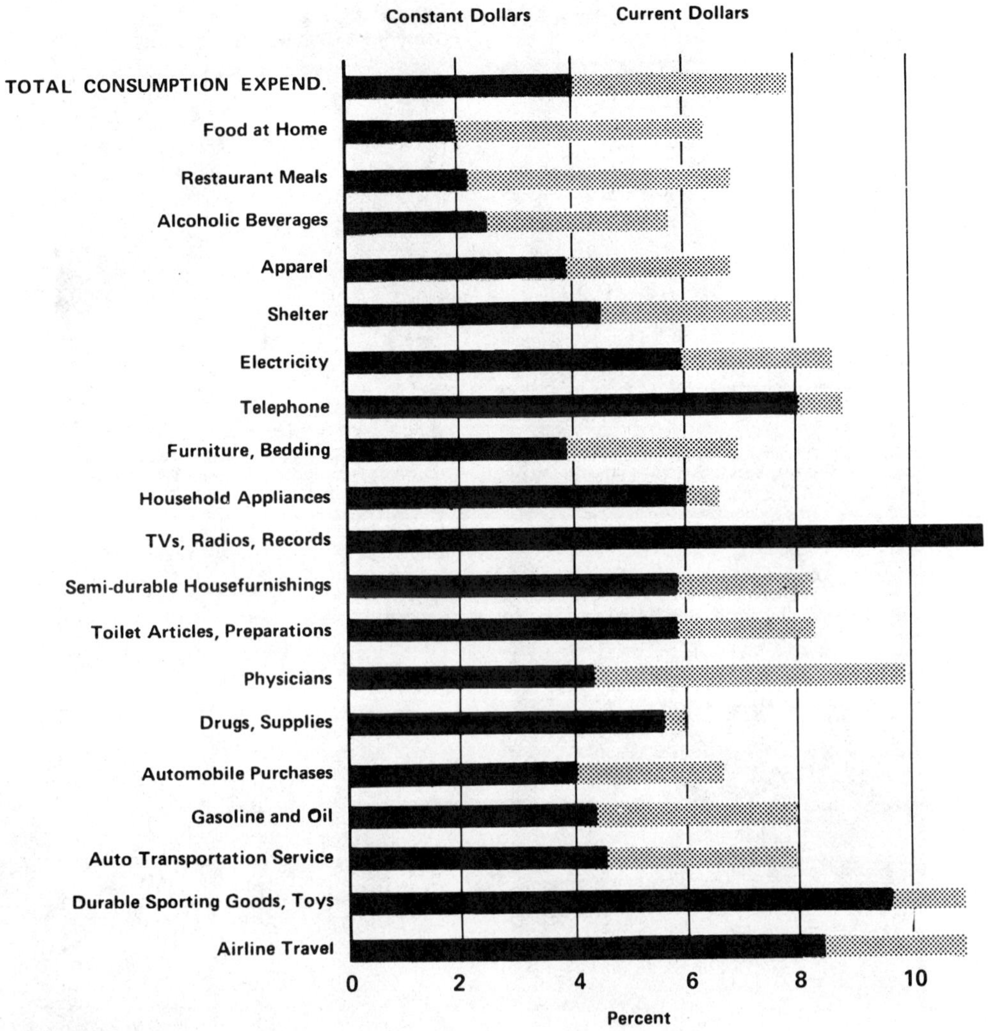

Source: The Conference Board

FIGURE 1-6
Patterns in U.S. consumer spending: 1960–1975. Reprinted, by permission, from *Fact Book on Direct Marketing, 1984 Edition*, p. 78. © 1984 by Direct Marketing Association Inc.

True-to-life vignette

Being aware of new trends and finding that special niche in the business is not limited to new marketers. Case in point: What do you do when the market you've dominated for more than 30 years is no longer pulling the response you need to keep your head above water. Sink or swim? The Lew Magram catalog, faced with such a predicament five years ago, is now riding the crest of success, thanks to a bold, risky, but ultimately

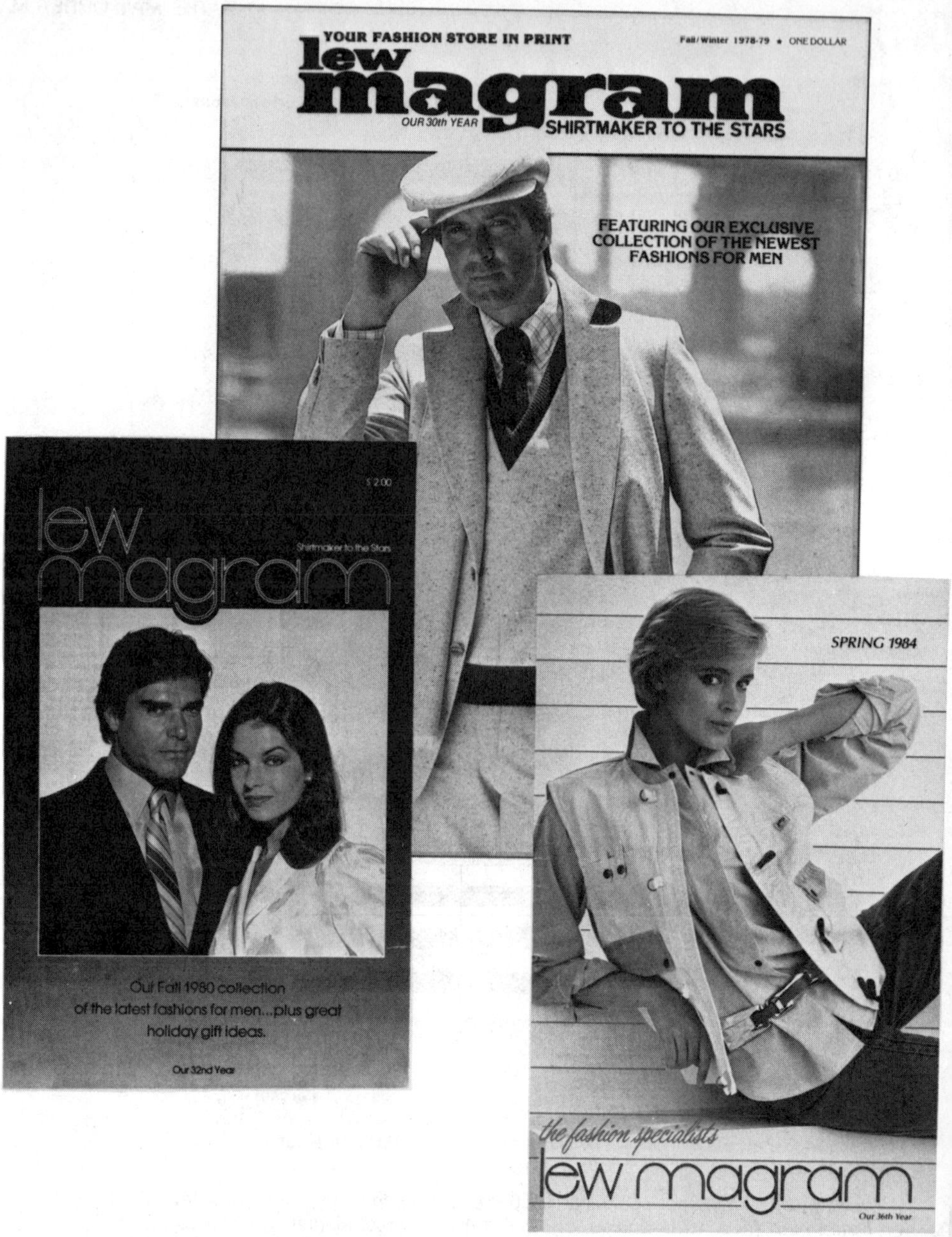

FIGURE 1-7
Lew Magram's 1978–1979 catalog specialized in "Shirtmaker to the Stars" men's clothing.

A woman shares the fall 1980 catalog cover as Magram begins to incorporate women's wear into its product line.

Repositioned as "the fashion specialists," Magram's spring 1984 catalog offered only women's wear. © 1978, 1980, 1984 by Lew Magram Ltd. and reproduced with permission.

rewarding transition from high-fashion menswear to upscale, high-fashion women's apparel.

Lew Magram Ltd. began in 1948 as a one-man business selling shirts out of a midtown New York storefront. Mr. Magram's entrepreneurial spirit paid off. The storefront soon expanded into a highly successful retail store. According to Erv Magram, Lew's son and vice-president of Lew Magram Ltd., almost every show business star you could name in the mid-fifties owned a Lew Magram custom shirt.

In the mid-sixties, the first Lew Magram "Shirtmaker to the Stars" catalog was produced. As high-fashion menswear flourished into the mid-seventies, so did the catalog. Then, according to Erv, menswear became more traditional and the market dramatically decreased. Not only did it become more difficult to merchandise the catalog, but the items themselves were no longer selling.

Caught in a Catch-22 situation, the Magrams took a bold step. Armed with their in-house "secret weapon"—Melanie, an experienced buyer and Erv's sister—the Magrams added five women's apparel items to the spring 1981 catalog. Not only were the items successful, but the move opened a floodgate of response from the men's list. Past buying history had indicated that women were buying for men. These results showed that the men's list consisted of a mail order buying household in which the wife had taught her husband to order by mail. Now, finding the opportunity to buy for herself, she did!

In 1982, the enthusiastically received women's apparel began to take precedence over the menswear. This trend continued until it was decided that the menswear, because it was not paying for its space in the catalog, should be dropped completely. Accordingly, the Lew Magram list has changed dramatically, with 80 to 90 percent women buyers in 1984 (see Figure 1-7).

From the original "Shirtmaker to the Stars" to the new "fashion specialists," the Lew Magram catalog is an example of an ingenious marketing strategy that turned a downward trend into a continuing success story.

WHY RETAILERS ARE GETTING INTO CATALOG MARKETING

As direct marketing sales were growing, retail sales were decreasing. Suddenly, retailers with businesses of all sizes were taking a fresh look at the benefits of a serious direct marketing program. Smart retailers knew they could no longer turn a blind eye to this upstart industry.

Some retailers, like J. C. Penney, Sears, Roebuck and Company, Spiegel, and Montgomery Ward had been in what they considered cataloging for a long time. But consumers had shown their dissatisfaction with the oversized, overwhelming books these companies offered by shopping from them less and less. Spiegel was the first to discover the joyful financial realities of diversifying into smaller, more tightly targeted catalogs designed to cater to the individual needs of specific segments of the population. From a catalog originally conceived for the homemaker, Spiegel has evolved to carry such designer names as Bill Blass, Norma Kamali, and Pierre Cardin.

Other recent successes include such stores as Sakowitz, whose Christmas 1983 catalog was 30 percent ahead of the 1982 Christmas catalog. And Bloomingdale's, which sends out 12 million copies of 24 catalogs, has had sales increases of more than 400 percent since 1978. As a matter of fact, Barry Marchessault, president of Bloomingdale's by Mail, predicts that their "Store 21" (the catalogs) will be the chain's biggest branch by 1986.

Wherever retailers have made a success of direct marketing operations, they have met three basic conditions:

- A true understanding of direct marketing and how it can be applied to retail.
- The willingness to adapt previously established retail methods.
- A firm commitment to a direct marketing program, allowing it to achieve its full potential.

Elements for success

The retailer has the right elements for potential success if it has:

1 A known name
2 A knowledge of merchandising
3 An outlet for unsold catalog merchandise
4 An understanding of the importance of customer service
5 Buying power
6 An existing fulfillment center
7 Statistical knowledge of customers' buying patterns
8 An existing catalog.

The key is to adapt these pluses to a true direct marketing strategy. Sadly, retailers all too often lack the experience or are unwilling to make these adaptations.

A known name

As direct marketing consumer catalogs become more and more prolific, the value of a respected and recognized name cannot be ignored. There will be a definite trend toward advertising consumer catalogs as a brand name in the same manner that general advertising now promotes products. A brand name will be essential to help ensure that consumers even select the catalog from the many available, much less buy from it. This selection will, in part, be based on the subconscious remembrance of a known name, perhaps a favorable past relationship with the store or a specific image that the store brings to the consumer's mind. One of the best examples of a store with a sensationally different-looking catalog, and effective image, was Bloomingdale's "Sighs and Whispers." Although not a true mail order catalog by industry standards, it certainly did get the customer's attention!

It's been more than 30 years since Neiman-Marcus came up with the truly brilliant, image-creating idea of an extravagant "His" and "Hers" Christmas gift. This idea, a real publicity maker, has been emulated, but never topped.

One of retail's consistent errors is to strive solely for innovation in graphics and ignore ease of customer ordering. Too many retailers attempt to establish themselves as standards of the right or avant-garde way, rather than understanding what the consumer wants—and what works in mail order. Hard as it may seem, because they usually have a pre-established image, retailers can be distinctive, please their customers, and create a unique market position by using established and successful direct marketing strategies. However, they must make use of the positive attributes they already possess.

A knowledge of merchandising

Having experienced buyers on staff means retailers have knowledgeable merchants, complete with reliable manufacturing sources, right at their fingertips. Yet, assuming that past retail merchandising expertise is sufficient for catalog marketing success is probably the most common, and often the first, pitfall for retailers just beginning a mail order catalog. Retailers naturally tend to believe that what sells in the store will sell in the catalog. This is not necessarily so. If a store is to succeed in the mail order business, both the retailer and the individual buyers must understand the bottom-line difference—the difference between buying for a store and buying for a catalog. It's not as hard as it seems, especially if buyers understand that their store is fully behind this new direct marketing opportunity.

A merchandise outlet

One of the most important things to learn in mail order is that a loser will always be a loser. Never rerun a poorly selling item. This, in effect, forces many catalogers to become retailers, opening outlet stores for unsold merchandise. Here retailers have a big advantage—if they will use it—because they can unload catalog merchandise on standard sales racks in stores. To persuade store/department managers to incorporate catalog merchandise into their sales program requires tact, diplomacy, an appreciation of the overall profits that can be generated from direct marketing (some of which go to their areas of responsibility), and a reasonable credit transfer program.

An understanding of customer service

The retailer first came up with the credo that "the customer is always right." In mail order, this philosophy is even more important. Once a customer is lost through bad service, it is virtually impossible to reinstate him or her. The retailer has the ability, if demand deems it necessary, to pull merchandise from the stores. Merchandise that is delivered quickly, returns that are processed courteously and promptly, and overall service help guarantee success.

Buying power

The merchandise buying power of most retail stores can be substantially higher than that of catalogs. This advantage allows the smart retailer to negotiate a better cost of goods, better delivery, and a better return policy (not all unsold goods need to wind up on sales racks). Many retailers have already discovered the economic advantage of importing their own goods, then labeling them with the store's name. When applied to mail order, the "house" name concept provides for the same low cost of goods, resulting in superior profits. The retailer not only has the sources for such items, but has determined which manufacturers are reliable.

A fulfillment center

Since most retailers have a version of a fulfillment center, with some adaptations, many retailers can use existing facilities and personnel for the initial catalog venture. The person in charge of fulfillment should already have the basic information required to run a cost-effective and customer service-oriented center. Additional space and personnel can be added as the catalog proves itself. (Fulfillment will be discussed in greater detail in "The Back End" in Part 8.)

Customer statistics

Stores offering credit cards have a built-in tracking system, by which they can readily determine a customer's buying patterns—by product category, recency, dollar amount, via mail, phone, or in-store. The basis for what could be, if properly used, the most powerful list catalog retailers can have —their own customers—is right at their fingertips. The use of these statistical data, however, is even more important than the possession of the actual data. Brooks Brothers, for instance, found that mailing to store customers who lived outside a 50-mile radius of the store gave superior results than mailing to the entire list. Sakowitz of Houston is using its list not only to make money for the company, but also to help the company identify clusters of Sakowitz customers for branch site planning.

An existing catalog

The complexities of putting together a catalog are "old hat" to many retailers; the only stumbling block is how to teach the existing staff the major, but not always evident, design strategies and production techniques so necessary to profitable mail order. The evolution from a catalog primarily devoted to traffic generation to one exclusively devoted to mail order sales does not have to mean a major adjustment on the part of the current staff. Proper guidance and understanding of the stores's policy and goals, plus a willingness to learn, are really all that is necessary to make this transition.

A separate profit center

It is important to understand that a mail order catalog and a store catalog are two entirely different selling methods. Those who attempt to achieve both goals with one catalog invariably fail. This does not mean that store sales will not be generated from a mail order catalog. In fact, careful testing has shown that additional store sales are indeed realized when a mail order catalog is mailed in the same regions as the stores. But smart retailers produce two different kinds of catalogs, one to generate store traffic and one to generate mail order sales, thus assuring themselves the best of two worlds.

Market penetration

Even the largest retailers cannot realistically aspire to total market penetration. The cost and the risk of opening stores in all the geographic regions retailers might like to address are astronomical. Direct marketing is the solution. Only through mail order can all the potential consumers be economically and successfully reached. The necessary tools are already at hand.

Part 2
RESOURCES

GETTING STARTED

The cart belongs behind the horse. Before considering what it takes to put together a successful catalog, you ought to know that no successful operation can start up until you have harnessed four basic resources: money, physical space, the right name/identity, and personnel.

Money

Catalogs today are costly. Although the return on investment can be substantially higher than in other industries, catalogs require large financial commitments (see Part 10, Economics).

For ventures that will be part of a corporate diversification plan, the usual procedure is to establish a budget through the corporate development or new projects office. As with any potential investment, a business plan must be developed. This will be reviewed in detail, with the profit potential considered in competition with other demands on the corporate financial resources. In recent years, many corporations have elected to purchase existing catalogs rather than to develop one on their own.

For the individual entrepreneur, the process is both easier and harder: easier because the individual has already made a singular mental commitment to the project, and harder because one person usually does not have the large financial resources available to corporations. The entrepreneur should prepare a business plan and evaluate it as stringently as a corporation would. If the project appears viable after analysis, where does the money to finance it come from?

- *Yourself.* You know your own resources. You may have no investable income or you may have large sums available from other successful business ventures. You must consider what you can afford to invest and the other possible investment opportunities you will forgo.

- *Friends and family.* Many major catalog companies were started with help from family and friends (one of the most famous being The Horchow Collection). They can often show you where your business plan or presentation is weak and how it can be improved. Even if they cannot or do not provide funds, friends and family know you, and can be a positive aid.

- *Venture capital firms.* Most venture capitalists require proof of some sort of track record. Have you managed another business successfully? Venture capitalists seldom invest in a pure startup, that is, an untested idea. They much prefer to put development money into already existing businesses that either have a history of success or show the potential for it. If, in fact, they do invest, they will require a strong measure of control, in both active participation and stock shares.

Many large banks have venture capital or merchant banking departments. See your banker; even if your bank has no such department, your banker can refer you to venture capital firms and other banks.

- *Suppliers.* Your prospective suppliers can help in two ways: credit and cash. The credit terms they give you can be used to reduce the "up front" cash required in your business plan. In addition, some suppliers have actually invested in new catalogs. But remember, you may become locked into that supplier even when you no longer think he is doing an adequate job.

- *Banks.* As a rule, banks will lend you money only when you have money. For startup ventures, most banks will not, without guarantors or security, lend more than you have already raised as capital. Therefore, go to the bank for funds only after you have other financing commitments.

There is one major exception to this. If you cannot obtain a bank loan, investigate the programs of direct loans and bank guarantees managed by the Small Business Administration (SBA) of the U.S. government. Under its bank guarantee program, the government guarantees 90 percent of the loan, and the bank is at risk for only 10 percent. The bank also obtains reserve requirement advantages, so many banks look with favor on SBA loans. For specific application requirements, see your banker or visit your local SBA office. Even if you do not need the SBA loan services, their specialists can assist you in writing a business plan and provide you with valuable information on opening your own business. Remember, SBA considers a business small even up to 500 employees.

Space

First, you'll need a warehouse and an office. By far the largest amount of space needed is warehouse space. Offices are usually in the same building as the warehouse.

One of the advantages of a catalog is that the catalog is the "store"; you don't need a fancy address or a location in a high-rent district to impress your customers. Your warehouse should be located in a low-rent area, easily accessible to both full- and part-time workers. Many catalog operations are located in small towns, where the space is not expensive and part-time labor is plentiful. Good examples of this are North Conway, New Hampshire, home of Yield House, and Hanover, Pennsylvania, home of Hanover House and its many catalogs. But do locate near major modes of transportation, UPS and USPS centers.

The amount of warehouse space needed depends on your merchandise and the volume of your business. This must be determined on an individual basis. Some catalogers really have two warehouses: one for bulk storage (reserve merchandise) and one for pick-and-pack operations (immediate-need merchandise). As the pick-and-pack area is depleted, more merchandise is brought from the bulk storage area.

Remember to keep shipping and receiving areas separate to reduce pilferage (see "The Back End" in Part 8). Also, for a small catalog, close proximity of the office space to the warehouse means that some people will be able to do two or more jobs at the start.

Another factor to bear in mind when selecting space is future growth. As your catalog business grows, you will need room to expand. Planning for this in advance will keep the cost of expansion to a minimum. If you have carefully shopped for space and the per-square-foot rate is reasonable, try to commit for more space than you initially need.

Name

Shakespeare said "What's in a name?" For catalogs, a great deal. The name should be easy to remember and/or allow the prospective customer to identify immediately with the person or company behind the catalog.

Many catalogs owned by entrepreneurs use the owner's name, such as Leichtung Inc. This is not an ego trip, but one way to make customers feel that someone they "know" stands behind the catalog. Catalogs such as Adam York, Charles Keith, and A. B. Lambdin, which bear fictional names, are using the same marketing strategy.

Retailers generally use the name of their store, or a modified version, such as Saks Fifth Avenue's Folio, Pier 1 by Post, and I. Magnin's Reflections. Once you select the name, see your attorney to determine if the name is available and how you can use and protect it. Insist that your attorney do the name research quickly. In more than one case, the name of a startup catalog had to be changed after the first catalog was issued, because it was discovered too late that the right to the chosen name was owned by another company.

Personnel

The most important resource of any catalog business is its employees. As many established catalogers have found, talented, experienced catalog personnel are rare and increasingly expensive. You really have four options: Use the services of an executive search firm (advertisements for such firms can be found in the direct marketing publications listed in the back of this book), run classified ads for experienced direct marketers, train an inexperienced person (preferably from within your company), or network through suppliers, family, friends, and such associations as DMA (Direct Marketing Association).

A list of job titles and functions one might find in a catalog operation follows. Table 2-1 shows the job functions for which an outside consultant or service can be used in place of internal staff. Obviously, many functions can be performed by the owner or other personnel assigned to more than one job. The job descriptions are not all-inclusive. They are meant to give an idea of the types of functions performed. In a large catalog operation, each job description might be a page or more in length.

Merchandising

- *Merchandise manager/vice-president of merchandising.* Supervises and advises buyers, negotiates contracts with major vendors, makes final selection of merchandise to be offered, determines merchandise pricing. Reports to vice-president of marketing or owner/president.
- *Buyer.* Sources merchandise, negotiates with vendors, arranges for backup merchandise, arranges delivery terms, and so on. Reports to merchandise manager.

Design

- *Creative director.* Responsible for design and graphic image of catalog. Works with merchandise manager to determine items to be fea-

TABLE 2-1
Job functions and outside service equivalents

Job/Function	*Outside Service Equivalent*
Buyer Merchandise Manager (Merchandising V.P.)	Buying Office Services
Copywriter Artist Creative Director Production Manager	Direct Marketing Agency or Free Lance
List Manager	List Broker/Manager
Statistician (Analyst)	Computer Service Bureau
Marketing Manager (Marketing V.P.)	Direct Marketing Consultant/ Direct Marketing Agency
Envelope Opener (Order Processor)	Fulfillment Service
Telephone Order Taker Telephone Manager	Telephone Answering Service In-WATS
Data Entry Personnel Office Manager (Data Processing Manager) Picker/Packer Receiving/Shipping Clerk Warehouse Manager	Fulfillment Service
Customer Service Personnel Customer Service Manager Operations V.P.	Fulfillment Service
Bookkeeper Accounting Manager/Controller	Accountant & Fulfillment/ Computer Service Bureau
Finance V.P. Personnel Manager/V.P.	Outside Accountant
Attorney	Outside Attorney
Owner/President	—
Secretary/Receptionist/Administrative Assistant	—

tured. May also supervise production. Reports to marketing manager/ marketing vice-president.

- *Copywriter.* Reviews merchandise and writes copy for catalog. Reports to creative director or marketing manager/marketing vice-president.
- *Artist.* Responsible for layouts and/or paste-ups. Reports to creative director.

Marketing and production

- *Marketing manager/marketing vice-president.* Has overall responsibility for creating, producing, and marketing the catalog. Reports to owner/president.
- *Production manager.* Responsible for scheduling, purchase, and coordination of outside services, such as photography, separations, printing, and lettershop. Works in conjunction with creative director. Reports to marketing manager/marketing vice-president.
- *List manager.* Projects mailing quantities based on past results and available names. Works with outside list brokers to select lists for testing and rollout. Either coordinates with outside list manager or is in charge of internal list management. Reports to marketing manager/marketing vice-president.
- *Analyst.* Uses historical and current data to project catalog sales, customer attrition rates, and inventory needs. Reports to marketing manager/marketing vice-president.

Office services/data processing

- *Office manager/data processing manager.* Responsible for all order processing/data entry staff and their functions. Reports to administrative vice-president/owner.
- *Envelope opener/order processor.* Opens and batches orders; may check for errors caused by improperly filled out order forms, missing checks, and so on. May be full- or part-time. Report to office manager/data processing manager.
- *Telephone manager.* Responsible for telephone order staff and script and order form development. Monitors calls. Reports to office manager/data processing manager.
- *Telephone order taker.* Takes phone orders, fills in order forms, and may attempt to sell more merchandise. Reports to telephone manager.
- *Data entry personnel.* Enter order data into computer or manually onto forms. May be full- or part-time. Reports to office manager/data processing manager.

Warehouse operations

- *Warehouse manager.* Overall responsibility for merchandise receipt and storage, order filling, and shipping. Reports to operations vice-president/owner.
- *Picker/packer.* Picks merchandise from shelves in warehouse, takes to packing area where merchandise is packed for shipment. Picker and packer may be the same person. Reports to warehouse manager.
- *Receiving/shipping clerk.* Receiving clerk checks incoming merchan-

dise shipments for quantity/quality, verifies vendor invoice data, inputs data to data processing/accounting. Shipping clerk verifies customer order output, handles USPS/UPS meters or manifests, inputs to data processing/accounting. Reports to warehouse manager.

Customer service

- *Customer service manager.* Supervises customer service staff. Is influential in establishing customer service policies. Reports to operations vice-president/owner.
- *Customer service personnel.* Handle customer requests, complaints, and inquiries by phone or letter. Must be pleasant and patient. Report to customer service manager.

Office operations

- *Operations vice-president.* Responsible for order processing, data processing, fulfillment, customer service, maintenance, and security. Reports to owner/president.

Finance

- *Finance vice-president.* Responsible for cash flow, profit-and-loss projections, financial analysis, and banking relationships. May also be in charge of long-term planning. Reports to owner/president.
- *Accounting manager/controller.* Responsible for accounting staff, accounts payable, accounts receivable, tax reports, and tax filings. Reports to finance vice-president.
- *Bookkeeper.* Responsible for keeping account books and systematic records of money transactions. Reports to accounting manager/controller.

Personnel

- *Personnel manager/vice-president.* Responsible for finding new personnel, salary recommendations and reviews, union relations, employee fringe benefits, training of personnel. Reports to owner/president.

Legal affairs

- *Attorney.* Usually an outside service, except in large corporations. Reviews contracts, advises on legalities of promotions (such as sweepstakes), on FTC regulations, and so forth; may review copy. If internal, reports to president.

The top

- *Owner/president.* "The buck stops here." In addition to running the entire catalog company, the president must provide time and effort for long-term planning. Reports to parent corporation/investors.

Administrative support

- *Secretary/receptionist/administrative assistant.* For a new catalog, this function can be the most important. A number of catalogs have been started by wife-and-husband teams plus one employee of this type.

With the aid of outside agencies and consultants, very small teams have efficiently performed many of the catalog functions listed here. All team members have, at times, served as order processors, buyers, pickers, packers, and more.

Areas such as list maintenance, merge/purge, printing, photography, and separations are not included in this job title list because, for the vast majority of catalogs, this work is performed by outside services. Finding the outside services you need is really a simple matter. Sources include the Yellow Pages, industry organizations, and trade publications. Be sure that, as you interview potential candidates, you comply with all the equal opportunity laws. Write to the Equal Employment Opportunity Commission in Washington, D.C., or your state's equivalent.

WHY SOME CATALOGS FAIL

No matter what the business, there are successes and there are failures. Direct mail is no different. Estimates of startup catalog failure range from 25 to 50 percent. And, since catalog operations involve a sizable capital investment, failures can mean major financial losses.

No one likes to talk about failure, so the reasons behind the downfall of a particular catalog are seldom really known, no matter what the press releases may say. But certainly there are some wrong ways to approach and/or operate a mail order business. Here's what to avoid—all are equally important:

1. *Undercapitalization.* Gone are the days when you could "make a million dollars off your kitchen table." It's a competitive world out there and there are some very big spenders in it. Unless you're prepared to invest a lot of money (estimates range from $500,000 to $2 million), don't even think catalog. There are unique exceptions, but those fortunate few are the ones who have either stumbled across a truly great product line or found a profitable niche previously untapped by anyone, which leads to the next situation to avoid.

2. *Overgeneralization.* Today, a catalog must have a unique niche or profile. Simply copying the latest shining star in the industry will not work. Some of the greatest success stories in our industry are of innovative catalogs that met a specific need.

3. *Ego investment.* Catalogs are created to make money, not impress friends. Investors who approach cataloging as a way of extending their own "good taste" may themselves become overextended. Harold Schwartz, president of the extraordinarily successful Hanover House, has a marvelous speech that spells out this peril loudly and clearly. Catalogers who insist on being the prettiest, the glossiest, the most gorgeous, often find they have a bottom-line problem. Getting customers to buy requires that products be presented attractively, but graphic awards benefit only the owner's ego, not the owner's pocketbook. Strive for an attractive catalog, but don't let high creative and production costs get in the way of profits.

4. *Inflexibility.* Times change and so do customers' needs. That niche you carved out for yourself may have been perfect when you began, but how has it weathered changing attitudes? For instance, stitchery catalogs were in abundance ten years ago. Not today. Women are working outside the home more, whether through necessity or desire, and haven't the time for needlework. Taking a more positive example, one cataloger started mainly with camping gear. Being in tune with consumers, the cataloger later discovered that camping gear was still needed, but the more active life-style of the eighties allowed a shift to general outdoor wear. The catalog's success, and sales, continues to grow every year.

5. *High customer-acquisition cost.* If your customer-acquisition cost greatly exceeds the profit you will make from the customer, you're in trouble. In essence, the initial cost of acquiring a customer must bear a relationship to the long-term profit to be derived from that customer. All methods of acquiring names must be carefully evaluated on this basis.

6. *Bad partnerships.* These have been the ruin of more than one business, and mail order is no exception. Know as much as possible

about the professionalism of the person you are considering for a partner and don't let friendship cloud your judgment.

7. *Corporate takeovers.* Large corporations are successful in many areas, but in some cases, running a mail order business is not one of them, for two major reasons:

- Profits are not sufficiently high to impress the parent company. Although the profits realized from some catalogs would make individual entrepreneurs extremely happy, to a multibillion dollar company, they may seem insignificant.
- Large companies cannot act as quickly as small companies. Corporations tend to have more complicated chains of command, resulting in slower decision making. Cataloging is a fast business, often requiring instant implementation of customers' needs. The methods that have worked well for other large corporate ventures too often do not work at all in mail order.

Direct marketing works

If you do the job right, catalogs can be both lucrative and rewarding.

Study the "how to's" carefully, and find your own way of adapting them to create a better and more distinctive catalog. Get the right kind of professional help and start mailing! After all, how many other businesses offer you the entire U.S. market (or more) without leaving the town in which you choose to live? And how many other businesses offer you the opportunity to develop loyal customers who, through correspondence, practically become members of your corporate family?

Part 3
MERCHANDISING

WHERE AND HOW TO LOOK FOR MERCHANDISE

Sourcing merchandise is relatively simple if you know where to go. A variety of "revolving" trade shows turn up in different centers around the country at different times of the year. These will be covered later in this chapter under "Merchandise centers (by city)." Besides these, there are specific subject shows noted for high attendance and merchandise variety. Be prepared to show a business card that states your company's name and your position within that company. Shows and showrooms are for buyers only.

Subject shows

The Atlantic City China & Glass Show

Features over 2,000 booths and showcases an international array of mostly china and glass but also offers buyers jewelry, silver, woodenware, paper goods, and much more. Located at the Convention Center in Atlantic City, New Jersey, the show takes place every January. Contact: George Little Management Inc., 2 Park Avenue, Suite 1100, New York, NY 10016 (212-686-6070).

The Consumer Electronics Show

Billed as the largest annual trade show in the world, this show boasts more than 1,300 companies exhibiting in more than 800,000 net square feet of space. Product categories include audio, car audio, video, computers and games, telecommunications, and personal electronics. Buyers are also invited to attend workshops, conferences, and exhibitions. The electronics show is held twice a year—in January (Las Vegas, Nevada) and in June (Chicago, Illinois). Contact: Consumer Electronics Show, 2001 Eye Street N.W., 3rd floor, Washington, DC 20006 (202-457-8700).

The National Mail Order Merchandise Show

The only merchandise show exclusively devoted to mail order marketing. At this compact show, more than 180 companies offer everything from leather goods to housewares to personalized giftware. It is held once a year at the Sheraton Centre in New York City. Contact: National Mail Order Merchandise Show, Division Expo Accessories Inc., 300 Allwood Road, Clifton, New Jersey 07012 (201-777-5802).

The Premium Incentive Show

The largest show of its kind, it features more than 1,200 exhibitors displaying more than 100,000 incentive products and services from around the world. This showcase for exchanging new incentive ideas and marketing techniques also offers a series of educational sessions, workshops, seminars, and conference programs. It is held annually in the spring at the New York Coliseum, New York, New York. Contact: Thalheim Expositions Inc., 98 Cutter Mill Road, Box 707, Great Neck, NY 11021 (516-466-2038).

Jewelers of America's New York International Jewelry Trade Show and Convention

The largest jewelry trade show in the country, this twice-yearly event boasts an international array of 1,100 exhibitors. The exhibition of fine jewelry offers the buyer the newest jewelry store products and services. The show also takes place once a year at the Chicago Expo Center, entitled appropriately Jewelers of America's Chicago International Jewelry Trade Show and Conference, with a list of 300 international exhibitors. It also takes place annually in New Orleans at the Hyatt Regency Hotel and features 300 exhibitors; that show is called the New Orleans Jewelry Trade Show and Conference. *Note:* To attend, you must provide identification showing that you buy fine jewelry at wholesale and sell at retail. Contact: Mort Abelson, Jewelers of America, 1271 Avenue of the Americas, New York, NY 10020 (212-489-0026).

Merchandise centers (by city)

New York City

The whole city of New York is a showroom! Here is just a small sample of merchandise categories with the approximate location or building address. Remember, the best way to find that extra special bestseller could very well be to knock on as yet undiscovered doors.

- *Women's clothing.* New York is noted as the fashion center of America, and Seventh Avenue and the surrounding garment district with its thousands of showrooms is deservedly famous. A few of the largest showrooms are at 1407, 1410, and 1411 Broadway and 485 and 530 Seventh Avenue. (For women's clothing directories, refer to the industry publications listed later in this chapter.)
- *Children's clothing.* 112 West 34th Street.
- *Toy center.* 200 Fifth Avenue and 1107 Broadway (two buildings connected by a skybridge).
- *Fur district.* Between West 28th Street and West 30th Street, and between Avenue of the Americas and Eighth Avenue.
- *Trimmings district.* Between West 36th Street and West 37th Street, Avenue of the Americas and Seventh Avenue. This district is great for baubles and beads, feathers and ribbons, distinctive accessories that you can make into unique jewelry, belts, and so on.
- *Jewelry district(s).* West 47th Street between Fifth Avenue and Avenue of the Americas. Also a block in either direction from the intersection of Canal Street and The Bowery (a street), located diagonally across from the Manhattan Bridge, near Chinatown.
- *Men's clothing.* 1290 Avenue of the Americas and the Empire State Building, located at 350 Fifth Avenue. Also check the lower west thirties, between Fifth Avenue and Avenue of the Americas.
- *Gifts and decorative accessories.* 225 Fifth Avenue and 41 Madison Avenue.
- *China, linen, and imports.* Along Fifth Avenue, from 23rd Street to 34th Street.
- *New York Coliseum.* Holds expositions and events such as the Na-

tional Fashion & Boutique Show, the National Men's Sportswear Buyers' Show (NAMSB), the International Leather Goods Show, the National Shoe Fair, and so forth. Some are open to the public; some are for buyers only. For a free six-month calendar of events, send a self-addressed, stamped envelope to New York Coliseum, Columbus Circle, New York, NY 10019 (212-757-5000).

Chicago, Illinois

The Chicago Mart Center is it. The two impressive buildings that house that hub of activity are actually comprised of three separate centers. Standing next to each other are the Merchandise Mart and the Apparel Center. Both house permanent tenants. On top of the Apparel Center is the Expo Center, which houses temporary exhibits. Bring your compass to the Merchandise Mart; each floor has 100 showrooms. Billed as the "world's first and largest design center," it showcases high-design residential and contract furnishings, floor coverings, lighting, giftware, antiques, and decorative accessories. The Apparel Center, the host of fashion for men, women, and children, also features an exhibition center, a 527-room hotel, and fine shops and restaurants. The Expo Center houses a variety of exhibits, from gift shows to toy and doll shows. For further information, call the Buyers' Service Department (312-527-4141). Or write The Merchandise Mart/Apparel Center, 830 The Merchandise Mart, Chicago, IL 60654.

Dallas, Texas

Typical of Texas, there are lots of marts for lots of product areas. The primary centers are Home Furnishings Mart, Trade Mart, World Trade Center, Menswear Mart, Apparel Mart, and the Infomart (called the "world's first permanent facility for computer hardware and software"). Farther down the road is the Decorative Center District and Market Hall, which houses temporary exhibits.

All in all, Dallas is one of the richest sources for merchandise in the United States: furniture, carpet, lighting, accessories, linens, jewelry, toys, cosmetics, apparel, footwear, sports equipment, and much more. One reason is that exotic imports arrive in Dallas via the Port of Houston. For more information, contact the Dallas Market Center, 2100 Stemmons Freeway, Dallas, TX 75207 (214-655-6259).

Publications

One of the rules of good merchandising is "Read everything you can get your hands on." Here is a brief list of publications that will be helpful.

CLOTHING DIRECTORIES

- *Buyers Guide to the New York Market,* Earnshaw Publications, 393 Seventh Avenue, New York, NY 10001. 212-563-2742.

- *Daily News Record's Directory Issue of Men's and Boy's Wear Firms at 350 Fifth Avenue and 1290 Avenue of the Americas,* Fairchild Publications, 7 E. 12th Street, New York, NY 10003. 212-741-4000.
- *Earnshaw's Infants, Girls, Boys Wear Review—Children's Wear Directory Issue,* Earnshaw Publications, 393 Seventh Avenue, New York, NY 10001. 212-563-2742.
- *Fairchild's Market Directory of Women's and Children's Apparel,* Fairchild Publications, 7 E. 12th Street, New York, NY 10003. 212-741-4000.

PERIODICALS

Men's Fashion

- *Daily News Record,* Fairchild Publications, 7 E. 12th Street, New York, NY 10003. 212-741-4000.

Women's Fashion

- *Women's Wear Daily,* Fairchild Publications, 7 E. 12th Street, New York, NY 10003. 212-741-4000.

Children's Fashion

- *Kids Fashion Magazine,* Larkin Publications, 210 Boylston Street, Chestnut Hill, MA 02167. 617-964-5100.

Gifts

- *Gifts and Decorative Accessories,* Geyer-McAllister Publications Inc., 51 Madison Avenue, New York, NY 10010. 212-689-4411.
- *Giftware Business,* Gralla Publications, 1515 Broadway, New York, NY 10036. 212-869-1300.

Toys

- *Toys, Hobbies and Crafts,* Harcourt Brace Jovanovich Inc., 545 Fifth Avenue, New York, NY 10017. 212-503-2915.
- *Playthings,* Geyer-McAllister Publications Inc., 51 Madison Avenue, New York, NY 10010. 212-689-4411.

Electronics

- *Consumer Electronics,* CES Publishing Corporation, 135 W. 50th Street, New York, NY 10020. 212-957-8800.
- *Leisure Time Electronics,* U.S. Business Press, 124 E. 40th Street, New York, NY 10016. 212-953-0230.

Jewelry

- *Executive Jeweler,* Talcott Communications, 310 Madison Avenue, Room 1505, New York, NY 10017. 212-661-1570.
- *Jewelers Circular-Keystone,* Chilton Co., Radnor, PA 19089. 215-964-4000.

Secrets of successful buyers

Be snoopy and be persistent. Ask vendors annoying questions, like "What have you got under the display table?" (at a show); "What are you hiding in the back room?" (at his showroom); "What's new that no one else has yet?" "What's relatively new, but selling like hotcakes for [*catalog name*]?" *Note:* Don't always believe the answer to this last question. Some vendors are scrupulously honest and some have regrettable tendencies to exaggerate the potential of an item they want to sell you.

Take a good vendor to lunch. Instead of always expecting vendors to treat you like a valuable asset, remember that you're dependent on them, too. And maybe the next time a really great item comes in, you'll be the one notified first.

Be fair. Keep in mind that vendors are in business to make money, just as you are. Negotiate differences in a reasonable manner. You'll soon discover which vendors appreciate a fair shake and which ones will try to take advantage of it. Get rid of the latter ones; there's rarely any item worth that price.

Don't be shy about stealing ideas from your competitors. In essence, they've done the testing for you. If you see a particular item repeated frequently, a selling space enlarged, or an item moved to a high-selling area of the catalog (such as the inside front cover), it's usually a safe bet that you're spotting a winner.

Send for the product and hope the manufacturer's name and location are on it. If not, take a picture (clipped from your competitor's catalog, of course) to one of your loyal vendors (the one you took to lunch last week) and see if he knows from whence it came. He'll help not just because he's kind (that, too), but because it's good business. The more successful you are the more you'll be likely to buy from him.

Read every magazine and newspaper you can get your hands on. Take note of mail order ads that feature the same merchandise again and again. Many mail order firms never run an ad on an item until it's proven itself in a catalog.

Look for "What's New" columns, frequently on products discovered or offered by retail stores. *New York Magazine* and home sections in newspapers are great for this.

Be alert to when a product has run its course. Following a competitor's lead by offering the same or similar merchandise is an excellent strategy as long as you're quick enough to understand when an item has "had it." Do you really want to be caught with a large inventory of pet rocks, hula hoops, E.T. dolls, or push-button telephones?

Make friends with other catalogers (competitors or not) and compare notes. One of the best things about the mail order industry is its openness. Generally speaking, catalogers will readily trade information. Even though your product line may not be similar, an exchange of information can help both of you pinpoint trends, and thereby become better merchants.

Shop retail stores. Keep a pen and pad always at hand to jot down sources and relevant information. Be polite when the department manager asks you to leave. Mail order is serious competition for retail, you know.

Check the labels in your own clothes and . . . If you liked it enough to buy it—and wear it frequently—so might someone else. See what that particular manufacturer is currently offering. Sometimes you're your own best "market research."

Ask friends. Spot an item a friend owns and love it? Find out who made it or where it came from. Again, it could lead to newer and better things. Also, sometimes a friend's creativity can create a product that never existed before. Spotting seashells artistically arranged in a basket once helped create a bestseller with a bonus: the consumer really had no way of "guestimating" the cost of finding all the shells and putting them into the basket. This provided an item that gave the cataloger great markup, but—even more important—consumers felt the product well worth the price because either they weren't geographically located where shell collecting was possible or, alternatively, the "prepackaged" product saved them the time it would have taken to collect the shells themselves. Even if they had collected them, they might not have had the idea of arranging them so attractively in the basket.

Think creatively. What an item really is does not mean that it has to remain so. Long johns with flaps were children's pajamas. It took the clever people at Adam York to turn them into practical loungewear for adults—and a bestseller for many a year.

Roger Horchow learned of the revival of the Orient Express and not only offered a favored few the chance to take this romantic journey, but also found wonderful products reminiscent of the Orient Express itself!

Have lots of stamina. You can always spot experienced buyers by their comfortable shoes and oversized—but not too big—tote bags. The buyer who brings home the bestsellers knows that footwork is the main ingredient of success. There is no such thing as a good show or a bad show, only a show that wasn't worked properly. Even those shows that at first appear to be dismal (where nothing obviously stands out as a fresh new item) can be the chance to unearth a real gem of a product. Walking the shows, inspecting every booth, whether or not it initially looks promising, is the way fresh new products and bestsellers are discovered. The same holds true when working buildings. There are many well-known buildings that hold a cornucopia of merchandise and are especially reliable for that last-minute item you need to fill out a spread, but it's the unknown buildings that often contain the "finds." Pick a building you haven't been in before and start walking. Knock on unfamiliar doors. Ask questions. If that particular vendor doesn't have what you're looking for, he or she may know who does.

Think U—unique and useful. Think of what you yourself might need in your everyday life. Generally, you'll find that the two requirements for this unknown product are uniqueness and usefulness, something different that solves a unique need or desire. Not being able to easily clean cobwebs out of the corner of a room caused one buyer to take an ordinary feather duster and add an extended wand. Thus was the beginning of another bestseller.

True-to-life vignette

During a product-sourcing foray at a well-known importer's showroom, an Indian brass box was discovered. It was small, about 4″ × 6″, slightly bulging at the sides (it didn't sit properly on a table), but beautifully finished. The box itself was dark brass but a lighter brass delicately scalloped the edges. It opened down the center, hinged and closed securely with a clasp. What to do with it? It was too uneven for a table; customers would surely complain. Suddenly creativity came to the rescue. "Why not," someone said, "put a chain on it and make it into a purse?" If you've perused any catalogs in the last six years, you've consistently seen either the original or its brothers many times! And, as has happened frequently in recent years, retail has "borrowed" the idea from mail order, finding, we hope, as great a success with this item as catalogers did.

SELECTING THE RIGHT MERCHANDISE

Every item considered for your catalog should be scrutinized and judged by ten essential criteria. Before assembling samples from vendors, even before going into the market to source merchandise, the buyer ought to fix all ten firmly in mind.

A product selection checklist

1. *Quality.* Does the merchandise you have selected or plan to select reflect your catalog's image? Will the respondent be happy with the quality of the purchased item? Since a consumer does not see or touch the merchandise before purchasing it, but relies solely on the presentation of the item in the catalog, it is essential that the merchandise live up to or, preferably, exceed expectations. Keeping a customer is even more important than getting one, and feeling cheated quickly turns a good customer into an unlikely prospect for your next catalog offering.

2. *Price.* Is the item in the correct price range for your targeted audience? Consider the budgetary constraints or affluence of the audience you have targeted, not whether you or your friends would be able to afford the item, or find it too cheap. For a low-ticket catalog, this could be the opportunity to test the customer's profile by offering a few high-ticket items. Conversely, a high-ticket catalog may increase response and attain a larger customer base by incorporating a few lower-ticket items.

3. *Availability.* Is the item made or stocked in the United States? If not, does the supplier guarantee its delivery within the time frame necessary for you to meet your customers' needs? Have you found another backup source for the same item? If there is any doubt about sufficient inventory to meet a possible demand, it is never wise to offer an item, even if it has the potential to become a bestseller. Customers could ultimately become alienated by unfulfilled orders.

4. *Exclusivity.* Does any other catalog offer the same item? Can you negotiate a similar style, but an exclusive one? Or an exclusive color? As catalogs become more competitive, exclusivity will encourage shoppers to purchase from your catalog more and more over those of competitors.

5. *Uniqueness.* An item may be carried by other mail order companies, but not be readily available in the retail market. Uniqueness is the major principle on which the first mail order catalogs were founded. In recent years, this quality may have seemed less important but this is not true. Despite some element of risk in offering a unique, untested item by catalog, being the first to capture the direct mail market, and the demand, for a thoroughly different item can have abundant rewards in increased sales.

6. *Vendor cooperation.* Will the vendor offer two- or three-to-one backup, that is, will he hold 200 or 300 on your order of 100? This will keep your initial inventory costs down while protecting you from running out of what could become a "hot" item. Is the vendor easy to reach, and fast at supplying samples? Does the company have the manufacturing capabilities to gear up to demand? Will your orders be filled with the same speed as those of larger catalogs or retail chains? Will the vendor assist you in determining an honest sales projection until you have a history of your own on which to rely? Have the company's items proven good sellers (for you or other catalogers) in the past?

7. *Photographic potential.* Will the item photograph accurately? Too flattering a photograph can increase returns and create dissatisfied customers; a photograph to the product's disadvantage will reduce sales.

8. *Cross-sellability.* Will the product encourage sales of other items offered in the same catalog? For instance, if you wish to offer a necklace, does the necklace have matching earrings? Natural combinations such as this can help raise your average dollar order and please the consumer.

9. *Mix factor.* Are you sampling too many items of one classification, too few of another? During the selection stage, keep a running tally by category of the items you are sampling, so you'll know which areas need more samples while you're still in the market. This will help cut down on last-minute, sometimes frantic, sampling for that perfect item in a category that may be "light" at the time of pagination. It will also help eliminate one of the greatest merchandising evils—running a "so-so" product only because it's readily available. (Tally sheets and pagination are discussed in "The Final Selection of Merchandise" later in this part.)

10. *Profit potential.* Will the product provide the sales dollars necessary to pay for the allocated space? To determine that, see "Merchandising by price point" in "The Final Selection of Merchandise." Does it have a better than two-time markup? In other words, if it costs $10, can you sell it for more than $20?

A vendor selection checklist

The most important quality to look for in a vendor is the right product, and the vendor who has it may suddenly seem irresistible. But before you let your infatuation with a particular product overshadow your business sense, ask yourself the following questions:

• *What are the minimum-order requirements?* Stocking too much inventory on an unknown product can prove painfully inefficient. If your operation is a small one, can you negotiate an arrangement that will allow a minimal inventory investment? If you're new in the business, have you made it clear that you are sincerely committed to this venture, and that adaptability now will help ensure much bigger orders as you grow?

• *How willing is the vendor to return or exchange merchandise?* You can usually sense the way a vendor feels about the goods being offered. Does the vendor play up the quality of the goods and the fact that this quality is backed by the company? Your contract with the company (as explained under "Contract negotiation" later in this chapter) will give you the right to return unsatisfactory goods. But it is much better to deal with a vendor about whose products you can be confident, making merchandise return only a remote possibility.

• *Will the vendor offer backup?* Can you place a small initial order with a guarantee that two to three times that number will be available to you if you need it? Clothing manufacturers find it difficult to offer backup, as a particular style or fabric is often available to them for only a short period of time, but hard-goods suppliers are often able to offer this valuable service.

• *Does the vendor offer advertising allowances?* Be sure to get base prices before you ask this question. Some manufacturers have been known to answer yes, after adding the advertising allowance to the base price. If you don't know the base price and are unfamiliar with the ethics of the company, you may think you're getting a good deal when you're not. Advertising allowances can run anywhere from 3 to 15 percent off the base price.

Manufacturers sometimes require that the company's name be listed in the copy block for their product. Be certain of details before writing the copy; it is most disappointing to lose a promised advertising allowance due to ignorance of the specific conditions under which it was promised.

• *Is the vendor willing to give you a photographic allowance? Or supply a color transparency of the product?* Some manufacturers allow a credit of $100 to $150 per item to photograph their products for the catalog. It may seem like a small amount, but considering how many photos are needed for a catalog, even small amounts can add up to a significant sum. Other vendors offer a photograph of the selected product. If you are given a choice, it is often better to take the allowance than the actual photograph. Supplied photographs tend to range in size, forcing random focus separations, which can increase production costs. However, if the product requires location or model photography, and the vendor has an excellent photo showing the merchandise to its advantage, you may wish to ask for a duplicate transparency or make a copy yourself. Be sure to return the original in good condition, if you are asked, to show that you can be trusted to care for any future transparencies you may require.

Selecting samples

Whenever possible, make your final product selection from merchandise samples; photographs or manufacturers' sales sheets can be misleading as to color, size relationship to other products, quality, and so on.

The cost of sampling

However, it is sometimes better to review a photo or advertising flier on a product before sampling it. Many manufacturers and their representatives are most willing to let you sample their merchandise at no cost. Don't hesitate to ask for free samples. But not all samples are free, and excessive sampling can quickly add up to a considerable sum of money, especially when such costs as "in and out" freight, unpacking and repacking labor, and recording time are added for each sample.

The sample log

Even free samples are not returnable should they become damaged or misplaced; they may have to be paid for. Once samples arrive, they should be kept in a secure area and treated like the valuable investment they are. Unless otherwise specified, vendors expect free ("memo")

FIGURE 3-1
Sample request letter

ABC Catalog Company
123 Main Street
Anywhere, USA 00000
000-000-0000

To______________________________ Date ____________________________
(manufacturer/importer/distributor name)

Your product________________________is being considered for inclusion in our catalog________________________. Please furnish________samples at once for
(name, season, year) (qty.)
possible photography use.

Product description ____
Your style no. ____
Color ______________________ Size __________________________
Cost ______________________ Retail _________________________

It is understood that, if not used, the sample will be returned to you and, if used, will be paid for in accordance with the price and terms on the accompanying Merchandise Information Form.

Please follow these instructions:

1. Label each sample with the vendor's name, style number, and cost.
2. Mark the outside carton "SAMPLE" for________________Catalog.
   (season)

- -

For catalog company use only.

Date item received ______________________________________
Date item returned_______________________________________
Date item sent to photographer/agency _________________________
Date item returned from photographer/agency_____________________

---

samples to be returned in the same condition in which they were sent. Keep the outer cartons as well as any inside packaging, the warranties, instructions, and so on, and be prepared to return items promptly. Too often, samples are carelessly opened and, in general, poorly handled—their packaging lost and warranties misplaced.

Keep a log of all incoming and outgoing samples. One method is to use the letter requesting the sample as the form for your log (see Figure 3-1). Photocopy the letter before mailing it, alphabetize copies by vendor, and place in a ring binder. If you are on computer, you can adapt this same system to your data base. Be sure to keep the information up to date and make follow-up phone calls on merchandise that is not promptly received. Log the dates of the phone calls to use later to evaluate the vendor's reliability.

The merchandise information form

The Merchandise Information Form (Figure 3-2) is sent to manufacturers or left with them at trade shows or in their showrooms for items strongly

FIGURE 3-2
Sample merchandise information form

ABC Catalog Company
123 Main Street
Anywhere, USA 00000
000-000-0000

A Your product listed below is being considered to be featured in____________________during the period from__________to__________. Incomplete information will not be considered.

PRODUCT
Product/Mfgs. No.__________Item Name__________

B

MANUFACTURER	SALES AGENT
Name__________	Name__________
Address__________	Address__________
City_____State_____	City_____State_____
Tel. ( )_____Zip_____	Tel. ( )_____Zip_____
Principal__________	Principal__________

Our orders should be sent to _____ Manufacturer _____Sales _____Other _____ (specify)
To trace shipments, contact__________

Will you furnish us with free samples? __________
If not, specify charge per unit $ __________
How do you handle returns?__________
Prior approval_____Yes _____No
Return to__________

C PRICE STRUCTURE
"Going" retail price__________Usual mail order retail__________
Lowest net cost to us__________Per unit (ea. dz. pr. set) __________
Will you guarantee price for the period listed above?__________

D SHIPPING INFORMATION
F.O.B. point__________
What freight allowance is made__________
Quantity and weight per carton __________
Individual product carton size—each dimension__________
Individual product shipping weight__________
Is this carton shippable/mailable?__________
If not, can you provide shippers?__________
At what cost $__________

E PRODUCT DESCRIPTION
Country of Origin__________

Dimensions of products______L ______W ______H ______Depth ______Dia.
If electric, is it UL approved?________________________Fiber content________________________
Vat dyed________________________Sanforized________________________Machine wash ____________
Hand wash________________________No-iron________________________________
Size equivalents P ( ) S ( ) M ( ) L ( ) XL ( ) XXL ( )
Description of item (also include descriptive advertising material and be as specific as possible)

____

____

____

If item or part of item is gold-plated, specify:
______Karat ______Gold ______Gold-plated ______Electroplated

F DELIVERY AND AVAILABILITY
Shipping time required from receipt of our order ________________________________
Can you drop ship to customers__________add'l charges________________________
What is your normal on-hand supply____
Is this an item you will be continuing ____
This item will be available from__________to__________
Will you grant exclusivity to us for____
The manufacturer maintains liability insurance on this product in the amount of $__________
Carrier ____

G PHOTOGRAPHIC ALLOWANCE
If two black-and-white photos are not available or suitable, will you allow a credit for photography?
$100.00 for black/white__________$150.00 for color__________
Signature ____

PLEASE SIGN SELLER'S WARRANTY
This merchandise conforms with all laws, federal and state, as to labeling, brands, and so on. We agree to indemnify against any claims arising from violation of trademark, patent, or similar law, or from damage or injury to person or property caused by a defect, malfunction, or false claim for this product by the seller.
X____Date________________________________
(Signature and title)

SEND ABOVE DATA AND COMPLETE FORMS TO:
ABC Catalog Company
123 Main Street
Anywhere, USA 00000

ADVERTISING AIDS
Please return with completed forms any catalog sheets, descriptive material, and so on, that will enable our layout and copywriting staff to do a better job in presenting your product. You know your own merchandising best, its special features, uses, and so on, and we solicit your suggestions and comments.

being considered for upcoming catalogs. The information on the form is used to prequalify a vendor, to make the final selection of merchandise, to clarify prices or questions about a product during pagination, as a check against the vendor contract, and, later, to supply needed information to artists and copywriters. The thoroughness and speed with which the form is filled out are good indicators of a vendor's business behavior.

Filling out the form

Start by adapting Figure 3-2 to meet your individual needs, then preprint it with your logo. Here are step-by-step instructions on how to fill it out.

1 Fill in section A with the name, season, and year of the catalog in which you are considering offering the merchandise. Next, indicate the time period for which you wish prices guaranteed (verified by the vendor in section C). Have the manufacturer or vendor fill out the rest of the form.

2 Note that in section B the manufacturer of the item may not be the sales agent. Also note that the form specifically asks vendors whether they supply free samples. The information requested on samples will help keep track of sample costs. Knowing the return policy will eliminate such problems as vendors' refusing to accept returned samples without an authorization number for items that will not be offered in the catalog.

3 Section C will give you valuable insight into the current retail and mail order price structure. It will also serve as written confirmation of advertising allowances.

4 Section D requests the costs of freighting the item to your warehouse. The weight and size of the carton must be known to allow for proper warehousing of products. By knowing the costs involved in using the vendor's reshippable cartons, you can determine whether it is more cost-efficient to purchase your own outer cartons.

5 Section E requests the product information needed by the copywriter. It also serves as written confirmation of the particular benefits of the product, which, most likely, have been verbally discussed.

6 Section F provides essential information on the timing of orders. It also addresses the need for vendors to carry liability insurance on their products.

7 The last section, G, requests financial assistance to photograph the vendor's merchandise. Not all vendors will agree to this, but it doesn't hurt to ask, and the dollars go directly to your bottom line.

8 The warranty will help protect you from possible consumer lawsuits arising from a product sold in your catalog but is not meant as a substitute for a contract (discussed in the next section).

9 The last paragraph restates the need for any sales material the vendor might have relating to the product. As the copy says, no one knows a product better than the vendor.

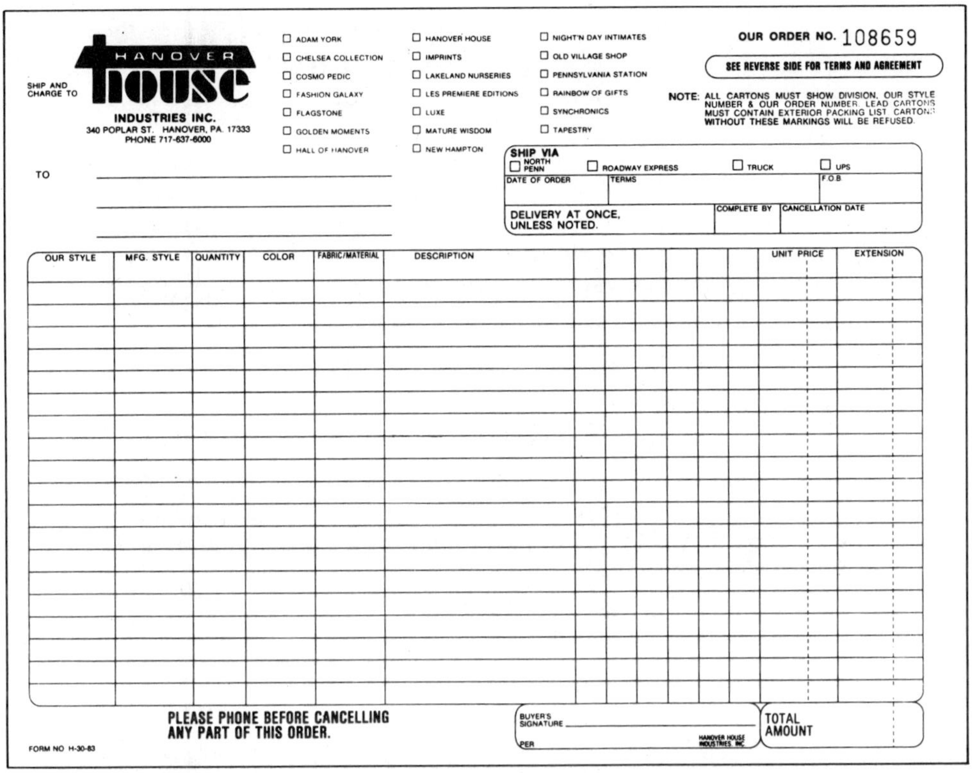

SHIP AND CHARGE TO
HANOVER house INDUSTRIES INC.
340 POPLAR ST. HANOVER, PA. 17333
PHONE 717-637-6000

☐ ADAM YORK ☐ CHELSEA COLLECTION ☐ COSMO PEDIC ☐ FASHION GALAXY ☐ FLAGSTONE ☐ GOLDEN MOMENTS ☐ HALL OF HANOVER
☐ HANOVER HOUSE ☐ IMPRINTS ☐ LAKELAND NURSERIES ☐ LES PREMIERE EDITIONS ☐ LUXE ☐ MATURE WISDOM ☐ NEW HAMPTON
☐ NIGHT'N DAY INTIMATES ☐ OLD VILLAGE SHOP ☐ PENNSYLVANIA STATION ☐ RAINBOW OF GIFTS ☐ SYNCHRONICS ☐ TAPESTRY

OUR ORDER NO. 108659

SEE REVERSE SIDE FOR TERMS AND AGREEMENT

NOTE: ALL CARTONS MUST SHOW DIVISION, OUR STYLE NUMBER & OUR ORDER NUMBER. LEAD CARTONS MUST CONTAIN EXTERIOR PACKING LIST. CARTONS WITHOUT THESE MARKINGS WILL BE REFUSED.

TO

SHIP VIA ☐ NORTH PENN ☐ ROADWAY EXPRESS ☐ TRUCK ☐ UPS

DATE OF ORDER | TERMS | F.O.B.

DELIVERY AT ONCE, UNLESS NOTED. | COMPLETE BY | CANCELLATION DATE

OUR STYLE	MFG. STYLE	QUANTITY	COLOR	FABRIC/MATERIAL	DESCRIPTION							UNIT PRICE	EXTENSION

PLEASE PHONE BEFORE CANCELLING ANY PART OF THIS ORDER.

BUYER'S SIGNATURE
PER
HANOVER HOUSE INDUSTRIES, INC.

TOTAL AMOUNT

FORM NO. H-30-83

FIGURE 3-3
Sample vendor purchase order. © 1984 Hanover House Inc. and used with permission.

Contract negotiation

Negotiating the prices of merchandise and hammering out the terms of a contract require tact, diplomacy, common sense, and a real understanding of how a contract should be structured. Remember: (1) get everything in writing, preferably in a formal contract, and (2) make sure that all papers are signed by the vendor and in your hands before you place an order (see Figure 3-3). The actual terms and conditions of purchase may vary, but here are the major points that should be covered:

1. *Price.* The order must be filled at prices no higher than those specified in your contract. Also, the vendor must hold to the price even if the quantity ordered eventually varies somewhat, whether slightly more or less. The price should include duties, excise taxes, commissions to representatives, and any other taxes.

2. *Quantity.* You should receive the quantity you ordered, not more and not less. If the quantity received is greater than the quantity ordered, the vendor must agree to allow overages to be returned at his expense.

3. *Delivery.* Since timely delivery is critical in mail order, the vendor must make delivery within the time specified in your contract. A vendor

who has delivery problems must inform you in writing of the last possible delivery date, at which point you have the right to reject the new delivery date, cancel your order, and hold the vendor accountable for any and all damages.

One of the alternatives you may wish to consider is having the vendor/supplier ship the merchandise directly to the customer. There are pros and cons to the drop ship method of fulfillment. For more information, see "Drop ship" in the chapter on fulfillment in Part 8.

4. *Warranty.* In addition to all warranties that are expressed or implied by law, the vendor must promise that each item will:

- be suitable for the use intended;
- be free from defects that could create a life-, injury-, or property-threatening hazard;
- be suitable for use, be manufactured, and be labeled and packed for shipment in accordance with and/or registered under all applicable federal, state, and municipal laws and regulations;
- not infringe on anyone else's rights, trademarks, and proprietary rights in general;
- possess all performance qualities and characteristics claimed by the vendor or advertisements for the product. The contract must assure you that the vendor has filed continuing guarantees with the appropriate federal agencies under all applicable federal statutes. The contract should also guarantee that the product does not violate any federal, state, or local statute, rule, or regulation and that you will be supplied with all current written warranties for the merchandise you purchase.

5. *Defective or nonconforming merchandise.* Merchandise that isn't "as advertised" by the vendor should be returned for refund of the full purchase price, repaired or replaced by the vendor, or repaired at the vendor's expense. The vendor must pay for all costs incurred in packing, shipping, and transporting the merchandise in both directions.

6. *Indemnification and damages.* The vendor, not the cataloger, should be held responsible for any claims, lawsuits, damages, judgments, and expenses (including those of attorneys) that might arise in connection with a product sold through your catalog.

7. *Insurance.* Require the vendor to supply you with a current certificate of insurance, which also insures you for any losses or damages for a five-year period following delivery of merchandise.

8. *Termination for default.* You can, in writing, terminate the whole or any part of an order if the vendor (a) fails to make delivery in the time specified; (b) fails to perform in accordance with the contract; (c) becomes insolvent or the subject of proceedings under law.

9. *Underwriters Laboratory listings and other approvals.* When it is

required by law, vendors must provide you with approvals and ratings of their merchandise from testing or rating institutions, at their own expense.

10. *Inspection and rejection.* You have the right to reject any merchandise that does not fit the specifications of your order. Shipping of unspecified merchandise is considered a breach of contract. You can either return the merchandise at the vendor's expense and risk for full credit of the order price, or require the vendor to replace the merchandise at no cost to you. You can also sue for damages on the rejected goods and cancel any unfulfilled part of an order.

Consult your attorney for the exact wording to be used in your contract before printing it on the back of your purchase order. And remember, a lawsuit is never a substitute for dealing with a reputable, honest supplier.

Backup vendors

Once you've found the perfect product, negotiated an ideal contract, and established an excellent relationship with the supplier, you may think you can sit back, relax, and wait for orders to come in. This is not necessarily so. Even the most trustworthy vendors can have problems.

One item placed in a catalog turned out to be an overnight bestseller. The vendor was reputable, personable, and always did everything in his power to keep to the letter of the contract. Unfortunately, the boat that was carrying the bestseller sank. The vendor frantically tried to have more goods delivered by air freight, but without luck. Orders kept pouring in and there was no product to fill them. That was a painful lesson in how valuable a backup source can be.

As you are sourcing product, make note of other suppliers who carry the same products or ones similar to those you are likely to run in your catalog. Although it is impossible to find backup sources for every item, it is possible for many. There is no need to tell a vendor that you plan to use him only as a backup source. Request all the other information you normally get from a prospective source, including how much inventory the vendor has available at any given time and the lead time for orders. Keep this information on record for emergencies, and you'll greatly increase your chances of never being caught without inventory on a bestseller.

THE FINAL SELECTION OF MERCHANDISE

The final selection of merchandise is made in the course of planning catalog pages or spreads (facing pages), a process commonly referred to as "pagination." Because the profit from a catalog is manipulated and controlled by what is offered on a page or spread basis, it is the bottom line—profit—that should determine which items you select from among the samples you have gathered. This section tells how to paginate for maximum profitability.

Pagination

The physical process involved in setting up for pagination begins with the assembly of all samples and proceeds as you organize them by likely pages or page spreads.

Preparing for pagination

Let's assume that you've already (1) requested and assembled samples of at least three times the number of products you plan to run in the catalog (see "Selecting samples" in the preceding chapter) and (2) kept a log by each manufacturer and item requested, with items logged by date and quantity as they were received. Next, (3) tag each item with the cost, anticipated selling price, advertising allowance, and any pertinent details, such as "limited quantities available" or "exclusive to us." Then (4) set up tables and shelves with the merchandise. Allow one large folding-type table per spread. Put as many similar products together as possible. For example, if you have several different kinds of wallets, put those together. This will allow you immediately to see all product choices per category. Keep several tables empty so that you can arrange and physically display merchandise as it will actually appear on the catalog pages.

Checklist of important pagination factors

- *Photographic potential.* Although photographic potential is one of the criteria for selecting an item in the first place, it is sometimes forgotten during pagination.
- *Theme.* Do items go together in such a way that they can sell each other? A spread can have a nautical theme, a kitchen theme, or a romantic theme, for example. Complementary items can be shown together in a response-encouraging, customer-pleasing manner.
- *Color.* Your catalog should attract the potential customer visually. When selecting merchandise, remember to plan color themes within the catalog to hold customer attention and invite page turning. Consider the season when selecting both color and merchandise, and be sure that the colors complement each other.
- *Complexity factor.* Products that have a multitude of features can sometimes also require a great deal of photographic and copy explanation. Carefully evaluate whether the space that must be allocated to properly explain the product will reap the necessary sales.
- *Position.* Historically, areas of pull, in order of strength, are: (1) front cover, (2) back cover, (3) inside front cover (IFC), (4) inside back cover (IBC), (5) center spread, and (6) around the order form.

The order of pagination

The inside front cover

Generally pagination starts with pages 2 and 3, also called the IFC (inside front cover). These two important pages should be a cross-section of all the items to come. They must not only grab customers' attention, but also must indicate the type of merchandise you offer and the price points at which it is available.

Since the IFC is one of the strongest selling areas of the catalog, be sure to include several items that have shown strong sales in the past or that instinct tells you will become strong sellers. Color is especially important here, for a consumer whose attention is lost at this point probably will not continue to look through the book.

Pages 4–5

The next spread, pages 4 and 5, should strongly reflect the reason your catalog exists. If yours is a gardening accessories catalog, this next spread should show down-to-earth gardening tools, such as trowels and spades. If it is a fashion catalog, pages 4 and 5 should show the most fashionable clothing you offer.

The order form area

Since customers often add items to the order as they fill out the order form, impulse merchandise is often selected from the area around and on the order form. View this area as a checkout counter at a supermarket. Notice how the counter invitingly shows such low-ticket items as chewing gum, razor blades, and magazines. Think about the impulse needs of your customer and offer products that naturally attract last-minute or add-on sales. Again, make sure that merchandise shown on a spread is always teamed to encourage multiple sales. Show the earrings that are perfect with a featured dress on the model wearing the dress and in a separate photo as well.

The inside back cover and back cover

The inside back cover (IBC) should be a "grabber," too. Many people read a catalog from back to front. Realize the importance of the inside back cover, and use it both to make a statement and to increase sales through the use of strong and inviting merchandise.

The back cover, all too often, is treated as a stepchild, even though it can be the second best selling area of a catalog. In fact, the back cover could be the first impression your potential customer has of your catalog; no one guarantees that the front cover will be seen first. Use this valuable area to promote enticing products that show value, uniqueness, and seasonal appeal. View the back cover as another window to your store. Show a tantalizing selection that compels the viewer to enter your catalog with the full intention of buying.

The cover

Because the cover is a reflection of the merchandise shown inside, it is often set up last. That way, it will accurately set the pace for all the items to come.

There is much discussion about whether to sell off the cover. This ultimately depends on the image you wish to convey. But this space is valuable and should be utilized whenever possible. Should you opt for product display on the front and/or back cover, select the product to be shown for its photographic reproduction possibilities, its sales potential, and the image it projects. The appearance of the cover in any case must be striking. A prospective customer who doesn't like the outside of your catalog will never open it.

Helpful hints

As you continue the process of pagination, don't feel locked into any one item on a particular spread. Rearrange merchandise freely to meet your goals, both graphic and financial. (Financial goals are discussed later in this chapter under "Merchandising by price point.")

Tally sheets

Tally sheets should be developed as products are selected. One sheet should segment products by category. Since merchandise selection can often be an emotional process, this will help determine whether there is an overabundance of certain product categories and whether others have unintentionally been overlooked. To prepare a tally sheet, break down your merchandise by category as in Figure 3-4. Make another tally sheet for price points, listing the number of products per $10 category, for example, $0–$10, $10.01–$20, and so on (see Figure 3-5).

When multiples are sold only as multiples, they are considered an individual unit. Refills are not included. When consumers are offered the option of purchasing a set, the individual piece price, not the set price, is tallied.

Spread record sheets

Spread record sheets (see Figure 3-6) will help keep you organized as you go along. For each spread, list the products to be shown (including the SKU—the stock keeping unit number—the name of the manufacturer, the manufacturer's product number, and the description of the product); the color, size, cost, and selling price of each item; and the advertising and the photographic allowances (if any), and any information you consider essential for layout artists to display the items correctly. Identify the spread by name and by page numbers, for example, "Traditional All American, pp. 10–11."

FIGURE 3-4
Example of merchandise categories

Home Furnishings and Accessories
- 11 Furniture, bedspreads, decorative pillows, floor coverings
- 12 Table accessories—useful
- 13 Table accessories—decorative
- 14 Linens—bed and bath
- 15 Placemats, flatware, napkins
- 16 Entertaining, food service
- 17 Desk accessories
- 18 Frames, mirrors, wall accessories, clocks
- 19 Bed/bath, soaps, sachets

Indoor Leisure
- 20 Planters, plants, silk flowers
- 21 Food
- 22 Books
- 23 Hobbies, games, toys
- 24 Paper goods

Women's Accessories
- 30 Clothing
- 31 Belts, scarves
- 32 Handbags, small leather goods, umbrellas
- 33 Fine jewelry
- 34 Costume jewelry
- 35 Intimate clothing

Men's Accessories
- 40 Leisure clothing, sportswear, loungewear
- 41 Jewelry
- 42 Toiletries
- 43 Clothing—other than leisure

Travel Accessories
- 50 Luggage
- 51 Business accessories, attaché case, portfolio
- 52 Travel accessories—business and leisure
- 53 Wallets, small leather goods

Children's Wear
- 60 Clothing
- 61 Accessories (nontoy)

Collectibles
- 70 Antiques
- 71 Limited editions

Outdoor Leisure
- 80 Sports equipment
- 81 Garden accessories
- 82 Pet accessories

Holiday Accessories
- 90 Stationery, gift tags
- 91 Tabletop
- 92 Hanging

Note: Numbers preceding subcategory listings are often used as the first digits of an SKU number for quick product category identification.

FIGURE 3-5
Price point tally sheet

Range	Number of Items
$0–$10	0
$10.01–$20	22
$20.01–$30	26
$30.01–$40	28
$40.01–$50	14
$50.01–$60	13
$60.01–$70	8
$70.01–$80	4
$80.01–$90	8
$90.01–$100	5
$100.01–$110	4
$110.01–$125	5
$125.01–$150	4
$150.01 or more	4

Preparing the artist and copywriter

If at all possible, have the artist and the copywriter present during the pagination. The information they accumulate (just from overheard comments) will be invaluable when they begin their respective jobs. Artists will have the opportunity to understand the size relationship between the items that are to be photographed together or on the same spread. Copywriters will hear directly from the buyers the all-important reasons that certain items were selected. They will have the opportunity to learn firsthand what makes a particular product unusual or desirable.

If it is impossible for your creative team to be at the pagination, be sure to supply the art department with Polaroids or photographic prints of the merchandise. Since you'll be the one taking these preliminary (for layout purposes only) pictures, be sure to include an easily recognizable item, such as a pen or a person's hand, in each photo so that the size of the item is readily apparent. Written measurements do not convey size nearly as effectively as a propped photo. One of our clients sometimes photocopies the actual product. This does not show color, but it gives a clear idea of size. You'd be surprised at how well even three-dimensional products photocopy.

Keep the Merchandise Information Forms, previously filled out by you or your vendors, in alphabetic order and readily available for reference. Any useful information added during pagination will be extremely useful to the copywriter.

FIGURE 3-6
Spread record sheet for "Traditional All American, pp. 10–11."

SKU*	Mfr.	Mfr.'s Product No.	Product	Color	Size	Cost	Sell	Advertising Allowance	Photography Allowance	Props/Comments
304-067	Able Products	49000	Two-Pocket Pant	Brown	6–18	$29	$65		$150	Show on model together with #7105 jacket in model's hand.
306-123	ABC Co.	72G44	Bow-Tie Blouse	Brown/Blue Plaid	6–18	$14	$30	5%	—	
305-720	Jones	7105	Single-Breasted Jacket	Rust	6–18	$33	$72		$150	Show on model—top shot only.
301-533	Smyth	3425	Crew-Neck Sweater	Blue	S,M,L	$23	$50		$150	Show on model—top shot only.
302-783	Any Co.	713944	Scoop-Neck Dress	Blue	S,M,L	$27	$70	10%	—	Both models should wear gold earrings #4618. One should carry portfolio shown on pg. 4.
307-400	Roberts Inc.	5362	Float Dress	Gold	S,M,L	$25	$64	5%	—	
346-470	Smith	4618	Shell Earrings	Gold		$18	$40	10%	—	Show close-up on model's ear.

*SKU = Stock keeping unit number, the number assigned items in the catalog to identify it.

Merchandising by price point

The term *price point* means selling price. The establishment of price points (price ranges) is critical to controlling profit. To achieve the correct price points:

- Predetermine your overall sales goal.
- Decide what response rate is realistic for your catalog.
- Determine what the average dollar order must be to achieve the overall sales goal.
- Estimate what the number of products ordered per person will be.

The sales goal

Without sales history or professional guidance, the number of products a customer will purchase per order is most difficult to determine. As a rule of thumb, higher-ticket catalogs have fewer items per order; lower-ticket catalogs have more.

To predetermine your overall sales goal, you can work with a one-, two-, or three-year plan that shows what your direct marketing profit center must generate in dollars to be profitable during the chosen time span (see "The Business Plan" in Part 10). Or, more simply, you can look at the initial, in-mail cost of a catalog and determine what you must generate in net dollars to cover that cost.

The response rate

If you are a first-timer with no history, you can start with the assumption that the higher the average unit price offered, the lower the response rate (this is not always true, but it gives you a starting point). For a catalog with no customer base and no known name, use response figures ranging from .05 percent to 1.25 percent for catalogs with an average unit price of $50 or more. Use .75 percent to 2 percent for catalogs with an average unit price of $50 or less. Responses may be higher, but these are realistic percentages. Higher percentage ranges can create overly optimistic expectations for an unknown catalog and can be morally and fiscally defeating.

Average dollar order per spread

Now add up the retail prices of all items per spread. Divide the total dollar figure by the number of items per spread. Multiply this number times the number of orders anticipated per person to get the average dollar order.

$$\frac{\text{Total Retail \$}}{\text{Total \# of Items}} = \text{Average Unit Price} \times \text{Average \# of Items Purchased Overall} = \text{Average Dollar Order Guide Figure}$$

Thus find the overall average dollar order by first adding the average dollar order per spread, then dividing by the number of spreads. Now take the anticipated percentage response times the quantity mailed. This will give you total anticipated orders. The number of orders multiplied by the average order will equal the gross sales. So average dollar order per spread of $78.30 with percentage response 1.5% × 500,000 (quantity mailed) = 7,500 orders × $78.30 = $587,250.

If this figure were to be determined for each spread (with the response rate factored in), the result should equal your overall sales goal. Let's use Figure 3-6, which shows the seven items on spread 10–11, as an example. The total of the seven retail prices is $391. If we divide this by the number of products (seven) on this spread, the average unit price is $55.86. Now let's assume that the average purchase (number of products per order) for the entire book is 1.4 per sale. Multiply this (1.4) by the average unit ($55.86) to find the average dollar order for this spread: 1.4 × $55.86 = $78.20.

Although formulas should be regarded as guidelines only and not as firm projections, they can temper emotional decisions with realistic financial objectives and can be especially useful in helping new catalogers toward a well-merchandised and profitable catalog.

Of course, not all spreads will perform evenly (in this case, at the 1.4 figure), but if you apply the formula to each spread, you will see a pattern developing. It may look like this:

Page	Average Unit Price	Average Order Guide Figure
2–3	$58.00	$81.20
4–5	54.75	76.65
6–7	85.50	119.70
8–9	62.50	87.50
10–11	45.00	63.00
12–13	52.00	72.80
14–15	73.00	102.20
16–17	48.00	67.20
18–19	64.00	89.60
20–21	69.50	97.30
22–23	81.25	113.75
FC–BC	75.00	105.00
		$1,075.90

Average catalog order

Now, add up the average order figures and divide by the number of spreads. In this case, the total average order figure is $1,075.90 ÷ 12 = $89.66. Common sense says that all of these factors are not constant in real life.

Therefore, if you were attempting to achieve a $90 average order and found the average order guide figure to be substantially lower than $90, this would immediately alert you to the need to rethink your merchandising selection.

Note: Don't confuse average items per order (the 1.4 number used in this example) with the response rate. Response rate is the percentage number of people who order from the quantity of catalogs mailed. For example, 2,000 orders generated from a 100,000 quantity mailing equals a 2 percent response.

With sales history, this formula can be refined. For instance, you may learn that customers who buy toys tend to purchase two items per order, but houseware customers average 1.2 per order. Obviously, you would adjust spreads featuring these products accordingly.

Evaluating individual products

Because individual response rates vary dramatically from product to product and are not predictable by the novice (or even by many experienced catalogers), a better method is to determine whether a product should be run based on profit potential. A rough estimate is made of the cost of the space the product will take and the dollars it will generate. A quick way to do this is to divide the total in-mail cost of the catalog (including creative and production costs, lists, postage, and all other expenses) by the number of pages. (For instance, a 24-page catalog costing $200,000 would have a per-page cost of $8,333.33.) Then divide by the number of photos per page. (If this catalog had five photos/products per page, each photo/product would need to generate $1,666.66 in *net* sales or $3,333.33 in *gross* sales if the catalog only had a two-time markup.) Then divide the net sales by the cost of the merchandise to determine the number of items that must be sold. Remember, this calculation too is rough, as products seldom have equally allocated space. Still, the exercise helps reduce the number of products included for emotional reasons.

For example, let's assume that everyone loves a stunning crystal vase that costs $37.50 and sells for $75. Using the previous figures, divide the net sales ($1,666.66) by the Gross profit per item ($37.50) to determine the number of vases that must be sold: $1,666,666 ÷ $37.50 = 44.44, meaning that 45 vases must be sold for this item to break even. The next question that must be asked is, "Is this a realistic figure?" Many potential disasters have been avoided because it was immediately obvious that the number of units needed to be sold was unrealistic. There is more detailed discussion of how to calculate response rates, average catalog orders, and space costs in the chapter "Catalog Analysis" in Part 9.

Repeat items

Determining which items to retain from one catalog to another depends in part on the mixture of products within your catalog. Obviously, a fashion catalog, which depends on the timeliness of its clothing styles, would be different from a catalog containing traditional home furniture. However, some guidelines hold true for all catalogs.

1 *Quality.* Has the manufacturer maintained quality? A decline in quality almost automatically means that the product should be discontinued. After all, the quality of merchandise you offer directly reflects the quality of your company.

2 *Reliability.* How reliable has the manufacturer/vendor been? It is rarely worth continuing a relationship with a vendor whose late delivery has caused customer dissatisfaction. But problems must, of course, be evaluated individually: Is the vendor consistently problematic or was there only one incident?

3 *Price.* Has the price gone up too much? If a price increase has become necessary due to increased cost of materials, is the higher price affordable? Or will the new retail price seriously discourage customers from buying? Also, has the vendor held to the price stated in the contract?

4 *The profile of the audience.* More conservative, less affluent customers tend to prefer having their choices confirmed by seeing them several times before actually making the decision to buy. Affluent audiences, on the other hand, want to be "the first on their block" to own a new item and will make the purchase the first time it appears. Knowing your audience's buying patterns is essential to determining how many repeat items you should offer.

Studies by the Direct Marketing Association show that hard-goods catalogers repeat 59 to 85 percent of their merchandise from catalog to catalog. Catalogers selling less-expensive soft goods show 37 to 43 percent of their products in more than one catalog.

Among the considerations that account for the difference are: (1) the cost of preparing the new photo, (2) the risk factor involved in attempting to find a new bestseller, and (3) the profile of the audience.

Part 4
UNDERSTANDING PRODUCTION

THE PRINTING PROCESS

Every part of the creative/production process is allocated a certain block of time in order to achieve optimum results and cost-effectiveness. Deadlines are determined by working backward from the time a catalog must be in the mail. Because in-mail deadlines are extremely important in this seasonally dependent business, missing any deadline in the process means that time must be made up somewhere; this can cost money and jeopardize quality.

Staying on schedule

Determine a realistic schedule and stay on it. The amount of time needed for the creative and production work depends on the number of pages in the catalog, the number of photos to be taken, and who will be doing the work. First, find out how much time the printer and the lettershop will actually need to print, label, tie, bag, sort, and mail the catalogs. Then, working the schedule backward, allocate time for separations or assemblies, photography, paste-up, typesetting, and so on. Figure 4-1 shows a typical schedule.

Keep in mind that the most expensive aspects of producing a catalog—the separations and printing—come toward the end of the production process. This, of course, is where time crunches usually develop. Being off schedule at this point can result in additional costs of 50 to 100 percent in overtime. If, for example, 100 percent overtime is incurred, separations quoted at $20,000 will cost $40,000. No one wants overtime. Suppliers dislike it because they must charge more for a job that, because of time limitations, too often is not up to their standards of quality. The cataloger, however, is the biggest loser, paying more for less because of the inability to stay on schedule.

To ensure that your catalog will look good and be financially worthwhile, schedule carefully, then stay on schedule!

Types of printing

It may be a surprise to learn that printers can do much more than just put ink on paper. Many offer separation services; most have the ability to make any last-minute changes in paste-ups that may be needed. Most printers can also bind in order forms, apply mailing labels, and oversee or actually provide a great variety of services designed to help get your catalog into the mail efficiently.

Before beginning to design a catalog, you need to have a basic grasp of the capabilities of different printing methods and their effect on costs and creative workup.

Because we hear so often of a new press that is said to outperform other presses, the choice of presses may seem unlimited. Yet all presses have some specifics in common. All presses are either sheetfed (print one sheet of paper at a time) or web (print from a continuous roll of paper). All also print either single color or multicolor, usually requiring a completely separate printing unit for each color.

There are three major types of printing.

1 *Letterpress.* Seldom used in the catalog industry, it mostly prints such items as stationery and cartons.
2 *Offset.* The most common form of print for catalogs, offset is often best

for runs up to approximately one million impressions (depending on number of pages and overall dimensions of catalog).

3 *Gravure.* Extremely cost-effective method of printing 4-color catalogs with long runs.

Sheetfed versus web presses

Sheetfed presses feed one sheet of paper through the press at a time and print only one side at a time. Compared with web, sheetfed is a slower process, but, because it allows for more control over the movement of the paper as it goes through the press, printing quality can be superior. Web printers will argue that through updated technology web presses not only hold their own in quality, but can be even better than sheetfed. But it really depends on the expertise of the people operating the presses. Whether sheetfed presses print better is moot. Except for small runs (usually 50,000 or under, depending on the number of pages and dimensions of the catalog), sheetfed is rarely a cost-effective method of printing a catalog.

Web is not only faster, but because the paper is in roll form rather than in sheets, printing efficiencies not available on sheetfed presses are provided. All catalog web presses have on-line folders, which fold the printed material into signatures, all in one continuous, money-saving process. Additionally, some web presses can perforate, paginate, cut, and slit. Since every piece of equipment has make-ready time—with a corresponding charge—the more functions one press can perform, the less expensive the total job.

Offset versus gravure

In offset printing, catalogs are printed on perfecting presses, which print two sides at one time. Standard offset presses can print four basic colors on top and four colors on the underside—commonly termed "four over four." For a special effect, such as a matte black finish or silver border, a press that can print five colors is needed.

A major difference between web offset and gravure is that web offset prints with a smooth surface and gravure prints from a surface etched with wells on a copper cylinder or wraparound plate. The copper cylinders used in gravure are more expensive than the metal plates used in web offset, but they are also more durable. This durability makes them excellent for long runs, because it is unnecessary to change plates as often and do make-ready (get the color right each time the plates are changed) as is necessary on web offset. One way to determine whether a catalog has been printed gravure is to check for tiny dots in the printing. Although virtually invisible to the naked eye, the screened effect of the entire image is easy to spot with a magnifying glass. (Compare the letters in Figure 4-2.)

While gravure has many advantages, the high cost of the copper plates means that it is cost-efficient only for high runs—which translates into large-quantity mailings. In addition, there are many more offset than

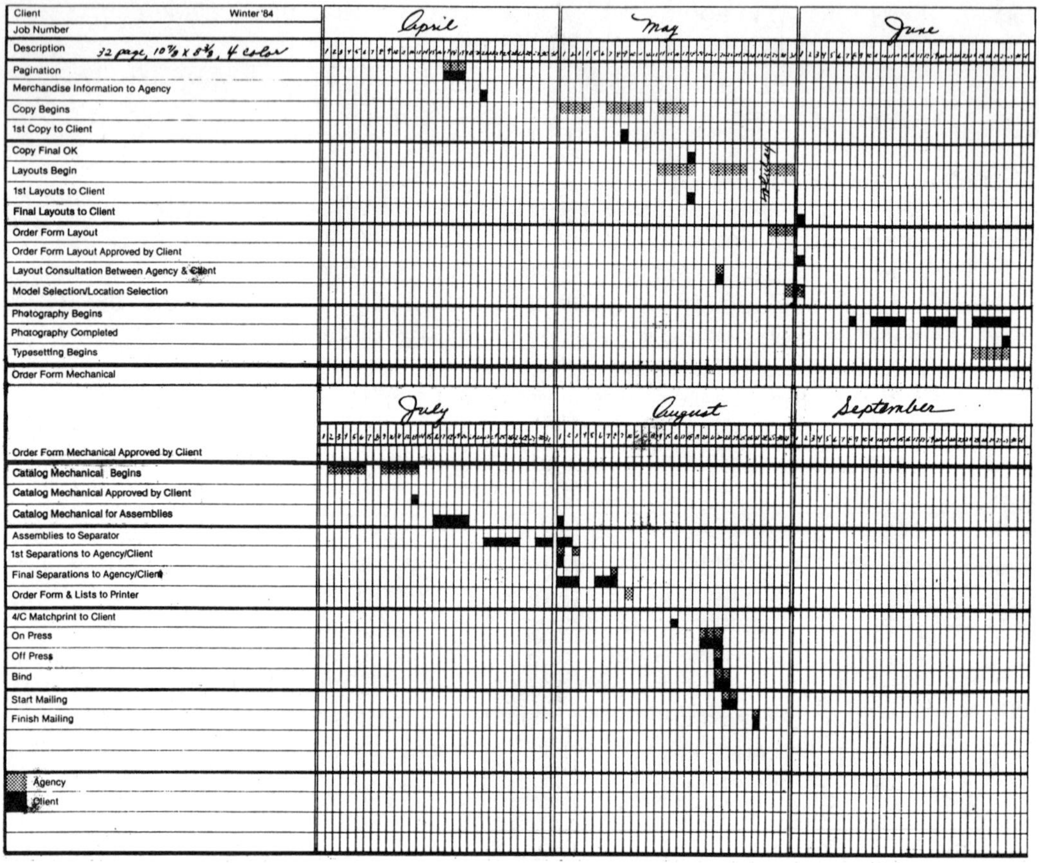

FIGURE 4-1
Typical creative/production schedule for a catalog.

gravure printers. With more printers come more options—such as the dimensions of the catalog and competitive price quotations.

Another difference between web offset and gravure is that while web offset prints with wet inks, gravure inks dry almost instantly, permitting each succeeding color to be printed over a dry color. Generally speaking, gravure nets more good impressions per hour than does web offset.

Signatures

Paper starts through a web press as one long roll, usually 34" to 38" wide. After it has been printed, it goes through dryers, where heat sets the inks. It is then cut ("slit") and folded into smaller, workable sizes, such as 8½" × 11". Once it is folded, it becomes a signature. The size of the paper after cutting and its final folded size determine the number of pages in the signature.

The standard number of pages from a web-offset press is 16 (see Figure 4-3). Therefore, most catalogs consist of several 16-page signa-

FIGURE 4-2
Recognizing printing processes.

tures. Assuming that one image is being printed per unfolded sheet, commonly called "one-on," two 16-page signatures make a 32-page catalog; three make a 48-page catalog, and so on. A 24-page catalog would be printed in one 16-page section and one 8-page section. One 16-page signature would be printed one-on and one 8-page signature two-on. For a total run of 100,000 catalogs, 100,000 impressions of one signature and only 50,000 of the two 8-page duplicate signatures are printed. This is because printing two (images)-on produces two of the same signature per press impression.

This may seem confusing at first. Select a reliable printer and rely on his experience. Most printers gladly answer questions and welcome the chance to help you better understand how to get the most out of the services they offer.

FIGURE 4-3
A 16-page imposition before and after folding.

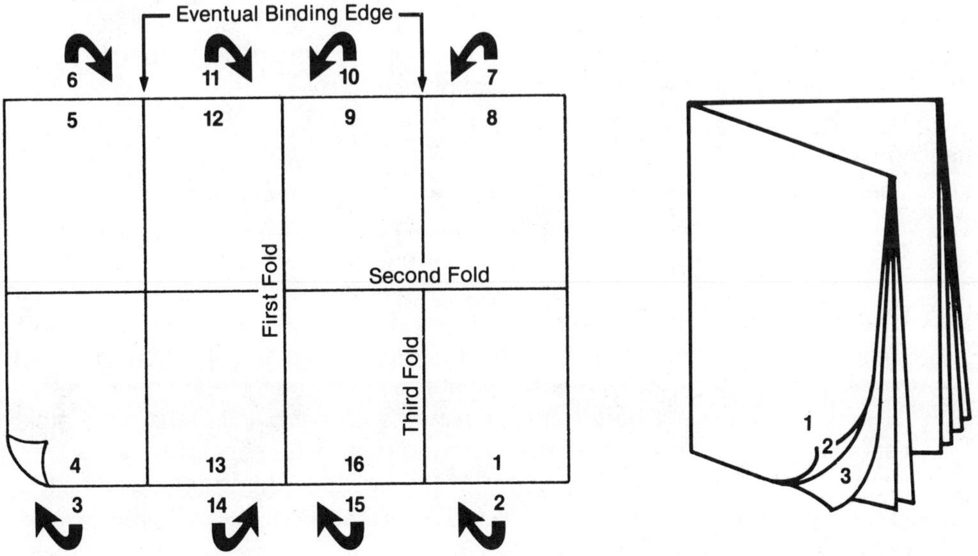

Covers

A catalog can have a self-cover or a separate cover. The less expensive is the self-cover, which is printed as part of the body signature.

A separate cover, as the name implies, is printed apart from the body of the catalog. An example of a separate-cover catalog is one which would have two 16-page signature bodies with a 4-page cover and would total 36 "pages." One advantage of a separate-cover catalog is that a higher priced, image-building paper can be used for the cover, and a lower priced paper can be used in the body of the book.

Number of pages

One of the questions my agency is asked most frequently is how many pages to put in a catalog. Because you now have an understanding of how a press works, you know that it is financially advantageous to work in signatures. However, you've also learned that you can divide signatures in two and that you can add a separate cover. So what at first seems restrictive can be adaptable.

The most important consideration when deciding on the number of pages to run is how many pages of strong merchandise you actually have. During pagination, there is a tendency to overmerchandise a catalog. Don't let this happen. Start with more pages than you need to meet press requirements, and cut to fit. Paginate your catalog, then sleep on your selections and delete marginal items the next day. "I have cut," you say, "and I still have enough strong merchandise for a 28-page catalog. Now what do I do?" Consider one 16-page signature, one 8-page signature, and one 4-page cover. Presto, you've got a well-merchandised 28-page catalog.

A successful cataloger quickly learns to run only the best merchandise on the correct number of pages for optimum press efficiencies. Never let the constraints of a press force you to run additional pages for which you do not have salable merchandise.

Ensuring quality printing

How can you be sure that the printing will be what you expect?

1. First, interview three to five reputable printers. Be sure to ask for recent samples and references from current clients.

2. If you are buying separations from a source other than the printer, make sure that the separator, the printer, and your production coordinator meet. During this meeting, they should agree on the specifications that the separator must meet to ensure that the printer can properly print the film. There are many horror stories, with the printer blaming the separator and vice versa when something goes wrong on press. Such problems can be avoided if the two suppliers have the opportunity to discuss their needs and capabilities. Have them follow up by sending each other written specifications, with carbons to you.

3. Don't buy on price alone. There is a saying in the printing industry that you can't have price, quality, and service all at once. More often than not, this is true. If the price seems too good to be true, it probably is. What you'll save in printing dollars, you'll lose in quality and consumer sales. But don't go for the highest price either. Printing needs to be of adequate quality only. Leave award-winning printing to people who can afford it and publications that require it, such as corporate annual reports.

4. Go to press with your job and, if time permits, stay for the entire run. Be there to check every press-form as it comes off the press. Listen to the advice of your salesperson or the press foreman (who knows best what the press can do). Realize that some compromises may have to be made, but don't hesitate to tell the press foreman if the color doesn't match your product. You know best what the product should look like. (For more on correcting color, see "Correcting on press" later in this chapter.) Once the job is running at full speed, monitor the work in progress. You don't want to discover, too late, that the latter part of the run was too red, water spotted, or defective in some other way.

Your printer's responsibilities—and yours

Your printer is responsible for a printing job that meets the quality standards of his samples and recommendations. Your responsibility is to stay on schedule and provide separations to the printer's specifications.

Remember, the schedule can mean the difference between a successful catalog and one that fails. If you follow the schedule from the printer for receipt of film, order forms (which you will probably purchase from a different printer), and mailing lists, then it is the printer's responsibility to see that your catalog is in the mail by the agreed-on date. If you don't, remember that delays in receipt of your materials can result in much longer delays than the time by which you are late. A good printer is probably a busy one with a tight schedule. If you are three days late with the film, don't assume that you will be on press three days later than you anticipated. The printer may have someone who has stayed on schedule booked for those days and have to fit you in when possible. Sometimes this can be weeks later.

The printer should check the separations when they arrive and alert you to any potential problems immediately, not once you're on press. The printer should also provide paper that prints well. (We'll go into more detail on paper later.) Even if you buy the paper directly from the mill, the printer should test it before actually going on press. If the paper appears to be a potential problem, replace it with stock the printer has on hand or get the mill to replace it. Once the presses are running, there will not be time for making this critical change.

It is common practice to have the printer mail the catalog, in which case the printer is responsible for preparing the catalogs properly for bulk third-class mailing. (This is covered in greater detail in "Binding and Mailing" later in this part.)

Correcting on press

To get good-quality reproduction, you must have good photographs, good separations, a good printer, and good paper. The best printer in the world can't make up for poor photographs, bad separations, or bad paper. Yet, some improvements can be made even during a press run.

First, let's discuss what to expect when you go "on press." You will probably review forms against your chromalins or press proofs as they come off press. During this reviewing process, the press will be running at a reduced speed, but it will still be running. While you are making corrections, it will be eating up paper. A certain amount of press approval time is built into the price quoted by the printer, but if you take too long, more paper may be used than was included in the quoted price. The result: a higher bill.

When making corrections, be aware of the way in which ink flows. Any color corrections directly affect all photographs in the same ink flow line. A correction to one item in the line could adversely affect other photographs in the same ink flow line.

So, for best results, be sure to provide the printer with quality separations and minimize the time spent approving press sheets. Some corrections can be, and often are, literally made at the last minute. Your pressman will attempt to guide you then, but use your best judgment, learn from experience, and attempt to provide even better separations the next time around.

The right paper

Paper is one of the most important, and least talked about, components of a successful mail order catalog. The way a catalog feels in a prospective customer's hands says much about your company. Remember, it's the customer's first and only physical contact with the company. Tests have shown that if the paper is of high quality, glossy, and of heavy weight, the customer perceives the catalog as offering top-quality, high-ticket products before even looking at the merchandise selection or prices. If the stock used is of a lower grade, light in weight, and coarse to the touch, a customer instantly assumes that the merchandise offered is lower priced—not specifically of either high or low quality, but definitely budget-oriented. Therefore, the choice of paper stock should be taken as seriously as the merchandise and lists selected.

Since paper can account for half of your printing costs, you must decide whether the benefits of offering the customer an immediate top-quality image will compensate for spending more on paper. How do you learn enough to make this essential decision?

Printers can be helpful. They have a working knowledge of paper and have a supply of paper at their printing facilities. They can make recommendations based on availability and price. Get samples of the paper along with prices, and keep the samples to check the paper after printing. Some printers have been known to switch papers on unsuspecting clients.

More helpful even than printers are paper salespeople. They are the paper experts and represent a multitude of different paper mills, so they offer the greatest variety and have the experience to know which paper is best for each job. They will supply you with important information on basis weight, grade, and bulk. Get quotes and paper samples from them and compare. Even if you don't buy their paper, they know that you can specify their paper to the printer, and that when your business grows in size you may purchase directly from them.

When paper is purchased directly from the paper manufacturer, the printer often charges a small (sometimes negotiable) paper handling fee. Even with this fee added to the price, the paper still usually costs considerably less than if bought from the printer. The availability of paper changes, so be sure to check with both the printer and the paper company before you commit. (See the Paper Distributors section in the Yellow Pages or ask your printer.)

Paper characteristics for good print quality

All of the following are important characteristics for good print quality.

- *Color.* Paper color directly affects the color of the merchandise portrayed. Paper with a yellowish cast makes a white product appear ivory. Type is most easily read against a soft white paper, and color reproduces best on neutral white paper.
- *Brightness.* Brightness is a function of paper shade (color) and whiteness. The brighter a paper is, the more the ink colors will stand out in contrast to the paper stock. If a catalog contains heavy, solid coverage on one side of a page, brightness need not be a prime consideration.
- *Opacity.* Opacity is a paper's ability to resist show-through. In general, the heavier or bulkier the paper, the more opaque it will be.
- *Smoothness.* Smoothness refers to the evenness of a paper's surface. The smoother the surface, the greater the clarity of the printed image. As smoothness decreases, print clarity decreases, especially in solids and halftones. Type is rarely affected.
- *Gloss.* Gloss is tied to smoothness and is a "measurement" (the amount of light reflected) of the amount of coating on the paper. Coated papers hold the ink on the surface, making the image clearer.

Last thoughts on selecting paper

A catalog should have sufficient weight or bulk to convey a feeling of substance to the customer. Because a small book, such as a digest, doesn't bend as easily as a larger one, the paper stock need not be as heavy. Tests should be conducted to determine the right paper appearance and weight needed to generate sales of the merchandise. For instance, tests for one high-ticket catalog have proven that catalogs printed on 60- or 70-pound paper produce better sales than when printed on 50-pound stock.

If your catalog has a good percentage of white space, you're probably better off using a free sheet (one without any wood pulp in it). You'll not only receive better reproduction in ink coverage areas, but the catalog in general will convey a cleaner, richer look than if printed on a stock containing ground wood.

For catalogs with fairly solid coverage on the pages, look into lower grade papers, making sure they will still offer the desired quality of reproduction. Another approach is to use a slightly lower grade and weight of paper for the body, with a cover of better stock. The savings gained on the body paper can be applied to the additional cost of a separate cover.

The price quote

One of the most common problems with printing quotations is misunderstandings regarding specifications. Be sure that each printer receives the same specifications, in writing, and insist that price quotations be submitted in writing as well.

Here's what your quote should contain:

1. *Quantity.* The number of pieces to be printed plus a cost per thousand for additional thousands over the original quantity.
2. *Number of pages.* Also indicate whether the catalog will have a self-cover or a separate cover.
3. *Paper.* The type of paper to be used by name brand as well as weight.
4. *Copy prep or film assembly.* The cost for such preliminary presswork as revisional typesetting, paste-up, assemblies, or separations should be definitively outlined. If you are supplying the film, the quote should specify the form in which the film must be received by the printer.
5. *Proofs.* It is a good idea to have the printer pull a proof of supplied film before going on press to make sure there are no problems. The quotation should indicate whether these proofs are included in the cost of printing the job.
6. *Color content.* How many colors in the job.
7. *Ink coverage.* The amount of ink coverage that your job will involve.
8. *Binding.* The cost of gathering, trimming, and binding (generally saddle-stitching for catalogs).
9. *Mailing.* This includes the cost of applying labels, sorting, bagging, tying, and delivering to the post office. You are responsible for supplying the labels or tapes for ink jetting; the printer's lettershop puts the catalogs in the proper order for postal discounts.
10. *F.O.B.* The charge for shipping unmailed catalogs and the location from which they will be shipped.
11. *Schedule.* You and the printer should agree on a definite mailing date and schedule.
12. *Terms of sale.* The method of payment.

All quotes should contain a written agreement or contract outlining the printer's responsibilities and yours. Read it carefully before you sign. Although you'll be telling the printer in what form mailing lists will be received (i.e., tape, Cheshire, pressure-sensitive), he will specify how packages must be marked. This will help avoid any confusion as to which code numbers belong with what lists. Confusion can occur because lists tend to look alike once they are removed from the carton in which they are sent. Although there should be codes both on the lists themselves and on the outer carton, this is often not done. Instructing brokers to code both helps eliminate confusion.

SELECTING TYPE

There are more than 10,000 typefaces available today—a bewildering number from which to choose. But the single most important criterion to have before you when selecting type is readability. You should be aware that the two main groups of typefaces (styles) that relate to the needs of catalogers are serif and sans serif. Serifs are short cross lines at the end of a main stroke. Sans (without) serif, as the name implies, has no serifs. Most books and newspapers are printed in serif type. Sans serif faces are often reserved for headlines or other such embellishments and serif typefaces are used for the body copy, but both can be used creatively for either purpose. This book is printed in a popular sans serif face, Helvetica.

Each typeface comes in a variety of point sizes, usually 6 to 72 point (see Figure 4-4). A font is a full set of characters in a given point size of any style of typeface, such as Helvetica. Each style has variations within it, such as light, bold, extra bold, italic, expanded or condensed, all of which are only thinner, thicker, fatter, or longer versions of the same typeface.

Readable type

The typeface reflects the personality of the catalog. A light, feminine typeface would be as inappropriate for an electronics catalog aimed at men,

FIGURE 4-4
Point sizes, from 6 point to 72 point.

6 ABCDEFGHIJKLMNOPQRSTUVWXYZ
8 ABCDEFGHIJKLMNOPQRSTUVWXYZ
10 ABCDEFGHIJKLMNOPQRSTUVWXYZ
12 ABCDEFGHIJKLMNOPQRSTUVWXYZ
14 ABCDEFGHIJKLMNOPQRSTUVWXYZ
18 ABCDEFGHIJKLMNOPQRSTUVWXYZ
24 ABCDEFGH JKLMNOPQRSTUV
30 ABCDEFGH JKLMNOPQR
42 ABCDEFGHIJKLMN
48 ABCDEFGHIJK
60 ABCDEFGHI
72 ABCDEFGI

as a bold, heavy typeface would be for a fashion catalog aimed at women. A more graphic, bolder type style can be used in headlines for impact, but body copy should be simple and easy to read. A number of factors affect the readability of type.

- *Line width.* A line of copy that is too wide or too narrow (requiring too many word breaks) can make reading difficult. If it's too narrow, the breaks in the words will dominate the look and cause discomfort in reading.
- *Word and letter spacing.* Too much word and letter spacing can cause a sentence to look "strung out." Too little can make sentences appear as one long word. Both can be discouraging to the reader.
- *Indenting and leading.* Indented paragraphs invite the reader to "read on." Leading (pronounced lĕding), the horizontal space inserted between lines of type, should be appropriate for the type size. Insufficient leading can make type appear "bunched."
- *Weight.* Consideration must be given to the effects of different printing processes on type. For example, because gravure screens all images on the plate, small point sizes and delicate, wispy fonts should be avoided to ensure clarity and definition.

When type prints on top of an image, or drops out of the background (white type), either the type must be larger than that normally selected or the photoplatemaker must be asked to spread the type visually, making it appear larger. The background from which type is to drop out must have color density of at least 50 percent. When surprinting, check to see that background colors have a density of *50 percent or less,* depending on the type size.

Character count

The person who has selected the typeface and size will divide the desired number of characters per line into the total number of characters in the original copy. Each and every character of the typewritten copy is literally counted, as are the spaces between the words. The total number of lines of copy is the dividend of this formula. At this point the copy can either be cut (if it is too long) or lengthened (if it is too short). Doing this after the type has been set means additional expense.

Typesetting

Most typesetting today is done by the phototypesetting method. There are many different types of phototypesetting machines, all of which operate like a personal computer. The typesetter sits at a keyboard in front of a display screen, types the copy, and visually checks it; the computer produces typeset copy on reproducible quality paper. As copy and typographic commands are read and analyzed by the computer, patterns of the selected characters are called out of the memory section and imaged

MARK	MEANING OF MARK	MARK ON ROUGH DRAFT	CORRECTED COPY
∧	Insert word or letter	Close the∧when you leave. (door)	Close the door when you leave.
⊙	Insert period	Send the manuscript to me∧⊙	Send the manuscript to me.
∧,	Insert comma	Later∧ if you have time∧ come to see me in my office.	Later, if you have time, come to see me in my office.
(:)	Insert colon	I have the following∧coffee, sugar, and cream.	I have the following: coffee, sugar, and cream.
;	Insert semicolon	Stay calm∧do not panic.	Stay calm; do not panic.
?	Insert question mark	When will the new forms arrive∧	When will the new forms arrive?
!	Insert exclamation mark	What a beautiful office∧	What a beautiful office!
’	Insert apostrophe	Didn∧t we have five reports when we left the meeting?	Didn't we have five reports when we left the meeting?
=	Insert hyphens	An up∧to∧date handbook is essential.	An up-to-date handbook is essential.
“ ”	Insert quotation marks	Susan said,∧How long will the meeting take?”	Susan said, "How long will the meeting take?"
*	Insert asterisk	Table 4-5.2 indicates the amounts spent for manuscripts last year.∧*	Table 4-5.2 indicates the amounts spent for manuscripts last year.*
♪	Delete	The speaker wore a green ~~and lace~~ tie.	The speaker wore a green tie.
(tr) or ∩∪	Words transposed	The conference was short too	The conference was too short.
Stet	Retain material as it was originally stated. Let it stand	The speech was ~~beautifully~~ (Stet) organized and delivered.	The speech was beautifully organized and delivered.
≡	Set underlined letter as capital	the time has come to develop a handbook.	The time has come to develop a handbook.
☰	Set entire word(s) in capitals	He will never do that again!	He will NEVER do that again!
(lc) or /	Set letter lowercase	Susan returned to College this year.	Susan returned to college this year.

FIGURE 4-5
Proofreader's marks and marked copy.

MARK	MEANING OF MARK	MARK ON ROUGH DRAFT	CORRECTED COPY
#	Insert space	The artwill be ready by noon.	The art will be ready by noon.
]	Move copy to right	A Handbook of Policies & Procedures	A Handbook of Policies & Procedures
[	Move copy to left	A Handbook of Policies & Procedures	A Handbook of Policies & Procedures
][	Center copy	A Handbook of Policies & Procedures	A Handbook of Policies & Procedures
[/]	Insert brackets	Mr. Robert Moss 1846-1937 lived a long and happy life.	Mr. Robert Moss [1846-1937] lived a long and happy life.
(/)	Insert parentheses	The United States of America USA is a great country.	The United States of America (USA) is a great country.
⌒	Close up space	The handbook coordinator will attend that meeting today.	The handbook coordinator will attend that meeting today.
run-in or	Run material in with material on line above	We hope to be going to Europe this year.	We hope to be going to Europe this year.
¶	Start new paragraph	. . . . The ten horrible days had passed. All were relieved. On the eleventh day, when everyone was. . . .	. . . . The ten horrible days had passed. All were relieved. On the eleventh day, when every- one was. . . .
no ¶	No paragraph	The decision was made to prepare handbooks for all programs. All participants were delighted with the decision.	The decision was made to prepare handbooks for all programs. All participants were delighted with the decision.
sp.	Spell the word out	The managers & supervisors were gathered for the meeting.	The managers and supervisors were gathered for the meeting.
	Move copy up	We were all waiting for the book.	We were all waiting for the book.
	Move copy down	I hope more information will be found.	I hope more information will be found.

in correct size and precise positions. One advantage of this method is that the computer retains the copy in its memory and changes can be made without physically resetting the entire copy. Only changed copy is reset, affording superior cost-efficiencies over older methods.

Keeping typesetting costs down

Because type is set by a computer, which must be programmed, it is best to submit all copy for typesetting in complete form. Each time additional information is given to the "type computer," there is an additional setup charge. So be sure to include prices, product sizes, stock keeping unit numbers (SKU), or any other vital information, rather than adding it at a later date.

Preparing copy for typesetting

Errors and costly changes can be avoided by making sure that the copy for the typesetter is produced as follows:

1 Use clean, white paper in the standard 8½″ × 11″ size.

2 Type copy blocks neatly, using double spacing and allowing wide margins. Type on one side of the sheet only.

3 Keep corrections to a minimum. Print them carefully in ink or use a typewriter. Changes that are scribbled illegibly or on attached slips of paper can result in costly mistakes.

4 Identify the job on each sheet of paper, for example, "Spring 1985 Lady L's Catalog, pages 2–3."

5 Number the pages in consecutive order.

6 Give the typesetter clearly understandable specifications.

Proofread typewritten copy carefully. Even though it should have already been checked and double-checked by the copywriters, check it again. The more eyes that see it the better. The time to catch errors is before the type is set, not after.

Correcting proofs

Once the copy is typeset, but before it is actually pasted onto the boards, you will see galleys, which show how the type looks. Galleys should be thoroughly checked. Correcting errors at this point means resetting charges, but a savings in the cost of extra pasteup time.

Proofreader's marks

The accepted system for correcting type copy is proofreader's marks. They are simple to learn and wonderfully efficient. Even more important, these marks are used universally and will be readily understood by your art team, the typesetter, or anyone involved in graphic arts (see Figure 4-5).

PHOTOGRAPHY

The photographs in your catalog are your "store display." They are the only visual presentation of your merchandise that customers see before their orders arrive. They are critical sales tools. So it is essential that your catalog photographs be tantalizing and realistic.

Selecting a photographer

Selecting a photographer is, to a large extent, a matter of personal taste. Nowhere else in the creative process of cataloging does the saying "Beauty is in the eye of the beholder" hold more true. However, a few guidelines can help keep objectivity in the process of choosing who will make your photographs.

• Check the photographer's samples. If he or she is a fashion photographer, be especially careful to note black-and-white clothing photographed in four-color. Can you see the individual folds of the black dress or the embroidered stitches of the white? Or is the clothing so poorly lighted that details are lost? Or perhaps the photo is too "hot" (has been lighted too heavily), resulting in loss of detail?

Does a photographer who specializes in still (nonfashion) photography add life to basically lifeless products? Is steam coming from the coffee in the cup? Are there bubbles in the cold liquid in the creamer? Is the monogram easily readable on monogrammed items?

• Ask current mail order clients for recommendations. Is the photographer easy to work with? Does he or she stay on schedule? Have mail order experience? Editorial fashion photographers may have exciting samples, but too often they go for effect, forgetting that the major purpose of mail order photography is to show the product clearly. Will the photographer work with you on reshoots, accepting the blame for some?

• Take a look at the studio. Does it seem large enough to work on your project concurrent with others, or will yours be put aside to shoot other products/clients' because of lack of space? Does the photographer do the shooting? Is it done by a knowledgeable assistant under the careful supervision of the photographer, or is the unsupervised work turned over to someone else once it is in the studio? Does the studio appear to be clean and organized? Sometimes the appearance of the studio can be a good indicator of how well the photographer will actually keep to schedule.

Keeping photography costs down

Nothing is as frustrating as discovering, too late, that your photography costs are considerably over budget. Here are a few pointers on how to make sure this doesn't happen to you.

1. Get a written quote from the photographer and understand exactly what you are buying. Film and processing should be included in the cost of each photograph. Leaving film and processing as an open expense can encourage unnecessary Polaroids (most photographers shoot Polaroids before the final shooting) and unanticipated expenses in the use of film. Be certain that there are no hidden charges. One photographer attempted to add a charge for studio rental and use of the telephone (for

local calls) during the shooting! There may be an added expense for feeding models. Get an estimate of how much this will be. And don't allow the photographer to buy lunch for the whole staff at the same time! Props are additional, so get an estimate with a minus or plus 10 percent ceiling.

2. Make sure all merchandise arrives on schedule. A written, hourly schedule can then be made up for the photographer to follow. Backgrounds should be included in the timing to avoid unnecessary set changes. This system will allow the photography to "go like clockwork." But if one cog (item) is missing, if merchandise does not arrive when expected, the whole system can come undone, resulting in extra expense.

3. Order duplicates, especially of breakable merchandise, to avoid frantic last-minute attempts to replace an item broken in shipment.

4. Have models try on clothing before the day of photographing to be sure that garments fit perfectly. This will save a great deal of time and frustration later.

5. Go over the layouts in detail with the photographer before the shooting. Give as much input as possible. Should chemise dresses be shot with or without the belt, or both? Is there a certain way an unassembled item goes together that is different from normal? What is the right age for the child model using a particular product?

6. Use tags or stickers to code all products to match the layouts so that the photographer's assistant can set up the shots before you arrive.

7. Discuss usage prior to shooting. Photos shot to be used only in a catalog sometimes may not be legally shown in other promotions. Be aware of what limitations, if any, the photographer has included in the estimate.

Fashion versus nonfashion products

In mail order, still photos (nonclothing items) are almost always shot same-size, that is, the image you see in the photograph is exactly the same size as it will appear when printed. This is done as a cost-saving measure. Photos shot same-size can easily be assembled (explained in "Separations" later in this part), then sent to the separator, where they will be separated on a per spread basis, rather than individually.

Fashion photos are generally shot random focus (with many different image sizes), using a 35mm camera, a Hasselblad, or a similar camera that shoots a 2¼″ × 2¼″ size. Since these are lightweight and mobile, they allow more freedom of movement for the models and photographer, resulting in better photos.

The camera used for same-size photography is very large and hard to move. It is an excellent cost saver for still photos, but is too bulky to use when action or fluidity is required, as in fashion photography.

Location photography versus studio photography

Location photography can add excitement and intrigue to your catalog. It can also add expenses not associated with studio photography, such as the cost of lodgings, travel time for models, and food for the whole entourage. Then too, if it rains, the hourly or daily rates for models, stylists, and photographers must still be paid.

Location photography poses other problems as well. Lighting isn't controllable and sometimes can be detrimental to the photos of the garments. If the sky is too overcast, clothing and the photo in general can lose their brilliance. If it's too sunny, models get hot, makeup looks shiny, everybody gets irritable. We once photographed a fashion catalog for winter clothing, fur coats and all, on a 99° day! Try to look cool and fabulous wearing a fur coat on one of the sunniest, hottest days of the year and you'll get some idea of how difficult location photography can be.

Yet location photos can set a mood and establish credibility (if shot in a realistic and glamourous location) that cannot be duplicated in the studio. And sometimes arrangements can be made with airlines and hotels wherein these normal costs are waived in exchange for promotion within the catalog. Even under these conditions, extra expenses are generally incurred. Be aware of all the costs involved and the potential problems of shooting on location, balance this against the image you wish to present, and make your decision.

Studio photography provides controllable lighting and weather conditions, two big pluses for catalogers. The cost, including props, is usually considerably less than going on location. Yet studio photography can be boring. Here's where a good creative team—your art director and the photographer—can make all the difference. Selecting the right backgrounds and props to create a memorable photograph, without overpowering the merchandise, is challenging but entirely possible. And, don't forget, sometimes the solution is to keep the photographs wonderfully simple, allowing the design and graphic elements in the catalog to create an overall favorable impression.

A good compromise might be to shoot some photos on location, some in the studio. Properly coordinated, this can give you the best of both worlds.

Selecting models

Models reflect your catalog's image. Here are some points to keep in mind as you review your choices:

- How old should the model be? Are you appealing to a young audience or a more mature one? Customers not only identify with models, but want someone they can respect. To be on the safe side, choose models who look slightly older than your targeted audience.

- How versatile is the model's expression? Sadly, some of the most attractive models seem to have the same frozen smile locked into place. Check the potential model's portfolio carefully to find out if he or she can adapt to the image of the product that is to be modeled.

Sometimes a wholesome, outdoor look is in order; sometimes a smoldering yet ladylike (or gentlemanly) look is required. But models should always look happy about the products they are wearing. High-fashion models are allowed distressingly sophisticated expressions (sometimes the models look like they are in real pain), but mail order sells fun, status, and just plain enjoyment, and the model's face should convey this.

- Is the model mobile? Or stiff and inexperienced? Since a customer will not actually touch the garment until it arrives in the mail, the model must make the product come alive, seem to zoom off the pages and into the customer's life-style. Fluidity of movement (or the lack of it) can make or break an item of clothing.
- How experienced is the model? Experience in front of a camera saves valuable hours of shooting time. Don't be tempted to use that good-looking next-door neighbor. Chances are she'll freeze in front of the camera, cause the photographer to take many more rolls of film than anticipated, and, even then, give unsatisfactory results. The only exception to this is child models. Unprofessional children are as good as, and sometimes better, than their professional counterparts. The inexperienced child model can bring a naturalness to modeling that some of the more experienced children, unfortunately, have lost.

In all cases, have models come for a "look see" before committing to them. The head sheets sent to you from a model agency do not always reflect how a model looks *today.* One of our clients selected a male model for his mustache. Imagine our surprise when he showed up on his "look see" sans mustache! The mustache in his photos was a fake. In another instance, a model who was supposed to be a size 8 showed up 20 pounds over her normal weight. She could never have fit into the clothes we had planned for her to wear.

Get a signed model release for every model, professional or not, that you use in your catalog. A model release, in essence, says that the person who posed in the photograph has no further interest in the use of the photograph. This allows you to use the photograph in a future catalog issue, in a space ad, or in any way you choose, without paying additional fees to the model (but don't forget to check usage rights with the photographer). Your photographer should have forms on hand for the models to sign. Be sure that they are used, and that you get a copy. Should the photographer move to another location, or should you change photographers for some reason, you will have a copy of the signed release in your files.

Retouching

Even with the best photography, the time will come when you have to resort to retouching. Perhaps a garment simply wouldn't iron properly and the wrinkles need to be "ironed out" through the magic of retouching. Or perhaps an item had to be held in position with a string, which now needs to be deleted from the photo.

Retouching can be done (1) directly on the transparency or (2) on a color print (dye transfer). The first is preferable, although more difficult, as it does not take the original art a step away from its original quality. To retouch directly on the transparency, the artist must have a delicate hand and full understanding of the chemicals used for the corrections. If the retouching is not done properly, the scanner used in separations may not pick up the correction from the transparency, or it may pick up a "bloom"—a shiny or hot spot caused by retouching on the transparency.

If you choose the second method, don't be tempted to use anything but a top-quality print of the transparency. Each successive step away from the original automatically means a reduction of quality, so don't compound this problem by opting for a less than perfect print. Here, again, the artist can run into blooms. However, because the print is generally larger than the transparency, the retouched area is easier to see and easier to correct. The print must wrap around the cylinder used by a scanner (separator), so don't allow the print to be mounted on board any thicker than .006″.

Some corrections can be made in the separation process. Before committing yourself to retouching, talk to both the separator and the retoucher. Clearly define the problem and rely strongly on their advice.

Be there

Your presence, or that of a knowledgeable representative, during the actual shooting is essential. No one knows the benefits of the merchandise, or how it should actually be shown, as well as you do. This is your final chance to make any changes in the positioning of the product as shown in the layout. And, if there was any doubt in your mind as to how the product would actually look when photographed, this is the time to ask questions, while you can still make adjustments.

Being there also helps eliminate reshoots. Be alert as to what is going on around you, and don't hesitate to speak up if you have questions about the way an item is being photographed. Identifying a problem before the shooting is avoiding a problem.

True-to-life vignette

Setting up the Stack'n' Store Bins for a photograph for a toy catalog was a painstakingly long process. The client, who lived in another state, had chosen not to be at the photography session. Every bin had to be assembled, then correctly propped. To compound this, the photograph was to include a child playing with a toy train in front of the bins. No one was more surprised than we were to learn that the client was greatly upset when the photo arrived. The bins were not stacked correctly! The client had manufactured special wooden dowels with which to assemble the bins in a totally uncommon manner. Trying to explain the way the bins actually went together over the phone was impossible. What's more, all scheduled photography was complete, and there was precious little time to reshoot the photograph. The solution: The client took a photo showing how the bins should look. We used both the original photo and an insert of the client's photo to show that the bins could be used in a variety of ways. A potential problem was turned into a benefit, but the importance of the client being present at the photography session was clearly demonstrated.

SEPARATIONS

Most consumer catalogs are printed in four colors. But how does one piece of film, the four-color photo, become the four pieces of film necessary to print? The step between the four-color photography and the actual printing of the catalog is the separations.

There are several ways to separate, but for catalogers this is the most economical method. Four-color transparencies are placed in front of the filters in an electronic device often called a scanner, which screens out color. A red filter produces a negative recording–a red separation negative—of all the red light reflected or transmitted from the photo. When a positive is made from this negative, the silver in the film corresponds to areas that do not contain red, but hold the other two colors of light, blue and green. The negative has taken away the red, leaving blue and green, called cyan. A green filter leaves red and blue, called magenta. The blue filter records all blue, leaving red and green, which produces yellow.

The three colors, cyan, magenta, and yellow, plus black, are the four primary colors used by printing presses for color reproduction. The separator produces a piece of film for each of the four colors. Using plates from the film, the printer can reproduce each of the four colors on press.

The scanner used in separations provides speed, economy, accuracy, and sharpness. Yet it has one major drawback: it separates exactly what it sees. If the color in the photograph is inaccurate, the color in the separation will be as well. Although the scanner can be programmed to make color adjustments in the four primary colors, it changes the overall look and can affect areas you might prefer left alone. So take care to provide the separator with photos that truly represent the products depicted.

Viewing separations

The film itself, whether in negative or positive form, is not the form in which you view the separations. To do this, you can select from a variety of proofing systems.

• *Color keys* are the least desirable and least expensive proofing system. Each color is shown on a relatively thick acetate sheet, one on top of the other. One advantage is that color keys do show exactly how much of each color will be printed. But because of the thickness of the acetate, colors may be somewhat distorted from the way they will actually print. Color keys are best left to those who have been reading separations for years and know how to compensate for the inadequacies of this form of proofing.

• *Chromalins* are a relatively inexpensive and often used method. Colored powders, which represent the colors to be printed, are laminated to sensitized film. Even though the film is composed of four different sheets, it is very thin and appears to be in one piece. One color lies on top of another, as it will when printed, giving a relatively accurate indication of how the finished piece will print. But because heavy paper stock to which the powders adhere is often whiter than the printing stock, the final printed piece may appear yellower (if the paper has a yellowish tint) or in some way different from the chromalin. Trans keys (also called transfer keys) are a similar method made by a different manufacturer. Some chromalins can now adhere directly to the printing stock.

• *Matchprints,* one of the newest printing methods and not yet available from all separators, follow the same principle as chromalins, but they always adhere directly to the printing stock. Colors are therefore truer to the final printed piece than with either chromalins or trans keys.

• *Progressive proofs (or "progs"),* the most expensive proofing method, are actual printed proofs of the film (separations), which show as accurately as possible how the printed catalog will look when it goes to press.

Each progressive proof comes in a "set," which shows exactly how much ink there will be per color on separately proofed pages. This helps check color accuracy. For instance, if you think that the separator has not made the red heavy enough, you need only look at the sheet containing the red to determine if this is true.

But progs are printed on a sheetfed press, and you will most likely be printing on a web press. Since a sheetfed press prints more slowly than a web press, inks are trapped differently, resulting in a slightly different look from the web-printed piece. Also, the paper used to print the progressive proof must be the same as that for the printing. Too often a progressive proof is printed on a heavier, whiter stock, so that the image produced in the proofing stage cannot possibly be duplicated on press.

Choosing the right proofing system depends on your budget, your separator's capabilities, and the requirements of the printer. Work closely with your suppliers, and be sure to let them know your needs and desires. Above all, don't be afraid to ask questions. Separations are one of the most confusing aspects of production. The more questions you ask, the more you'll learn and the better the overall job will be.

Buying separations

Generally speaking, separators separate and printers print. But some printing plants have excellent separation facilities. How will you know when to use the printer's separator and when to use an independent firm?

Get samples, price estimates, and recommendations from your printer's separation facility just as you would from an outside separator. Also, bluntly ask the printing salesperson how the company's separations compare with those of outside sources. Some separation facilities located within printing plants are there for last-minute changes only, while others are excellent.

Buying separations from your printer eliminates possible confusion over what the printer needs from the separator. Still, since not all printers have separation facilities that are as good as outside sources, you may choose to purchase your separations from one source and your printing from another. Ask your separator to talk with the printer's production manager. If necessary, have the production manager visit the separation plant. It is in their best interest (and yours) to know each other's equipment and how they can make the best use of it. Contrary to stories of animosity ("The color's not right because the separator's film was inferior"), true professionals work well together; they know it is the only way to get the best results.

Your separator and printer should agree on the following:

1 Screen specifications
2 Dot angle
3 Density
4 Percentage of overall coverage
5 Ink hues and order of color laydown
6 Form in which film is to be received
 - negative or positive
 - reader's or printer's flats
 - plate-ready or intermediate
 - progs, color keys, chromalins/trans keys, matchprints
7 Press layout
8 Scheduling
9 Paper being used

Assemblies

Assemblies, the actual cutting and piecing together of the original, same-size photos or transparencies of your product, are cheaper by far than individual separations. In this process, all transparencies are arranged in position exactly as they are to appear on a spread, then held in this position in an acetate sleeve. In a combination fashion and nonfashion catalog, any fashion photos that were shot random focus are duped (duplicates to the correct size are made) and incorporated into the assemblies. The separator then separates one spread at a time, rather than one photo at a time. The disadvantage is that the scanner will see the overall color, rather than treating each photo as a separate element. Some trueness of color will invariably be lost, but cost will be held to a minimum.

Even though the reproduction quality of individually separated photos is superior to that of assemblies, individual separation is seldom used for mail order catalogs because of its high cost. If the cost of separating one photo is $150, to separate each of the ten photos in a spread individually would cost $1,500. But because the scanner views an assembly as one photo, the cost of separating the same ten-photo spread as an assembly would be only slightly higher than $150. Even with the extra expense to prepare the assemblies and any necessary dupes, you can easily see why assemblies are generally favored over individual separations.

The exception to this is a fashion catalog, which is almost always separated on an individual-photo basis. Since fashion photos are usually shot random focus, the cost of duplicating and assembling every photo in the catalog would most likely exceed any savings generated by using assemblies. Accuracy of color is also extremely important when dealing with clothing.

Price your catalog both ways. Be aware of the color discrepancies that can occur with assemblies and decide whether budget or absolutely perfect color is more important. Remember, the consumer needs to know how the product looks, but may not remember the exact shade of, say, a brass pot. As long as the color of the reproduction is not misleading, the consumer will be happy with a purchase whether it is an exact color match or not except, of course, in the case of clothing.

Paste-up, mechanical, finished art

A confusing aspect of the advertising business, even to those already in it, is that so many words are interchangeable. Paste-up, mechanical art, finished art, and "boards" *all have the same meaning.* For four-color work, that process is the final assembly of position art and type, ready for the separator. The type and position-only photostats are pasted to a stable surface, such as illustration board, in the exact position in which they will appear when printed.

The photostats, often called "stats," are inexpensive, nonreproducible black-and-white photos. They are pasted on the boards to show the separator the position and cropping of the photos to be separated. Usually the edges of the stats are wavy or "trapped" and the words "for pos only" are written across the top of the stat. Let the filmmaker know that the stats are for position only and are not to be used as art. A tissue overlay attached to the mechanicals will indicate any nonphoto areas to be colored, such as key letters or colored borders.

BINDING AND MAILING

After your beautiful catalog is printed, you must get it in the mail. This is where a bindery (or lettershop) comes in. Often, the bindery is part of the printer's facilities. When it is not, catalogs must be shipped to the bindery, and they must arrive in the condition in which they left the printer: flat and undamaged.

- Find out exactly how the lettershop wishes to receive the materials. This includes how the catalog is to be physically packed. For instance, should it be banded on skids or in cartons?
- Does the bindery agree with all your specifications? If not, what is its preference? Consider having the printer talk directly to the bindery, but be in on the conversation so that you are aware of any expenses that may be incurred.
- Make sure every shipment includes a detailed packing slip. Mark cartons legibly. For example:

  Description: XYZ Catalog, Spring 1985

  Source Code Format: Code 123

  Contents: 10,000 catalogs

  Version: Cover A

Basic information for the bindery

Regardless of where it is physically located, the bindery's (lettershop's) responsibility is to sort, bag, and tie the catalogs to qualify for all possible postage deductions according to the rules and regulations of the post office. Your responsibility is to see that the bindery has the necessary information to do its job right. Be explicit on each of the next six matters.

1 Mailing date (or dates if a scheduled series) and any changes in the schedule.
   - Quantity to be mailed per mailing date.
   - Codes for each list and/or list segment.
   - Any changes in printed material: Is there more than one cover? Does a certain segment require an outer envelope? Or a different order form?

2 Total number of catalogs to be mailed. Are leftover catalogs to be mailed? If not, are they to be stored or sent to you or your agency by mail or truck? Nobody is happy if the lettershop mails surplus catalogs to do you a favor and as a result you are left with too few catalogs to fill such needs as inquiries from magazine ads.

3 Where and by what method catalogs are to be shipped.

4 What postage format to use. If indicia, who supplies the permit number, you or the bindery?

5 Description, source code format, and expected arrival date of mailing lists. Identify the contents on the outside of the package. Also, indicate the quantity contained within.

6 Where the address label is to be positioned.

Remember, both your printer and your lettershop want everything to go smoothly. The more information they have before they receive your catalog, the better they can do the job. When all the team members have the same information, teamwork can be one of the most important factors in a successful mailing. For a discussion of postage costs, refer to the section on bulk-rate mailing in "Other Factors Affecting Profitability," in Part 10.

3602s

Good lettershops automatically provide you with a copy of service form 3602 from the U.S. Postal Service. Two copies of this form are completed: one for you and one for the post office. This is your receipt for entry of mail into the postal system. It includes the following information.

1 *The date the catalog was taken to the post office.* Lettershops have been known to misrepresent actual mail dates, showing instead the date the client wants to see. The 3602 prevents this from happening. But it is important to note that the 3602 shows the date the catalog goes into the post office. The date it leaves depends on the efficiency of the individual bulk-rate center and its current work load.

2 *The cost of postage.* Since you most likely prepaid the postage to your lettershop, check the 3602s against the amount you paid. Sometimes the mailing quantity changes slightly and there can be discrepancies or oversights on the part of the lettershop.

3 *The number of catalogs mailed.* Because spoilage can occur during label application, this figure may differ from the one your lettershop provides. They are not trying to be devious; inaccuracies often occur quite honestly, so use the figures on the 3602s, not those of the lettershop.

4 *The number of catalogs in each mail category.* This information will be most helpful in future analysis of response rates and average orders from carrier route, five-digit presort, and residual bulk third-class mailings. This can also be an additional check on postage costs.

Make it a point to get 3602s from your lettershop. They are a valuable receipt!

Part 5
THE CREATIVE AREA

CATALOG DESIGN: FORMAT AND LAYOUT

Once you achieve an understanding of both the potential and the limitations of catalog production, you are ready to let those creative juices flow. You want the best-looking, highest-quality catalog possible. But, remember that you must account for every dollar you spend. Will those fancy rounded edges pay for themselves? Or will they look great, but fail to generate added sales?

The direct marketing catalog professionals you hire or have on staff also want a great-looking catalog. Their challenge is to design, layout, and write a visually commanding, articulate, *and* sales-oriented catalog for which there is no preset formula. A definitive idea of the targeted market and the budget are two important steps toward success. Understanding the creative language of artists is another.

Format

The format of the book is the shape and size and overall general approach including such elements as typeface, quality of paper, and, of course, design. For instance, a mail order catalog can have a magazine format. Another important design element is the size of the catalog. Some people think that a smaller-size catalog will wind up on top of a pile of larger books. Others prefer oversized books, which they think will bury the smaller catalog. Unusual catalog sizes have become increasingly popular as the number of catalogs has multiplied and as printing capabilities have expanded to allow for new cost-effective formats without wasting paper.

Work with your printer, your art staff, or your creative agency to determine the size for your product line idea. Think in terms of the production options that are economically viable and the importance of standing apart from the competition. Square, tall, oblong, side-stitched 8⅛″ × 11″ are some of the more exciting choices. Then choose the format that best suits your merchandise. If yours is a fashion catalog and has tall, long photos, you'll probably opt for a tall and narrow format so that the artist who lays out your catalog will have the right-size space to show off clothing to its best advantage. Conversely, in a square catalog, photos must be smaller and do not allow fashion to be shown to its best.

The design concept

Choose your design concept carefully. It must be adaptable to potential changes in consumer buying habits. Too many graphics in your very first catalog may lock you into a format that will not pay for itself. Begin with a simple concept. More complex adaptations can be tested in the future when the catalog has paid for itself and funds are available for experimentation. Don't be caught in the ego trap of designing a catalog that's great for showing off to country club friends, but hasn't a chance of realizing a profit.

Here are a few good rules to remember:

1 Make sure the design represents your company.

2 Work with a professional direct marketing artist who knows the difference between award-winning and sales-generating graphics.

3 Select a design that will fit your budget; it can always be adapted to something more elaborate in the future.

4 Select a design that is adaptable to changing consumer needs.

Finding a design concept that is both unique and versatile enough to withstand changes in marketing strategies usually takes many hours of brainstorming. For one of our clients, an importer of foreign goods, our concept was to use postcards showing actual products and a foreign stamp. We used valuable selling space primarily to sell products, but also incorporated foreign flavor through the use of the canceled stamps. In this same catalog, we also showed telexes written by the company's buyers. Their humorous stories added credibility to our imported-goods story and reinforced the image of the importer as a friendly company that went to great trouble to supply its customers with imported goods (see Figure 5-1).

Your company image

Before you sit down with your designers, know your potential market and the image you wish to convey. Are you targeting an affluent market used to the better things in life? Then your design must reflect this life-style. Perhaps you want high-quality paper, contemporary graphics, and bold and colorful visuals. Or do your products appeal more to middle America, an older audience with less income, determined to buy only products that represent true value? Then think "Norman Rockwell." Use lesser quality

FIGURE 5-1
By reproducing telexes from buyers in far-off places, Pier 1's catalog played up the company image of going to any lengths to find special merchandise. © 1983 Pier 1 Imports and reprinted with permission.

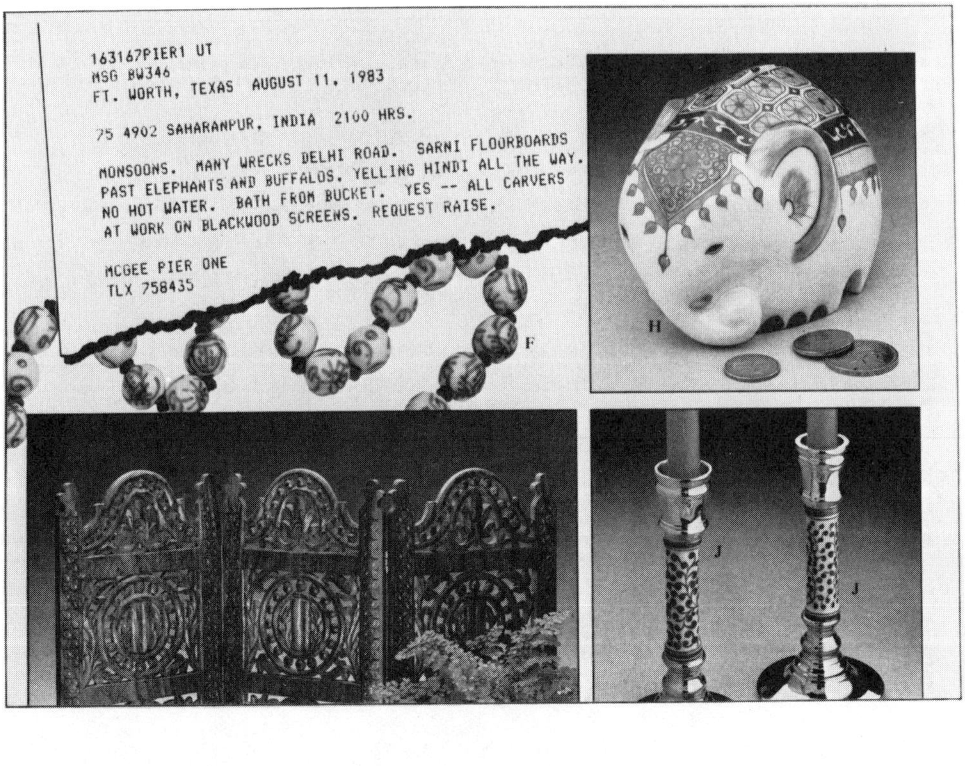

paper, but not a low grade. Show the benefit of the merchandise (for instance, a mother receiving a gift from her child bought via mail order) and use clear photos with callouts (lines of copy describing features of the product) that spell out the quality and value of the product.

Layout

Layout is the rendering of pages to show the position and space allocation of photography and copy and to indicate the general feeling or "flow" of the catalog.

During the layout stage, the cataloger should provide general input and make desired changes in the space allocation or copy to avoid later costs for photo resizing, type resetting, and so forth.

Layouts may be in four-color or black and white. At least two spreads should be in color, so that the cataloger can better visualize the actual product. The remainder of the layouts can be done in black and white with color indicators. Since it takes less time to produce a black-and-white layout, this can be an important cost saver.

Working with artists

Give your artists as much information as possible about the merchandise they are expected to portray. Include:

- *The size of the item,* so the product can be positioned and propped correctly.
- *Unusual features,* so the item can be shown "in use," if applicable, or alone, if necessary for photographic effect.
- *Previous sales history,* to determine if the space allocated should be enlarged or decreased.
- *The price of the item.* If no previous sales history is available, this can allow the artists to give higher priced items more dominance.
- *Featured items in each spread.* The reasons for selecting merchandise may not be known to the layout person. Let him or her know why some items might be more important than others.

Feel free to express both compliments and constructive criticism, but be specific. Make both your positive and negative feelings plainly understood. What don't you like? Do you have another catalog that may give the artist a better idea of what you like? Are the photographic areas too small? Does the fashion, as depicted, seem lifeless? Most artists welcome input and, if possible, will act on it. But be willing to listen to what they have to say as well. Let their experience help you create a professional catalog—one to which customers will eagerly respond—the first time or the fiftieth.

Color

Before beginning the layout, it is important to understand how the ink will flow and where pages will be in relationship to each other on press. To select background color compatible with the ink flow, the artist must see a signature from the printer. For example, it could be disastrous to make pages 5 and 6 red and pages 11 and 12 white. If page 5 actually were to be printed next to page 12, the ink from page 5 would flow onto page 12, producing a pinkish page instead of the desired white one.

Balancing color in layouts for printing is an area too often overlooked by artists. Some compromises may have to be made in the position of merchandise, but proper layouts can minimize on-press problems.

Props and backgrounds

Props are necessary to establish size relationship. Even when written size specifications are provided, consumers still tend to order merchandise on the basis of a preconceived desired size. Propping allows the potential buyer to know, at a glance, if the item is the desired size; this reduces returns.

Colorful backgrounds can put life into a catalog and emphasize a season. Red and green are naturals for the winter holidays; pastels for spring. But remember that a product will often take on some of the background color. Think twice before shooting a white vase on a red background. The red could give the vase a pinkish tint. Because consumers tend to buy what they see, you could have orders for a pink vase, when in reality you are offering the vase only in white. Also, use colored type carefully. It can distract the customer from the merchandise.

Mood shots and overly propped photography don't belong in mail order. Customers should be able to see the merchandise clearly.

To avoid loss of time and misunderstanding, the display of the merchandise and the necessary propping should be clearly illustrated on the layouts. The layout artist should contact the photographer before actually beginning to choose props and backgrounds. Considerable expense can be avoided by using backgrounds and props available in the photographer's studio.

Eye flow

Through graphic illustration and subtly controlled layouts, the consumer can be subconsciously encouraged to see every item on every page. Designs should flow effortlessly across a spread, with intermittent "hot" spots (through the use of color or product space allocation) that grab the customer's attention. This can be accomplished through a variety of methods. One of the most common is a line drawn graphically from the left side to the right side of the page.

In Figure 5-2 the line is a bold banner of color, appropriate to the merchandise and mood of a children's catalog. The banner pulls products together and visually invites the customer to view each product. In this example, photos are also cut into each other, effectively forcing the eye to look at more than one photo. The large building block set creates an attention-getting hot spot.

A more subtle version of eye flow is illustrated in Figure 5-3. Here the artist uses the actual products to encourage customers to see and, it is

FIGURE 5-2
A color band at the top of the spread pulls products together and visually invites the customer to view every product. © 1981 Wonders Inc. and reprinted with permission.

hoped, buy every item. The garden markers point downward toward the book and the smoker grill. The hand turning the lobster on the grill leads the eye to the strawberry pot. The props in the strawberry pot redirect the eye back to the smoker grill, where the napkin forces the eye to the binoculars. Here the position of the binoculars and prop direct the eye to the croquet set. The hand above the croquet set leads the eye to the trowel, which moves the eye to the basket. The pea pod sculpture forces the eye to look at both the basket and the croquet set. In every case, the customer's eye is to be directed to another product. This is a good example of effective eye-flow technique.

When using eye flow, make sure that the products and the models face into the spread. If they face off the page, the potential buyer will

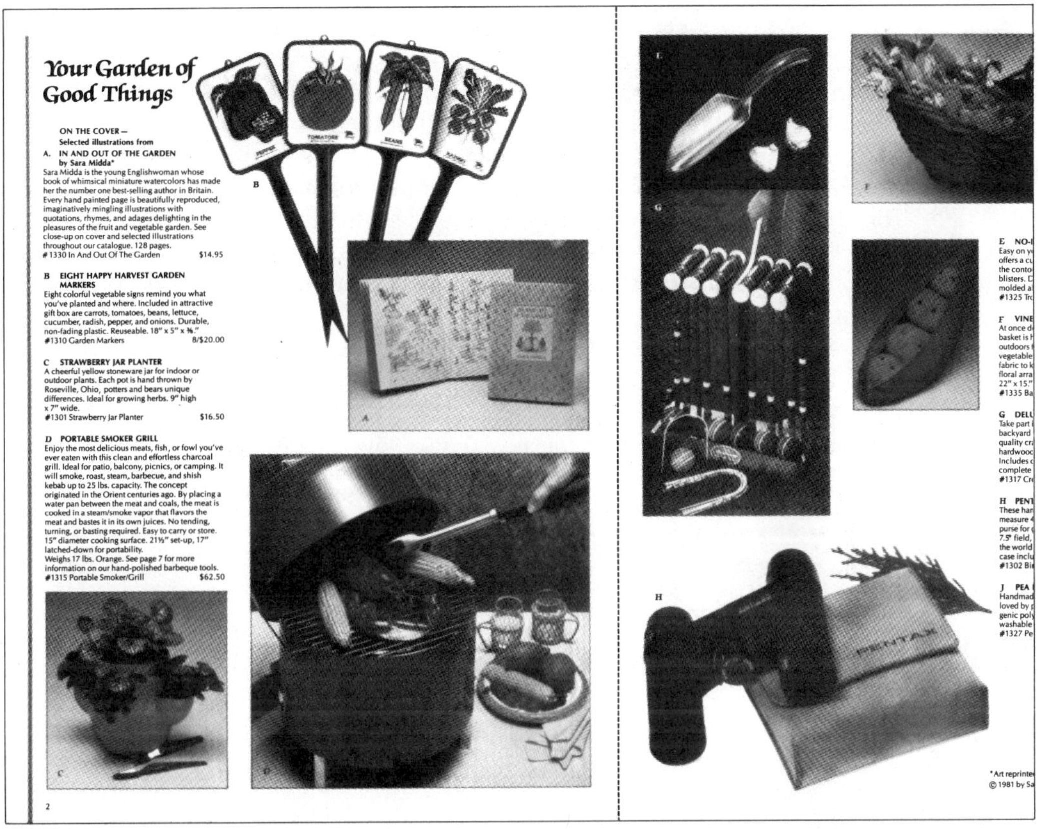

FIGURE 5-3
On this spread, products are effectively positioned to point in directions that encourage eye flow and multiple purchases. © 1983 David Kay Inc. and reprinted with permission.

subconsciously be encouraged to turn the page, possibly resulting in lost sales.

Space allocation

The space allocated to a particular product undoubtedly is related to the sales generated for that product (see square-inch analysis in the chapter on catalog analysis in Part 9). Therefore, an understanding of how space should be allocated is necessary. Here are some pointers:

1. Allocation of space should not be based *solely* on sales of one product. In a split test on space allocation, Spiegel Inc. discovered that increasing the space allocation of one clothing style by 50 percent increased its sales only 36 percent. But the reduction in space of other styles in the same spread resulted in less than proportionate loss of sales. The result was that overall demand for merchandise in the spread rose considerably.

2. When everything is treated equally, nothing is really featured. The illusion of dominance can be created by visually increasing the space for

one or two products. They do not actually take up any more space or dominate the spread, but appear to because the other products on that page have had their space allocations minimally reduced. This can have the effect of increasing overall sales without making one product pay for a large increase in its space allocation.

3. When one color of an assortment is dominant, that color generally outsells all other colors. If one color is to be featured, select the color that has the greatest sales potential. The one exception to this rule is when color selection is a major sales point; then showing the entire assortment is preferred.

4. When one product is to be featured, the product should be one with broad appeal. If the product has a poor sales history, increasing its size will generally not benefit overall sales on the page. Unless a significant increase in sales has already been realized through an increase in space, giving it even more space is of no benefit. In fact, it can have a negative sales effect.

COPY

A great-looking layout and effective design elements can help guide customers through your catalog, but won't motivate them to buy. That's the copywriter's job. But descriptions alone don't sell. The copywriter must convince the customer to buy the product.

Effective copy

Here are some pointers for writing effective catalog copy.

1 It's not what you write, but how you write that makes a sale. Be scintillating and motivating. Remember, today's audience is often in a hurry. If your copy doesn't immediately grab and hold the customer's attention, other waiting catalogs will!
2 Be direct. Make sentences short and enthusiastic. Don't generalize. Get to the point. Unlike many space ads and most direct mail packages, you are working within a severely limited space frame. Learn to be a nitpicker and you will get the sell across quicker.
3 State benefits, not fluff. Benefits, substantiated by facts, sell products. A noted copywriter once wrote:

    Tell me quick and tell me true
    or else, my love, to heck with you.
    Less how this product came to be,
    more what the darn thing does for me.

   Think of customers asking themselves, "What can this item do for me?" and "What makes it unique?" "How will it improve the quality of my life?" If your copy is powerful enough to convince the customers that they will be prettier, richer, happier, healthier, and so on, you've practically ensured the sale.
4 Suggest ways of using the item that the consumer would perhaps never consider. For instance, we found that a terry cloth turban, normally used to protect hair while applying makeup, could convert into a shoulder carryall. We included this idea in the copy. The surprise element ("What a great idea!"), coupled with the extra selling point, made the product a bestseller.
5 Encourage the potential customer to act in a specific manner. For example, "Buy one for a friend and one for yourself!"
6 Don't make the product sound too good. You'll not only get returns, but you may lose a valuable customer.
7 Make your copy flow. It should have rhythm and sound pleasant to the ear.
8 Don't be too clever. By the time the reader deciphers your meaning, the momentum will be broken. Be creative, not elusive.
9 Read the copy without the photo. Does it demand attention, arouse interest, and call for action? If so, congratulations! You didn't use the picture as a crutch. Photos can add life to your words, but even the most vibrant photo can't make a product come alive. The copywriter must do that, and make the consumer want to own the product, too.
10 Don't forget cross-sell. Does one product on the spread go well with another? Then state it in the copy!
11 Use captions, especially to describe the hidden features of a product and emphasize special details (see Figure 5-4).
12 Let consumers know if a product is exclusive to the catalog.

B.
ESPN
THE TOTAL SPORTS NETWORK
Lightweight cooler straps on back or hangs over shoulder!
ESPN
C.
B. BACK PACK SOFT COOLER Don't let bulky coolers cramp your style. Waterproof, heavy duty nylon soft cooler travels light on your back or over your shoulders. Keeps food and drink refrigerator fresh for 24 hours! Just add ice or icepack. Foam insulated, hi-tech rustproof hardware. In red with white panel, white back and shoulder straps. Great for all sports events, picnics, hiking and bicycling. 14"H x 13"W x 6"D.
#313 Soft Cooler $24.95
C. FRISBEE The authentic frisbee with a new twist! Red with white ESPN logo. Double your fun—buy 2 and save $2!
#402 Frisbee $3.50 ea 2 for $5.00
CREDIT CARD HOLDERS CAN ORDER THEIR SELECTIONS BY PHONE
Use our Toll-Free Number, 24 hours a day, 7 days a week
1-800-544-1000, Operator #1
ESPN TM
13

FIGURE 5-4
Caption used to highlight a special feature. © 1983 ESPN TM and reprinted with permission.

13 Answer every question the customer is likely to ask (see Figure 3-2, the Merchandise Information Form). If you are not an expert on the product, ask questions and find out the answers. Otherwise, the information necessary to convey the product's benefits will not be in the copy and sales will be lost.

14 Get in the right seasonal mood. In catalogland, if it's July, it must be Christmas! Even if you are still recovering from 100° temperatures on the Fourth of July, play Christmas music to help you get in the mood for tantalizing holiday copy. Make a file of advertisements that pertain to the season, holiday, or special event (wedding, graduation, and so on). By speaking the language of the season, you will increase sales.

15 Always turn to your Merchandise Information Form for help. Does the product have an interesting story behind it? Play it up and give the customer even more reason to buy.

16 Consider writing the copy in a frankly personal manner. Figure 5-5 makes the reader feel part of a family that cares about his or her well-being.

The three good Ps

Determining the exact copy approach to take depends on the three "good" Ps: personality, people, and product. (The three "bad" Ps—or at least the most costly Ps—in the catalog marketing business are paper, printing, and postage.)

Know the personality of your catalog, the identity you want it to project. Just as Bloomingdale's invokes an image of refined elegance, your catalog should be readily defined in a category. Write the copy to reflect this personality.

Know the people to whom you are writing in terms of gender, age, income level, marital status, and life-style. What is important to them? What do they want from life? Love? Health? Success? Status? Financial security? The copywriter's job is to pinpoint customers' most prominent needs.

Joe Sacco, writing in the January 1983 issue of *Madison Avenue Magazine* (p. 31), states that "sensitivity to the needs, problems, moods, experiences, [and] language of others stands highest among human faculties. It is perhaps the most difficult state of awareness to achieve." He speaks of two copywriters, one of whom is me-oriented, the other not, and of how they approach selling a new product—a disposable insulin syringe featuring a new sharp needle.

The "me" copywriter has no desire to explore the world nor any curiosity about the person behind the customer. The quick and simple ways to express the benefits of the needle that come to mind are "hurts less" and "the gentle way."

The not-me copywriter, on the other hand, reads books on the subject of diabetes and observes that the word "sharp" pops up frequently in interviews with prospective customers. "No injection can be comfortable,

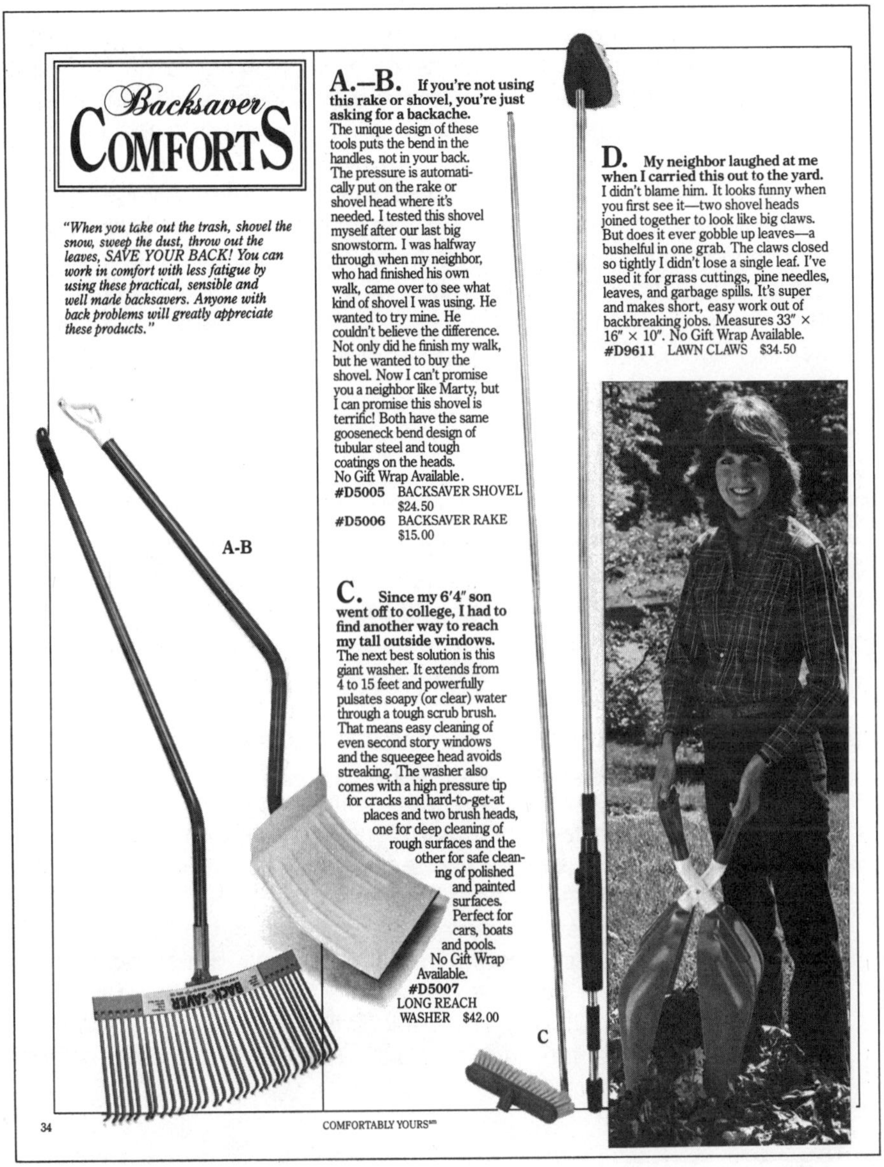
Backsaver COMFORTS
"When you take out the trash, shovel the snow, sweep the dust, throw out the leaves, SAVE YOUR BACK! You can work in comfort with less fatigue by using these practical, sensible and well made backsavers. Anyone with back problems will greatly appreciate these products."
A.–B. If you're not using this rake or shovel, you're just asking for a backache.
The unique design of these tools puts the bend in the handles, not in your back. The pressure is automatically put on the rake or shovel head where it's needed. I tested this shovel myself after our last big snowstorm. I was halfway through when my neighbor, who had finished his own walk, came over to see what kind of shovel I was using. He wanted to try mine. He couldn't believe the difference. Not only did he finish my walk, but he wanted to buy the shovel. Now I can't promise you a neighbor like Marty, but I can promise this shovel is terrific! Both have the same gooseneck bend design of tubular steel and tough coatings on the heads. No Gift Wrap Available.
#D5005 BACKSAVER SHOVEL $24.50
#D5006 BACKSAVER RAKE $15.00
A-B
C. Since my 6′4″ son went off to college, I had to find another way to reach my tall outside windows.
The next best solution is this giant washer. It extends from 4 to 15 feet and powerfully pulsates soapy (or clear) water through a tough scrub brush. That means easy cleaning of even second story windows and the squeegee head avoids streaking. The washer also comes with a high pressure tip for cracks and hard-to-get-at places and two brush heads, one for deep cleaning of rough surfaces and the other for safe cleaning of polished and painted surfaces. Perfect for cars, boats and pools. No Gift Wrap Available.
#D5007 LONG REACH WASHER $42.00
C
D. My neighbor laughed at me when I carried this out to the yard.
I didn't blame him. It looks funny when you first see it—two shovel heads joined together to look like big claws. But does it ever gobble up leaves—a bushelful in one grab. The claws closed so tightly I didn't lose a single leaf. I've used it for grass cuttings, pine needles, leaves, and garbage spills. It's super and makes short, easy work out of backbreaking jobs. Measures 33″ × 16″ × 10″. No Gift Wrap Available.
#D9611 LAWN CLAWS $34.50
34
COMFORTABLY YOURS℠

FIGURE 5-5
Chatty copy puts readers at ease and pulls them into a catalog "family." © 1984 Comfortably Yours SM and reprinted with permission.

but a sharper needle makes it easier." This copywriter determines the major product claim to be "sharpness" and the benefit, "unequalled injection ease," with which the customer can enthusiastically identify.

Exploring the outside world and discovering what is important to the person to whom you are writing isn't easy, but the success of your catalog is worth the effort. Think of this awareness as a photograph being developed in a darkroom. The more you learn about the person, the clearer and more focused the person becomes. But if you open the door too soon, the photograph will not develop. So, do your research. Talk to your merchandise buyers. They know the audience for which they are buying. Study any market research available on your company's targeted or existing market. You'll soon discover a successful approach.

Finally, know your product. That's where the Merchandise Information Form (Figure 3-2) can be useful. Properly filled out, it can save phone calls, money, time, and frustration. Even more important, it provides the vital information necessary to make that sale. Make sure the merchandise buyer fills in the form completely and sends you a copy. You should both keep the form on file for when such questions arise as fabric content, size, color, and so forth.

Master the three good Ps and your copy will make you, and your company's accountant, proud.

Headlines

A headline must immediately attract the customer's attention, convey a benefit, and offer incentive to read on. Remember that self-interest is a strong motivator. Consider using such key words as "free," "new," "exclusive." Whatever you do, don't be negative. Think positively and so will your audience.

Words like "bonus" or "free" get attention in headlines because they appeal to consumers' natural desire to save money. If you're offering a special value, state it clearly and boldly.

"New" is a magic word, too. People still want to be "the first on the block" with that new electronic gadget, fashionable dress, or toddler toy. Use "new" to help a customer who receives your catalog regularly to quickly spot items not seen there before.

If an item is exclusive to your catalog, say so in the headline. Don't hide this important selling feature in the body copy. Better yet, display a company logo by your headline (see Figure 5-6). Not only will you call attention to the product, but (1) you'll look like a forerunner among the competition because you have products not available to other companies

FIGURE 5-6
Eddie Bauer uses its famous logo to highlight exclusives. © 1982 Eddie Bauer® and reprinted with permission.

Eddie Bauer®
NEW! GOOSE DOWN SLIPPER SOX
Designed as the ideal complement to our lady's goose down robes, these light-as-a-whisper Slipper Sox will keep your feet warm and cozy. Bauer Goose Down insulation is quilted in vertical tubes. Sole is tough, long-wearing Cordura® nylon. An excellent choice for wearing around the house or cabin. Hand or machine wash and tumble dry.
Sizes. Women's S(5-6½), M(7-8½), L(9-10½).
#0746B Colors. Navy or Wine to match #0745B Button-Front Robe. Fabric is nylon taffeta...$19.95
#0699B Colors. Rose, Light Blue or Salmon to match #0439B Wrap Robe and #0766B Zip-Front Housecoat. Fabric is a blend of polyester, nylon and cotton...$19.95

and (2) you'll satisfy a human need to have something not available to everyone else.

Copy is the most personal touch your catalog has with its customers. Make the lead-in easily identifiable with the product. Don't make lead-ins so clever or cute that the customer misses the point and has to hunt for the corresponding copy block. You could easily lose the reader's attention—and the sale. If customers open your catalog, they have, in essence, let you into their home. Your copy should convey the warm, friendly, yet never boring attitude of a welcome guest who's there to enchant and inform. Don't let your customers down and your catalog will always be welcome.

Sales tools

Such sales tools as toll-free numbers, endorsements, and catalog owners' letters are important incentives to buy that too often are simply dropped in at the last minute. Figure 5-2 shows one way attention was drawn to the toll-free number by incorporating a complementary design element.

Endorsements from satisfied customers can say more about a product than any amount of professional copy. Use them liberally and creatively. A standard method is to sprinkle them throughout the catalog, in which case they should be short and to the point. A potential customer should be able to get the message at a glance. We have most effectively used them as attention-getting headlines.

Quotes from famous authors can also be used to establish credibility for first-time catalogs. Figure 5-7 not only succeeds in doing this, but also ties in with the name of the catalog ("Wonders") in describing the wonder of being a child. This example also illustrates how a family portrait, combined with an honest, open letter, can add personality and believability to a catalog. Although valuable inside front cover space should generally not be used for the catalog owner's letter, sometimes, as in this case, the story behind the catalog is so important that the letter belongs where it will immediately be seen by the customer. Before running endorsements or testimonials, read about pertinent FTC regulations in Part 12.

The catalog letter

One of the best ways to establish credibility for your catalog is to include a personal letter. In this manner, you can let customers know something about the people behind the catalog. Consider showing photos. People like identifying with someone they "know."

Explain how the catalog came to be (if it's a new one), what makes it different, and what outstanding qualities it may possess (for instance, information about a special customer service representative).

If the catalog is an established one, give some history and accentuate the number of years it has been in business.

Use the letter to highlight particular products and trends within the catalog: "Customers tell us they've looked everywhere for a stepping stool that's lightweight, compact, and sturdy, all to no avail. Well, we've

"If I had influence with the good fairy who ... presides over ... children, I should ask that her gift to each child ... be a sense of wonder so indestructible that it would last throughout life... "*

Rachel Carson
A Sense of Wonder

Thank you for sharing our first WONDERS catalog.

Our parent company, Environments, Inc., has been producing successful catalogs of toys and other educational materials for schools throughout the country for eleven years. Our customers know they will receive only the best - and that their orders will be handled quickly and efficiently.

It has been our dream to present a collection of fine classic toys for the home. We learned after having our own child five years ago how difficult it is to find things as special as she is. We understand the need for assurance that a plaything is of superior quality, and that it will bring many hours of fun and discovery.

What feelings about children guided our selection of these few toys from the thousands that we reviewed? We let Rachel Carson and others speak for us in the quotations throughout our catalog. We do hope you enjoy it, but most of all, our wish for you this season is that you and the children in your life experience the joy of sharing a gift of wonder.

Beecher Hoogenboom, President
WONDERS, INC.

Irene and Beecher Hoogenboom with daughter Caroline

P.S. Please remember that you can be confident in your gift selections. We assure you of the quality, safety and age-suitability of these toys.

2A ***The House that dreams are built on.*** Our limited edition classic Plantation is magnificent. Step up onto the gracious verandah and through the stately columns. Turn the brass doorknob, and enter the world of enchanted play! See the beautifully designed interior on page 20, so spacious that it invites many hours of furniture arranging and Southern hospitality. This unique doll house is very sturdy and playable, and ready to move into when you take it out of the box: all wood construction, completely assembled, painted, and wallpapered, with carpeted stairs. We're happy to be able to offer a doll house of such durablility, craftsmanship, and careful attention to detail. Unfortunately, there are only 48 of these houses available, a quantity so limited that we would not have catalogued it had we not thought it so perfect. Six rooms, 1" to 1' scale; 27" high × 26" wide × 21½" deep. From 6 years.
#313-001WT ***Plantation House*** $185.00 (*)
* This item must be shipped by truck. Add $35.00 for shipping and handling, and disregard shipping and handling charges for all other items on this order being sent to the same address as the Plantation House.

• Reprinted by permission of the Marie Rodell-Frances Collin Literary Agency Copyright © 1956 by Rachel L. Carson

2

FIGURE 5-7
Wonders Inc. used quotes from famous authors and an informal portrait of the company president's family to establish credibility.
© 1981 Wonders Inc. and reprinted with permission.

found one. See page 17 for that wonderfully practical stool that meets all needs!"

The most common location for the owner's letter is on the order form, but no matter where you choose to place it, this essential element should be in every catalog. Even if customers don't read every word, and they seldom do, they want to know that a real person is behind the catalog. It helps to assure potential buyers that someone will receive their order and ensure their satisfaction.

Restate positive attributes like your money-back guarantee, quick delivery, easy toll-free number ordering, and so forth. Put a letter in each catalog. Without it, catalogs can seem cold, barren, and impersonal. Let customers know that this catalog company cares. Just as you would automatically include a P.S. on any well-written direct marketing letter, you should do so in your catalog letter. Use it for something special: a reminder of a particular gift-buying season or one of the pluses of your catalog.

Part 6
GENERATING SALES

SALES FACILITATORS AND INCENTIVES

In the catalog business, there are ways to increase sales, both in numbers and in dollars per order. Some—like bouncebacks, market research forms, and toll-free numbers—are facilitating techniques that take advantage of opportunities inherent in selling by direct mail. Others are outright incentives to buy: premiums, discounts, twofers, and sweepstakes among them.

Bouncebacks

Promotional materials included with outgoing orders, or bouncebacks, are an excellent opportunity to make additional sales without incurring the cost of postage. A customer who is happy with a purchase is often in the mood to buy again. Be sure to provide the opportunity.

Some catalogers include order forms or catalog extras from their current mailing with all outgoing orders. Others preplan an overrun of just the order form and include only that.

One way to almost guarantee that customers will notice your catalog and/or order form when they open the package is to have a savings offer boldly displayed on the front of the catalog or order form. Before going to press, check with your printer on the most cost-effective way to add a special savings message to a portion of your print run.

For those on really tight budgets, consider reprinting current or recent product advertisements. The art for the ad can simply be reproduced by a local printer. Since advertisements printed on white paper may be mistaken for packing material, be sure to use colored paper.

Whatever you decide to include in your outgoing packages, make sure the graphics are bright enough to attract attention. A strong offer, such as savings, a bonus gift, or a sweepstakes, works better than a standard product offer. Be sure to include a method by which customers can respond. And never use a manufacturer's sales sheet. Newcomers are sometimes tempted to use this cost-saving shortcut, but it only confuses the customer and gives your competitors the name of your source.

Market research forms

The market research form is a very effective method for finding out who your customer is. The information obtained often shows a considerably different customer profile from the one suggested by customers' buying patterns.

A market research form can be enclosed as a bounceback, be part of the order form, or be designed to answer specific questions about a particular segment of the market, such as inactive customers, and can be mailed bulk rate. Customers are generally willing to share their thoughts without an incentive (such as a bonus gift). However, if the targeted market is inactive, you might offer a discount coupon on future purchases in return for filling out the questionnaire. In either case, a postage-paid envelope will increase the response.

The market research form should immediately convey to your customers that you need their help to do a better job for them. It should explain that any information they divulge will remain confidential and be used only to improve service. All questions should be concise and to the point.

Solid information on your customers will allow better segmentation of your house list, by product category, sex, and so forth. Category selects are worth extra dollars in rental fees and make your list more appealing, both of which will substantially increase its rental value.

Here are some of the types of information you'll want to solicit:

- Is this a first-time customer?
- Is this a multibuyer?
- If so, how many purchases has this customer made during the last year?
- Does this customer usually purchase more than one item at a time?
- Does this customer buy from other catalogs?
- Which catalogs?
- How long does this customer retain your catalog? (Be sure to give multiple choices ranging from days to years.)
- Is this customer happy with your service?
- If not, why not?
- Do other catalog houses offer services this customer would like to see you offer?
- If so, which services?
- Does more than one person in a household order from the catalog?
- Of which products would the customer like to see more? (List individual categories or be specific.)

You don't want essay answers, so supply multiple-choice answers. For example:

> Do you purchase from other catalogs? ☐ Yes ☐ No
> If so, please check *all* catalogs from which you have recently purchased (last 6 months): 1. ☐ Horchow 2. ☐ Serendipity 3. ☐ Adam York

and so forth. (The catalogs you list depend on the type of merchandise offered in your catalog.)

Such confidential information as the respondent's name, address, salary range, and so on, should be requested on the bottom of the market research form, preceded by a paragraph explaining that the customer need not fill out this part of the form. Experience has shown that most people will fill out the market research form in its entirety if they have the option of remaining anonymous.

However, since geographic data are becoming more and more important in list selection, zip information should be obtained. If you ask for the zip code only in the confidential area of the form, you might not get it. Therefore, place the request for the zip code within the body of the form. Should the respondent choose to remain anonymous, you still capture that all-important zip!

Keep the form simple and as short as possible. Response will be poor to a form that is too long or too complicated. Use typesetting or a word processor so that the form is visually pleasing and easy to read.

Use double spacing between the lines and slightly more space between questions.

Premiums

Defined as a price bonus or award given as an inducement to purchase, premiums can be extraordinarily effective in both raising your average dollar order and reactivating inactive customers. But even if you think a premium is a good idea, always test against a control group first.

Begin by choosing a premium that reflects the merchandise you are now offering. Also, make sure the premium is small and flat enough to fit into standard outgoing packages. Then decide what it should cost and the perceived value. As often as possible, the perceived value of a premium should be two to three times the cost. Such incentives as free postage and handling are less effective than a product, because customers do not immediately perceive the value.

Next, you must decide on the premium dollar requirement. This is done by determining your current average dollar order and the increase you realistically expect from offering a premium. For instance, if your average dollar order is currently $25, can you expect it to increase to $50, or would $40 or even $35 be more realistic? In truth, a $10 increase is seldom accomplished through one step, and there is no set formula for establishing the percentage increase for which to aim. Before you decide that a large difference between the premium dollar requirement and your current average is the method of boosting your sales order, check your sales history (if you have one). It best indicates whether your audience is ready to spend substantially more than it has been spending.

Generally it is more effective to increase the premium requirement dollar and product mix gradually. Let's assume that you decided to aim for a $35 average order. Find out the number of customers already ordering $35 worth of merchandise. Multiply this number by the cost of the premium you wish to offer to determine the cost of the premium for your current $35 customers (assuming customers order consistently from one catalog to the next). Adjust for seasonal differences in response rates.

The next step is to look at the number of customers ordering per price range: the $10–$20 customer, the $20.01–$30 customer, or however you decide to group your customers. Then project the percentage of customers expected to increase their orders to your premium offer requirement, and calculate the cost of the premium per category. (Note: Only history will give you accurate percentages of increase. Use common sense to dictate assumed percentage increases. Obviously, the customers currently ordering in the price range closest to the premium offer dollar requirement will be more willing to spend the required amount and will convert at a higher percentage than those in the lower price ranges.) Add the cost of the premium for current and projected $35 customers for the final projected cost of offering a premium.

By comparing final projected cost with the projected increased profits per price category, you will have a good guide as to whether a premium is your answer to increased profits.

If you are a first-time cataloger and renting lists, consider these other points: Does the list you intend to rent offer premiums now? If so, are those premiums of higher perceived value than yours? Will the list owner allow you to rent the list if you are offering a premium? (Some won't.) And, even if you do attract the customer, effectively increasing your response, did the customer buy only because of the premium, and will he or she remain loyal?

Premiums can be excellent ways to remind old customers of how much they enjoyed ordering from your catalog and to reestablish old buying (from you) patterns.

But be sure to test your premium first. If you offer it to everyone on your list, you won't really know whether an increase in the average order and response is attributable to the premium or to an overall change in the buying habits of your customers.

Discounts

Discounts give a specific percentage off the purchase price. They can be used to thank a new customer for requesting a catalog, to raise an average dollar order, as an incentive to those who order early, or in a wide variety of other ways. A major advantage is that you need not search for the perfect premium, invest in stocking it, and worry whether your customers will be receptive to it.

But discounts can do more than just give your customers "dollars off."

- The coupons in Figure 6-1 helped track consumer response both to Pier 1's new mail order catalog and to its stores. Store managers who had concerns about losing business to the new mail order venture were thrilled when thousands of customers showed up at their stores, coupon in hand. Not only was mail order benefiting the overall company, but the coupon proved conclusively that it was good for the individual stores, too. To avoid partiality, a redeemable mail order coupon was bound into the same catalog.
- Figure 6-2 shows a most creative, clever discount offer. Here Ric Leichtung of Leichtung Inc. gives his customers the chance to save big (up to $607.50 if they have all nine of his past catalogs), gives credibility to his company (celebrating ten years in business), and puts a real value on his catalogs. (Who will ever risk losing money by throwing one away again?)
- Figure 6-3 goes for the big spenders. The Sharper Image's latest offer is a smart adaptation of the bonus-points system made famous by the airlines. This approach encourages consumers who may have planned to buy a similar item through another catalog to shop exclusively with The Sharper Image and gain bonus points as well.

Discount offers can be right for your catalog, too. Be sure to track the results carefully to determine the loyalty of customers acquired

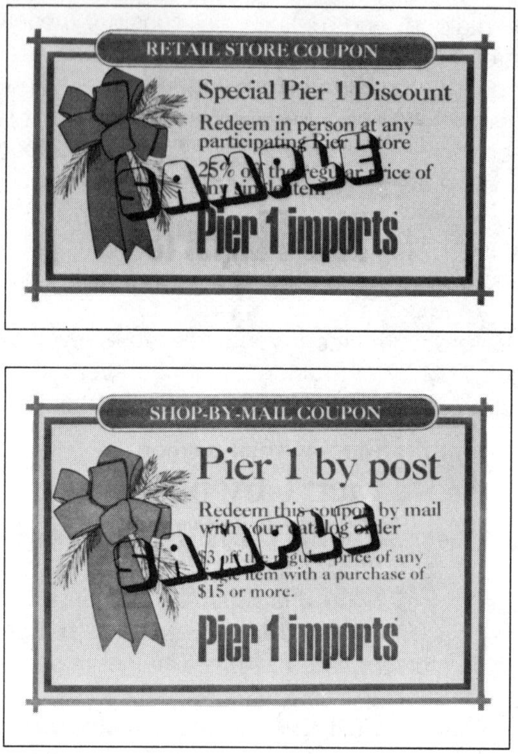

FIGURE 6-1
Pier 1 Imports tracks both store and mail responses through the use of bound-in discount coupons. © 1983 Pier 1 Imports and reproduced with permission.

through this method, as well as the immediate benefits. For maximum effectiveness, tailor the discount program specifically to fit the image of your catalog.

Twofers

Offering a multiple of any item at a discounted price is such a tried-and-true method for increasing sales that no catalog should be without it. Such offers give the customer the incentive to buy and also help raise the average dollar order.

Regardless of your merchandise mix, several items generally take readily to such an offer. Sometimes it's a natural grouping of items, such as bathroom accessories. Offer a "threefer" value that immediately conveys savings to a customer who purchases a tumbler, toothbrush holder, and a soap dish. And tell your customers (for example, in the copy line listing the price) that you're saving them money: "Save $5.00! Buy the set!"

Take a look at leftover merchandise from previous catalogs. Perhaps an item that was a slow seller would be a natural tie-in with a new product in your forthcoming issue. For instance, suppose you are planning to

Will You Sell Me An Old Leichtung Catalog For $250?

This is our 10th anniversary year and so we've come up with a fun idea: we'll buy certain old catalogs from you at the prices shown, until December 31, 1984.

All you do is send in as much of the specified catalog as you still have . . . but you must send in, at least, the whole original front and back cover to be eligible. Photostats or reproductions will not be accepted. For each qualified catalog you send to us, you will be given a credit which can be used as cash to pay for any orders which you may place with us at once or in the future. Here're the only catalogs eligible for credit, along with the amounts. (Only one catalog for each year may be submitted by each person. If you've got two, give one to a friend.)

Ric Leichtung,
LEICHTUNG, INC.

P.S. If you can return one of each, your credit will come to $607.50. Now, when your wife asks why you save all those old catalogs, you'll have a heck of a good answer! All catalogs submitted become our property and will not be returned to you.

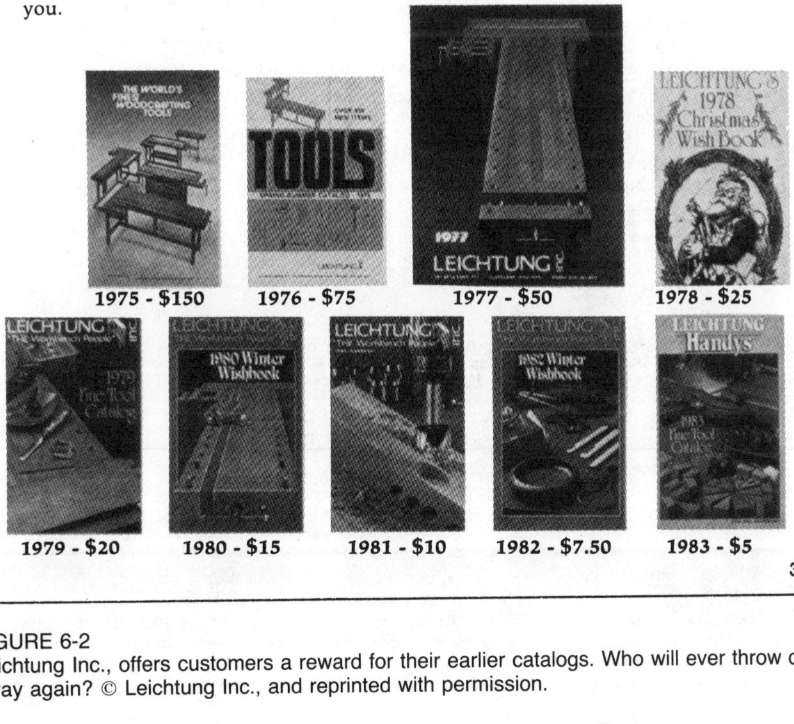

3

FIGURE 6-2
Leichtung Inc., offers customers a reward for their earlier catalogs. Who will ever throw one away again? © Leichtung Inc., and reprinted with permission.

We take our products seriously.

Your satisfaction means everything to us. That's why we choose only quality products. And why I test and use every one personally.

We also offer you a responsive ear. With toll-free customer service lines. Speedy refunds and credits. And now we've instituted the Frequent Buyers™ Reward. To thank the loyal customers who've helped our business continue to grow.

These are some of the principles we believe in. Our reputation with you is more important than any profit. Order from us with confidence. You'll be 100% satisfied—or we'll make it right.

Happy shopping!

Richard

Richard Thalheimer
President

P.S. We gladly accept returns. And we appreciate your cooperation in returning items complete with box and packaging materials.

Good news for good customers.

The Sharper Image introduces The Frequent Buyers™ Reward.

Good customers deserve a reward. Because your good will means everything to us.

Now, every product you buy from The Sharper Image earns you points toward valuable gift certificates. You receive one point for each dollar you spend between January 1, 1984 and December 30, 1984. And this is how your reward adds up:

750 points earn a $50 gift certificate.
1500 points earn a $150 gift certificate.
2500 points earn a $300 gift certificate.

How to claim your reward.

1. Save your sales receipts.
2. Use the Reward Form, included in all Sharper Image shipments.
3. Add up all merchandise points, not including sales tax and delivery charges.
4. Deduct all refund and credit points.
5. Return original sales receipts and completed form by March, 1985.
6. Enjoy shopping with your gift certificates.

Refunds are matched against original purchases. Points are earned when products are delivered, and are not transferable. Please save your original receipts (packed with items). They are your sole proof of points and must be returned by mail for redemption when requesting gift certificates.

$50
Gift Certificate
750 points earn a $50 gift certificate.

$150
Gift Certificate
1500 points earn a $150 gift certificate.

$300
Gift Certificate
2500 points earn a $300 gift certificate.

ORDER TOLL-FREE. 24 HRS. EVERY DAY.

800-344-4444

Canadian/Overseas orders 415-344-4444
Toll-Free ordering by credit card only.

Award Winner
Best in Catalogs®

FIGURE 6-3
The Sharper Image catalog order form explains an incentive for frequent buyers and heavy purchasers: gift certificates for the customer. © 1984 The Sharper Image and reprinted with permission.

offer a casserole as a new item, and the old, not-so-great seller is a ladle. Consider offering the casserole at your planned price and either offer the ladle as a free gift or at a greatly reduced price with the purchase of the casserole.

Study the economics thoroughly before offering twofers or bonuses. Determine how the additional anticipated response will affect your margin of profit. Test bonus and/or twofer offers minimally before proceeding with a greater percentage of such offers in each catalog. Experience demonstrates, however, that customers show a preference for a twofer over the single item.

If you have a high-ticket catalog and have concerns about how customers will perceive such offers, cease worrying. Customers appreciate good value, no matter how high the ticket. But the way you present your savings offer should be determined by the overall image of your catalog. Present the bonus offer as a gift, specifically targeted to a time of year. Using the example of the casserole and ladle, point out that the ladle is a natural with the casserole, and also has many other holiday functions, such as dipping into the wassail bowl or fruit punch.

Sweepstakes

Sweepstakes certainly get attention. Who can resist opening a catalog or package that promises riches, vacations, or dreams come true? As sweepstakes expert Jeffrey Feinman, president of Ventura Associates, so aptly says, "The threat that you may be throwing away $25,000 transforms junk mail to money mail."

Interestingly enough, focus groups have indicated that consumers have a high degree (91 percent) of trust in the honesty of the offer. Respondents buy not because they think it's the only way to win, but because they're basically honest people who feel guilty entering the contest without buying. And they really want to enter the contest. Everyone likes the chance to get something for nothing.

As there are different kinds of catalogs, so there are different kinds of sweepstakes. A general sweepstakes, such as those offered by Spencer Gifts and one of its offspring, Beautiful Beginnings, is ideal for a general audience (which they have). Other sweepstakes have a theme or a specific audience in mind. For example, an American Express sweepstakes was tied to travel. The company helped generate additional catalog orders by making the fourth prize 500 gift certificates of $25 redeemable through its catalog.

One note of caution, however. Some established catalog businesses will not rent their lists to a catalog offering a sweepstakes. Whether or not the respondent buys, the names of those who entered are retained, effectively cutting back the number of rental names needed—and the list renter's profits—in the future.

If you decide that running a sweepstakes might just be the ticket to increased sales, you'll need expert help. The legal considerations are discussed in Part 12, but professional help is strongly advised. Industry publications (listed in the back of this book) run ads of firms specializing in sweepstakes. The initial consultation is generally free, and the service fees are reasonable when you consider how complicated and legally dangerous sweepstakes can be for the novice.

Properly handled, sweepstakes do work. But be sure to proceed cautiously down the path to those riches.

Toll-free number

A major reason for the phenomenal success of mail order in recent years is consumers' lack of shopping time. The toll-free number places the means for shopping right at the customers' fingertips. It can be an essential element in the success of your mail order program and should most definitely be tested.

If you decide to use a toll-free number, give it a fair chance for success by advertising it from at least every other spread of your catalog. Provide at a glance the means to order a desired item. No one wants to search through a catalog to find the toll-free number. Also, be specific about the days of the week and the hours the toll-free service is available. If there is a different number for the state in which the service is located, give this less importance (it's only 1 state out of 50 and fewer people will use it).

Consider using a copy line that conveys a benefit of using the service, such as "For faster delivery, call toll free." And specify "Credit card holders call 000-000-0000." As impossible as it may seem, some people don't realize that they need a credit card to place an order by telephone. You can cut down on wasted time, cost, and customer aggravation if you make this clear from the start.

In-house versus outside service

One of your most important decisions is whether to use an in-house or outside service. An in-house service is costly, requiring round-the-clock, seven-day-a-week personnel and enough incoming lines so that customers don't get a busy signal. Patrick Moore of Chargit told us that for an in-house 800-number facility "the true costs for space, labor, training, management, heat and light, equipment, telephone lines and equipment, and other overhead items like recruiting and employee benefits [mean] you'll be lucky to get away with a total of $2.50 to $4 an order." No one can take better care of your customers than your own, in-house personnel, but using an existing service allows first-time catalogers to concentrate on other important areas, such as fulfillment and customer service. Investigate the costs, then decide which method best fits both your pocketbook and your company's philosophy.

Toll-free numbers are more than just an answering service. Many companies offer an upsell and/or cross-sell program that allows the customer the option of purchasing additional products while placing an order. This can be extremely effective in increasing sales. One major catalog allows the 800-number customer to purchase an item available only on the day of the call at a discount from its normal cost.

Whether you use an outside service or an in-house department, the person who answers the toll-free service phone represents your company. His or her attitude and handling of the customer can make or break a relationship. If you have an in-house service, give frequent "pep" talks to those who have phone contact with customers. Consider offering bonuses or some other form of recognition for a job well done. Monitor calls to hear exactly how individual operators are performing. If you are using an outside service, place frequent test calls to make sure the service is performing their duties as well as you expect.

WATS service

Depending on the merchandise you offer, you may wish to investigate an Out-WATS service. This can be excellent in following up mailings. A potential customer may have planned to act on an offer, but, for some reason, have forgotten to do so. An Out-WATS call may not receive a definitive yes or no, but can trigger another look at the offer. If presented as a customer service, the call can actually enhance the image of your company.

In-WATS service, used in conjunction with an Out-WATS program, can be even more effective. Its easy accessibility allows customers the time to review your freshly presented order (your Out-WATS people have courteously represented the offer by phone) and then quickly (via In-WATS) get back to you with an order. Such a combination has been known to increase sales by an impressive 75 percent.

Evaluating telemarketing

Here are some facts and figures that show why telemarketing has become so important.

- American Express receives about 50 percent of its 1.5 million yearly orders by phone. In the five years since the company initiated its telemarketing program, sales have risen from $29 million to more than $115 million annually.
- Selling desk-top supplies turned out to be a cinch for Great North American Stationers. Through the use of its telemarketing sales force, sales grew from $25,000 to $14 million in less than ten years.

But telemarketing doesn't have to mean toll-free. Listing your own telephone number is a viable alternative. A good idea is to use a toll-free number in the first catalog to give your potential customers every opportunity to purchase, then evaluate the cost of the service against the revenue generated. If you are not pleased with the results, consider a split test. Print some catalogs with the toll-free number and some with your regular phone number. Evaluate the results again and you'll be in an even better position to determine whether this service is for your catalog.

A gift wrap/card service

With more and more people relocating around the country, many customers prefer to have gifts sent directly to the recipient. Whether you offer a gift wrap/card service can be a deciding factor when the customer is ready to order.

To ease into this service, start by offering a gift card only. Make sure that your order form allows special areas for gift addresses and messages. Then simply transcribe the message from the order form to your gift cards, making sure the message is handwritten.

After testing the economics and working out the fulfillment details of the card service, you may want to attempt gift wrapping. You can give free gift wrap with an order of any size or only when a specific dollar amount is ordered. Or you can charge a small amount for standard gift wrap and offer a range of prices for fancier gift wrap. Before deciding which is best for you, investigate.

- How much will the gift wrap cost? This, of course, depends on the size of the packages. Use the average box size for "ship-to" items as a guide. Not all "ship-to" items are gifts, but their average is more representative for gift wrap purposes than the overall average of all packages. However, for now, determine the average size of the packages sent most often.
- How much time does it take service personnel to wrap an item? This, too, will vary according to size. Try several different sizes, and for the time being, use the average to determine the dollar value of the time spent.

Once you decide to offer gift wrap, monitor the exact cost of gift wrap and employee time closely. Keep the wrap simple in the beginning and avoid such costly additions as monogrammed ribbon until you have a firm hold on the economics of offering this service. This service has proven dangerously unprofitable for more than one catalog business.

Handwritten messages

Add a personal touch by handwriting headlines throughout the catalog, notes that point up special values, or even the toll-free number. Make sure the handwriting fits the audience, and keep it clear and crisp. Handwritten messages are a wonderful idea to personalize your appeal to the customer and give you the opportunity to highlight a particular benefit.

The back cover

Too often the back cover is perceived by catalogers as the tail end, not worthy of special treatment. Yet, it is one of the biggest selling pages in the entire catalog. Some people actually see the back cover before they see the front or inside.

Always consider showing at least one of the following on the back cover:

- Your toll-free or ordering number
- Your money-back guarantee

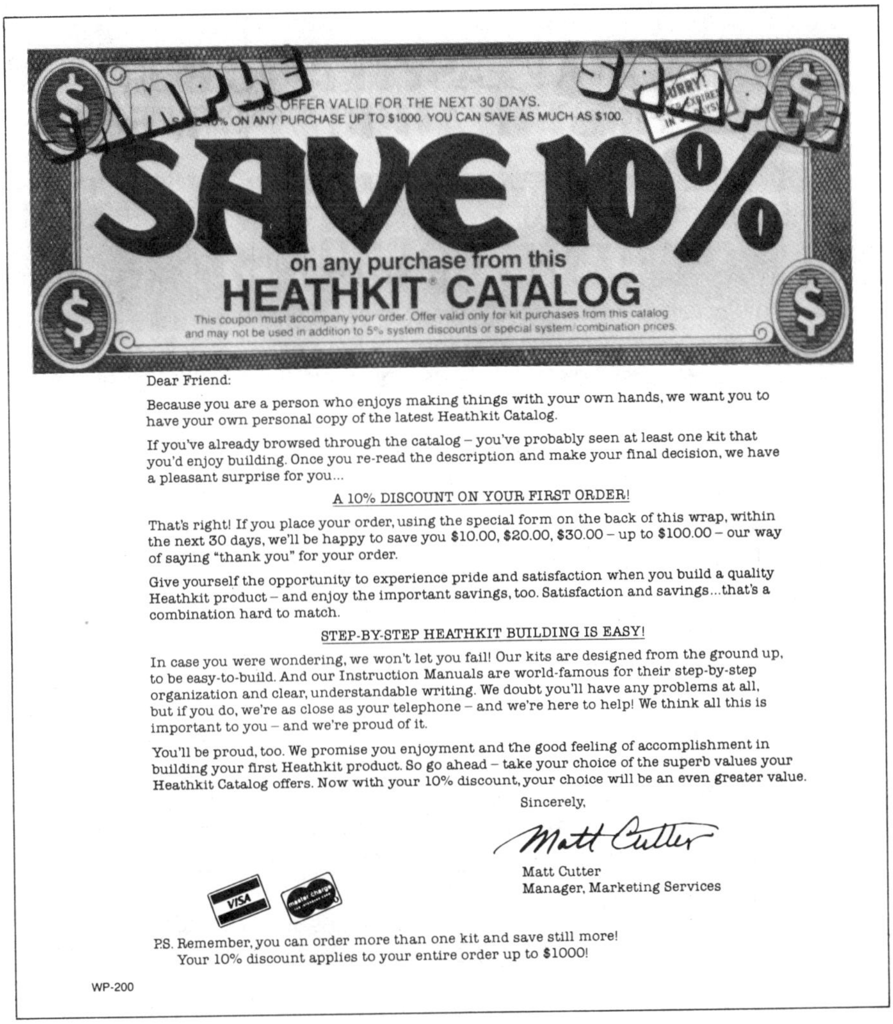

Dear Friend:

Because you are a person who enjoys making things with your own hands, we want you to have your own personal copy of the latest Heathkit Catalog.

If you've already browsed through the catalog – you've probably seen at least one kit that you'd enjoy building. Once you re-read the description and make your final decision, we have a pleasant surprise for you...

A 10% DISCOUNT ON YOUR FIRST ORDER!

That's right! If you place your order, using the special form on the back of this wrap, within the next 30 days, we'll be happy to save you $10.00, $20.00, $30.00 – up to $100.00 – our way of saying "thank you" for your order.

Give yourself the opportunity to experience pride and satisfaction when you build a quality Heathkit product – and enjoy the important savings, too. Satisfaction and savings...that's a combination hard to match.

STEP-BY-STEP HEATHKIT BUILDING IS EASY!

In case you were wondering, we won't let you fail! Our kits are designed from the ground up, to be easy-to-build. And our Instruction Manuals are world-famous for their step-by-step organization and clear, understandable writing. We doubt you'll have any problems at all, but if you do, we're as close as your telephone – and we're here to help! We think all this is important to you – and we're proud of it.

You'll be proud, too. We promise you enjoyment and the good feeling of accomplishment in building your first Heathkit product. So go ahead – take your choice of the superb values your Heathkit Catalog offers. Now with your 10% discount, your choice will be an even greater value.

Sincerely,

Matt Cutter

Matt Cutter
Manager, Marketing Services

P.S. Remember, you can order more than one kit and save still more!
Your 10% discount applies to your entire order up to $1000!

WP-200

FIGURE 6-4
An overwrap on a Heathkit® catalog got attention by boldly announcing a 10 percent savings on any purchase in the catalog. © Heath Company and reprinted with permission.

- The credit cards you offer
- Endorsements from satisfied customers
- The number of years you've been in business (if it's an impressive number)
- The locations of your stores (if too many, just a blurb inviting customers to visit your stores)

One good alternative to actually selling products off the back cover is to show a selection of products offered inside the catalog. This enticement should always state the pages on which the products are located.

Use the same care in picking products for the back cover as you would for the front cover. It can be the reason prospective customers do or do not open the catalog. Treat the back cover like the money-maker it can be and it will reward you with impressive results.

Overwraps

You may not know the term "overwrap," but you've probably seen them—the extra cover of coarser offset paper attached to standard four-color, glossy catalogs. More often than not, an overwrap announces something special about the catalog issue. Heathkit used an overwrap to present customers with a discount in Figure 6-4, getting extra mileage out of it by putting a second order form on the back.

Designed properly, overwraps can have the advantage of getting the prospective customer's attention. But they are relatively expensive and should be tested against a standard cover with the same message before being used in a full run.

Credit cards

Credit cards are an essential part of your business. Consumers like them because they make it easier to order. You will find that in most cases credit card orders have a higher average value than those paid by check.

Although many consumers will hesitate to write a check for more than $20, they will charge the amount. Credit cards also add credibility. One small mail order firm quadrupled its sales after it started offering credit card sales.

No catalog concern should be without Visa and MasterCard; American Express and Diners Club are also recommended. They cost more than the bank cards, but the higher average order they tend to generate is well worth the difference in cost. Test them to see which works best for you. (For how to handle credit card charges for your catalog, see "Credit card payment processing" in the chapter, "Order Intake," in Part 8.)

ORDER FORMS

This is it! This is where the sale is actually made or lost. The order form can either promote or discourage sales. If it looks unfriendly and confusing, that prospective customer may just decide not to fill it out. Remember, mail order is based on impulse buying. It is within your control to make it easy or hard to act on impulse.

The order form as sales tool

Put your order form to work. Tests have shown that bind-in order forms pay for themselves in increased sales. But they must be much more than just an envelope/order form for customers to fill in.

1 Generate additional sales by offering impulse items on the front flap and pocket.
2 Consider encouraging a high average dollar order by offering an incentive to purchase more.
3 Display your guarantee prominently. Give customers the reassurance that you'll be there if and when any problems develop. Be explicit.
4 Allow space for customers to list names of friends who would like to receive your catalog.
5 Show the specific sales tax, shipping charges, credit card options, gift certificate information, your customer service number (this should always be different from your toll-free ordering number), and easy-to-understand ordering instructions.

Designing the order form

Keep your order form clean and simple without wasting space.

1 Leave plenty of room between lines so that customers can write legibly to avoid incorrectly processed orders or calls to the customer for clarification.
2 Work with the data-entry personnel who will be using the form. Solicit their input and put it to use. Keep the information in the order in which your computer, or manual system, reads.
3 Use screened areas to attract attention or guide the consumer to specific spaces. But use them in moderation. Too many tinted areas can make the order form confusing and be self-defeating. Use black and white at first; it's less expensive and easier to work with. Simply have your order form printer screen black to achieve a gray tinted area.
4 Be sure to request the customer's phone numbers in the phone number information area. If you do have a problem with an order, you'll need to know where to get in touch with the customer, both day and night. Customers generally don't mind giving phone numbers if you specify why you need them.
5 If you are renting your list, display the mail preference service option. This will let customers know that you are ready and willing to take their name off the lists you rent to others if they so desire (see "Renting the house list" in the chapter, "List Selection" in Part 7).
6 List your toll-free number boldly. Even though customers who are reading the order form most likely intend to use it, they may choose to call the toll-free service. Give them this option.
7 Keep your mailing list up to date by asking for a change of address.

If space allows, you can leave an area for this information; if not, simply ask customers to make the appropriate corrections on the existing address.

8 Let customers know that you can't deliver UPS packages to a post office box number. Specify that you need a street address or a rural route number. (Note: not applicable if using USPS delivery.)

9 Include "Prices effective through (date)," so that customers who retain the catalog will readily be aware of the age of your catalog and to protect yourself against price increases. If you choose, you can add a line suggesting that customers call customer service to determine whether a product is still available after the expiration date of the catalog.

10 Clearly tell customers what the minimum charge order is. It is important to establish a charge minimum, as processing costs on low dollar orders are often prohibitive. Rather than discouraging orders, a minimum tends to encourage customers to order more so as to be able to charge.

11 If you have fast delivery, state the time it takes for your company to turn around a package. For example, "Orders filled within 48 hours of receipt." But don't exaggerate. It's worse to promise something you can't deliver than not to make a statement at all.

12 Do you ship outside the continental United States? Take a careful look at the cost. You may need to add a surcharge for items sent to Puerto Rico, Alaska, and Hawaii. And don't forget Canadian and foreign cities. Ask for payment in U.S. dollars only.

13 Plainly indicate "PLEASE PRINT." Some people need to be reminded to write their orders legibly. Valuable time can be saved when processing orders.

The order form checklist will help you ensure that your order form is complete. Before beginning your artwork, be sure to get a template from the printer. Because layout of an order form can be rather complicated, it is essential to use a template, which is literally a piece of paper or cardboard marked with imposition for the particular size and folds of your order form.

ORDER FORM CHECKLIST

- ✔ Company logo and address
- ✔ Credit card number/charge card logos (16 spaces)
- ✔ Expiration date (4 spaces)
- ✔ Signature line, with the words "required for charge orders" beneath the line itself
- ✔ Customer service information
- ✔ Ordering instructions
- ✔ Sales tax information
- ✔ Postage and handling information
- ✔ "Share us with a friend."
- ✔ Money-back guarantee

- ✔ Person ordering name area
- ✔ "Ship to" name, address, area
- ✔ Screened "Thank you for your order."*
- ✔ Gift certificate*
- ✔ Copyright*
- ✔ Price guarantee
- ✔ Mail preference service*
- ✔ Minimum charge
- ✔ Toll-free number
- ✔ Association logos*
- ✔ "Have you enclosed your check or credit card information?"
- ✔ In the ordering area:
    - Page number
    - Description
    - Item number
    - Size*
    - Color*
    - Monogramming information*
    - Quantity
    - Item or set price
    - Total charge
- ✔ "Items ordered together are not always shipped together. There is no additional charge for multiple deliveries."
- ✔ Method of payment information
- ✔ Client letter*
- ✔ "Please have your credit card handy since only credit card orders can be taken by phone."
- ✔ Customer telephone numbers: day/night-home/office
- ✔ Can't ship to post office boxes statement
- ✔ Time period in which orders are shipped (if orders shipped fast)*
- ✔ Address correction copy line
- ✔ Bar code*
- ✔ Misprint disclaimer

*Indicates may not be on all order forms, depending on catalog policy.

A double order form

To determine whether to use a double order form ask yourself three questions: Will your catalog have a high pass-along rate (such as a toy catalog)? Will it have a long life (such as a stitchery catalog)? Can you afford the additional cost at this time?

If your answer to these questions is yes, you should probably test a double order form. But don't sacrifice a full page of merchandise selling space for the second order form. Consider inserting it between signatures instead of the more common central insertion. This will enable the catalog to open naturally in three sections (two at order forms, one in the center) and can contribute to added sales.

A double order form should not be tested until a catalog is established. A note within the body of the catalog—"Order form missing? Simply call or write"—can eliminate the problem of a missing order form and help keep startup expenses down.

The order form printer

Order forms are printed on presses designed primarily for simple printing but complicated converting. They print from one to four colors at a time, then actually make an envelope, apply glue, and perforate, all in one continuous line. Catalog printers seldom have these capabilities; instead, they would have to do each of the functions separately, at far more cost.

Order forms are most often "gang" run, which means that several different order forms are run at one time. The result is even greater cost-efficiencies, but the order form printer must have your artwork when it is due. Otherwise, the press will run without your order form, and it may be some time before there is another opening.

If you supply the catalog printer with preformed envelopes or bind-ins, make sure the order form printer puts the following information on the outside of each carton:

1 Customer and printer job number

2 Code number, if used

3 Name and date of mailing

4 Quantity

Be sure instructions to the catalog printer include a request to check bind-in quantities by code as soon as they arrive. Then, if discrepancies exist, there will be time to remedy the situation.

Also, before ordering the bind-ins, check with your lettershop to determine the waste factor. Then order accordingly. Waste always occurs during insertion, so order extras. It's a small price to pay to ensure having enough order forms to complete a mailing.

Postage-paid envelopes

A major rule of cataloging is to make ordering as easy as possible for the potential customer. Therefore, a postage-paid envelope, which eliminates the need for a stamp, seems to make sense. Yet in random sampling of catalogs during the first few months of 1984, less than 30 percent included a postage-paid envelope. There are two major reasons why so many catalogs do not choose to prepay postage.

1. *Cost.* For prepaid envelopes, the post office charges the normal first-class rate plus an 18-cent handling charge if you pay by cash or have a postage-due account, or a 5-cent handling charge if you have a business-reply account, for which you pay a $75 annual fee. The cost runs from 25 cents to 38 cents each for prepaid envelopes compared to no cost for postage when the customer supplies the stamp. In one test of postage-paid envelopes, orders increased, but the increase was not sufficient to cover the cost of postage.

2. *Nonorder mail.* A postage-paid envelope seems to encourage such mail as letters from lonely people, consumers who see an opportunity to complain about everything in general, and political activists who want to share their message. Such mail is not only annoying (cutting down on efficiency), but also comes right off the bottom line. The postage is prepaid even if the return envelope doesn't contain an order.

First-time catalogers are not advised to use postage-paid envelopes. As their catalog and mailing quantities grow, they can consider offering a postage-paid envelope to a small test segment. But before the test, they should check with the post office for current charges. At the time of this writing, the post office is considering an increase in the handling fees to 25 cents for cash or postage-due account customers and 7 cents for business-reply account customers, and an increase for first-class mail to 23 cents. If this happens, even fewer catalogs may offer prepaid envelopes.

The use of color

Without a doubt, color affects buying decisions. According to a survey conducted by *Better Homes and Gardens* in 1982, 94.2 percent of its readers stated that color influenced their buying decisions when ordering by mail. However, color also costs more, and because first-time catalogers need to keep production expenses to a minimum, using color on the order form is not advised.

Instead, select products that do not need color to help sales. For instance, a silver key chain is just as attractive when photographed in black and white as it is in color. For the data-entry section of the order form, black tints can be used to highlight special areas. As sales increase, these areas can be highlighted in a second color, a relatively inexpensive move that can make the order form even more inviting. Then, as the catalog becomes more established, four-color can be tested against black and white. One of mail order's advantages is that an idea can be tested before investing substantial sums of money.

Part 7
MAILING LISTS

MAILING LIST BASICS

There is an internal debate in our industry as to which is most important: merchandise, creativity, or mailing lists. Ideally, all should work together, but the selection of mailing lists—the names and addresses of prospective customers who have something in common—is the cornerstone of the growth of catalog operations. Renting names is the fastest and most economical method both to obtain initial customers and to build a base of customer names. The names you rent can make or break your venture. The right names get orders; the wrong ones don't. Let's take a closer look at mailing lists and how you can put them to work for you.

Type of lists available

A mailing list contains the names and addresses of prospects or customers who have something in common. The mailing list you rent may contain the names of persons who have previously purchased by mail. These fall into several categories.

1 *Catalog mail order buyers.* Persons who have purchased goods from a catalog. Most often, these are the best respondents.
2 *Catalog respondents.* Persons who have requested a catalog, but have not purchased from it. These are not prime prospects.
3 *Space ad respondents.* Persons who have purchased a product through a magazine or newspaper advertisement, but are not necessarily catalog customers.
4 *Direct response customers.* Persons who have purchased a product through the mail, but not from a catalog or space ad. These can be good respondents, depending on the product offered.
5 *Subscribers.* Persons who have subscribed to a publication but are not necessarily mail order product buyers. If their demographic profile is extremely close to your targeted market, subscribers can be worth investigating.
6 *Compiled lists.* In the past, lists derived from secondary sources such as business and professional directories, telephone directories, and warranty registration lists were not highly effective. Recently, however, such lists have been distilled enough from general data and enhanced enough by demographic overlay information that they occasionally can be effective for customer acquisition.
7 *Fund-raising or political donors.* Persons who have responded to an appeal for contributions to a nonprofit organization. They are not necessarily open to purchase from a catalog but should be investigated as your catalog grows.

The mailing list profile

No matter what the category, a mailing list includes the names of consumers and their home addresses (3-line addresses) or their business addresses (4-line addresses). Each list also has a profile, which contains many or all of the following facts about the composition of the mailing list.

- Male/female breakdown.
- Source of names (mail order, space ads, inserts, and so on).

- Average order size in dollars. Be wary of this one. Average order size can be "cummed," meaning that it represents the average amount the person has spent with that catalog over a time period, or it can be the average amount of customer's last orders.
- Total size of the list (referred to as the "universe").
- Recency and number of names. The names on the list during certain time intervals (customers from the past three months, or six months, and so on).
- The rental price per thousand, plus the cost per thousand for "selects," the segments chosen over and above the base list price.
- Minimum name rental order amount.
- Merchandise categories, when available.
- Type of addressing (Cheshire, magnetic tape, pressure sensitive).
- State, SCF (sectional center facility—the first three digits of a five-digit zip), and zip code.
- Average dollar order of selects.
- Key coding and tape charge.
- Information regarding the product line offered by the list owner.
- Multiple purchasers.
- Demographics, if available.
- Foreign selects.

Mailing list brokers

All mailing list information is available on mailing list cards (see Figure 7-1) from mailing list brokers who work for mailing list brokerage firms. Other than the commission paid to the brokerage firm by the list owner for the rental of the list, there is no charge for the services of brokers. Their services are one of the best values in the entire mail order supplier spectrum.

The mailing list broker acts as an agent in the mailing list transaction and provides research services, professional judgment, and detailed recommendations on lists that may be profitable for you. A good list broker works with you to develop a marketing plan, which includes both testing of lists and recommendations for subsequent "rollout" (continuation phases) based on initial test results. In addition, a broker should ensure that the names you ordered are delivered to the right location on the right date.

The broker must also present your catalog to the list owner for approval (list owners have the right to refuse anyone). List owners clear the intended mailing date to see that competitive offers are not mailed at the same time. The broker bills the renter and transmits payment to the list owner/manager.

One of the greatest advantages a list broker has is daily contact with lists that work, valuable information to pass on to you, the client. Your broker may well recommend new lists, or special categories that have recently performed well for other mailers with offerings similar to your own. It is to a broker's advantage to recommend only lists that will give superior results, not only because he or she would like you as a long-term client, but also because brokers receive only a 20 percent commission on the lists they rent. Only through rollouts, seldom from small, initial tests, do they realize any profit.

When considering which broker to use, ask the following questions:

1 Does the broker's client roster include customers with products or markets similar to your own? Brokers tend to specialize in specific areas. Be sure to choose one with expertise in your market, not one who is trying to be all things to all people.
2 How did your initial mailing fare? Were the results reasonably good? If errors in list recommendations were made, has the broker taken obvious corrective action or continued to make the same or sadly similar recommendations?
3 Is the broker recommended by other mailers or catalogers?
4 As your program progresses, does your broker suggest new segmentation strategies and state-of-the-art demographic analysis?

Don't be dazzled by a personality. Ask hard questions of your broker and expect to see bottom-line results. As your mailing quantities grow, don't hesitate to work with several brokers. No one person knows everything. Valuable input can be gained by soliciting more than one recommendation.

The rental transaction

The basic list rental transaction is for one time only. The names you and your broker select are taken from another mailer's "response" list or a compiled list. Usually a minimum number of names (5,000 to 10,000) must be rented from a response file. Compiled lists, depending on their size, require either a minimum or, if small, a full rental. Response lists run from $45 to more than $100 per thousand; compiled lists cost about $35 per thousand. The selects often contained in response files can cost an additional $3 to $20 per thousand each. (See the section on selects in the chapter, "List Selection," later in Part 7.)

The list renter can be charged in two ways. "Gross payment" means a straight payment basis for the full quantity of names ordered. If you rent 5,000 names, you pay for 5,000 names, no matter how many are actually used. For instance, if you rent a list with a base cost of $60 per thousand and one select at $10 per thousand, the cost for 5,000 names would be $350. Gross payment is usually the only way you can rent names in the testing, or small quantity, stage.

However, in the rollout realm a price and quantity negotiation opportunity emerges, commonly known as "net name" basis. The list owner is often willing to offer some pricing flexibility in response to list broker prod-

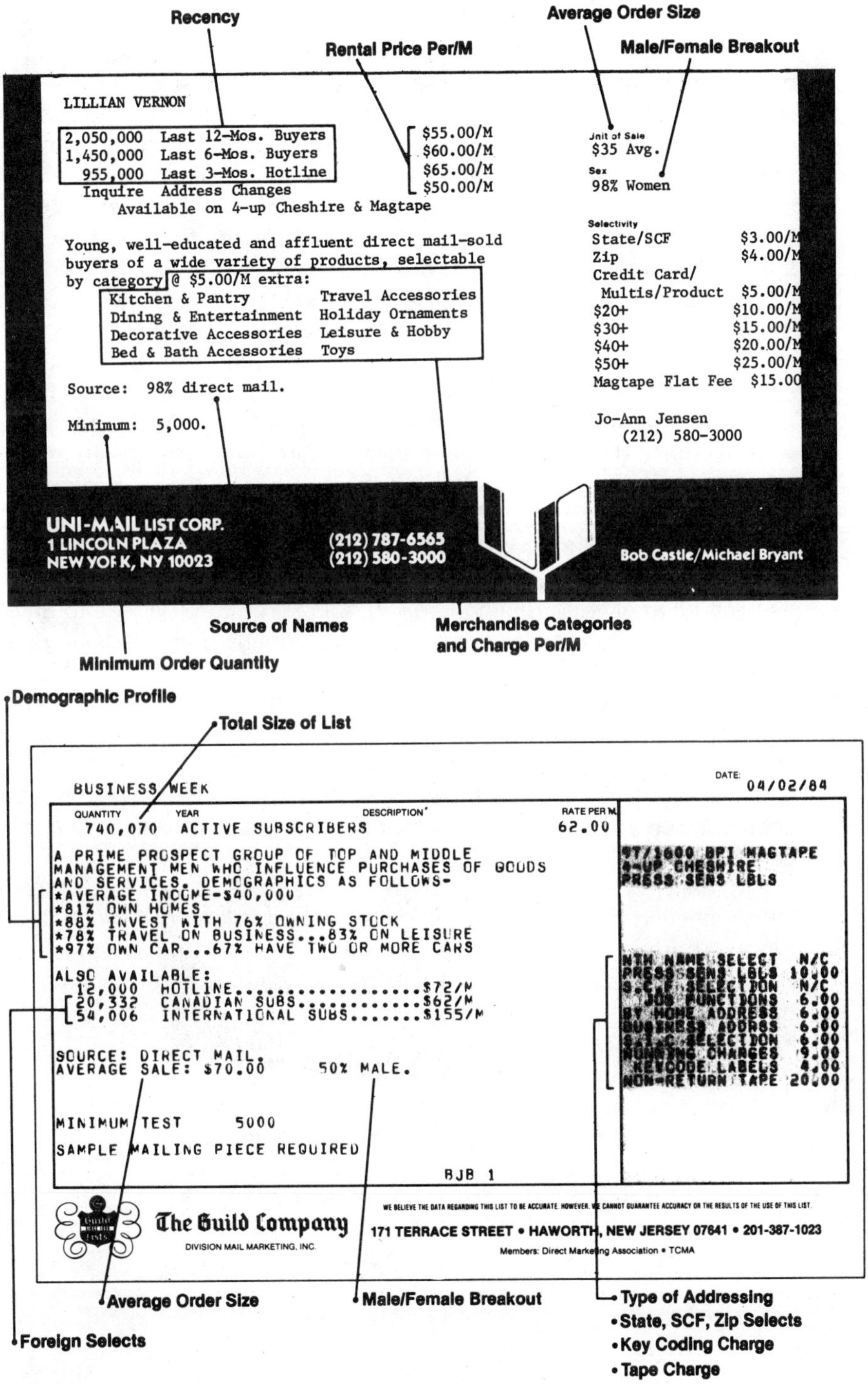

FIGURE 7-1
Typical mailing list cards from mailing list brokers. Courtesy Uni-Mail List Corp. and The Guild Company.

ding. Net name payment basis also makes sense because when you rent a large quantity of names from several mailers, a certain percentage of names is inevitably duplicated among files. The owner of each selected rental file wants to be paid on the most lucrative basis possible, but is usually willing to compromise for guaranteed payment for 85 percent of the names, regardless of whether the file is duplicated to a large extent among the files selected. Under this arrangement, even if you mail only 75 percent of the names unduplicated, you still pay for 85 percent. On the other hand, if you mail 92 percent of the file, you have to pay for the full 92 percent. With this agreement, the owner's revenue is protected regardless of overlap, and you don't pay fully for list quantities not used.

The duplicates that emerge between files are often not wasted. Duplicates represent true multibuyers of mail order products and as such are extra special mail order targets. If you are on a gross name basis, you may have the right to mail to them again (but check the remail date with the owner or broker before mailing to these names a second time). If you are on a net name basis, you should also verify that you have, in fact, paid for the name before remailing.

As your catalog grows and you acquire customer names of your own, an alternative to renting is exchanging. The approaches to an exchange of names vary from company to company, but the driving factor behind their viability is that appropriately exchanged names can outperform rented names. This is true for two reasons: (1) competitors who will not rent to you will sometimes exchange. Obviously, the more similar their market to yours, the better the chance the list will respond well. (2) Some established catalogers will allow rollout only if you agree to exchange once you have names of your own. If you plan to rollout a list, it's because it did well on its initial test.

Usually, one cost is involved: a brokerage fee of $6–$8 per thousand for negotiating the exchange, processing, and following through the order. (There is no broker's fee for selects either on an exchange or rental basis, and sometimes list owners exchange directly and avoid the base brokerage commission.) Exchanges save mailers upfront dollar costs, thereby lowering the in-the-mail cost on a particular list.

LIST
SELECTION

To develop the best possible list rental strategy, a mail order marketer must first determine the customer profile. All rented lists should be selected for their suitability for testing against the existing or targeted customer profile.

The customer profile

For catalogers with an existing house list, constructing the customer profile means research, careful response analysis, and scrupulous maintenance of the customer list. The same essential facts shown on other list owners' data cards, such as education level, hobbies, buying habits, and income, must be gathered for the house list. The customer list must also include transaction histories (purchase and payment performance) and be segmented according to source, frequency of purchase, size of purchase, category of merchandise purchased (see Figure 3-4), long-term value based on several buying seasons, recent purchases, and so on. The more you know about the people who buy from you, the more successful you'll be in hunting for more like them. But keep in mind that the customer profile may change with each new catalog response analysis, so be sure to update your records.

Other selection factors

Both newcomers and established catalogers need to ask themselves some critical questions before deciding which mailing lists to rent.

- What is the major thrust, image, or product of your catalog? What motivates customers to purchase? Is the catalog classic or high-tech? What makes it unique? Quality? Originality? Price? Is the merchandise geared to a particular life-style?
- What are the quantity limitations? Budget? Print run? Committed inventory? Have certain list categories been exhausted?
- What is the primary financial objective? Immediate dollar return using minimum-risk lists (which may have smaller universes for potential rollout) or marginal lists providing break even or slightly less return (which have huge universes and the potential larger rollouts)?

The answers to the first question will help you determine the list type, in terms of life-style, best suited to your catalog's image. For example, if you sell well-priced, traditional home furnishings, you would be more likely to rent a list such as Williams-Sonoma's, consisting of buyers of gourmet cooking accessories, than a list such as The Sharper Image's, consisting of buyers of electronic "toys."

The answers to the second question will help you identify your limitations. Budget, of course, is always a major consideration, but the size of the print run should be determined by the list quantities you select, not the other way around. Never choose the print-run quantity and then search for lists to meet its needs. Rather, determine the lists, and the quantities per list anticipated to be most profitable for your catalog. Then match your print run to this quantity.

Inventory, on the other hand, can be a decision-influencing factor. If the merchandise you intend to stock is readily available, the size of your mailing need not be restricted. However, if inventory is purchased from abroad, and availability may be restricted, it might be wise to mail less to avoid running out of merchandise. As more product category history becomes available, inventory commitments can be made with greater knowledge and mailings can be comfortably increased.

The primary financial objective should always be to make as much money as possible. Minimum-risk lists should always be tested first; you can later expand into marginal lists. Build a strong customer base, one that responds in hefty dollars, before testing marginal lists. Don't overlook long-term growth strategy, but make viable list selections so that you are still around to complete your long-term strategy.

Selects

Another important consideration in list selection is the available "selects," or descriptive categories by which the names in the list are grouped. The selects you choose can make or break your lists program.

1. *Merchandise categories.* Once you establish that a rental file contains names of people who have purchased goods similar to those you are offering, you can sometimes zero in on purchasers of specific product categories, such as home furnishings, dining/entertainment, or kitchen/pantry items or decorative accessories. For the most part, this detailed product selection option is available only from list owners with large universes, such as Lillian Vernon and Spiegel. If the universe is a large one, and a product category is not on the list card, ask your broker if one is in the process of being compiled.

2. *Demographics.* Most lists contain several demographic descriptors, all of which are critically important assessment factors, but only some of which are actually available to you as selections. A rental list profile often contains information breakdowns by male/female, occupation, marital status, incidence of children, income ranges, education levels, and home ownership. The gender breakdown is the one most commonly available for rental. Beyond this selection, however, demographic information consists of aggregates or averages and is therefore of analytical value only.

One way a renter can make practical use of demographic profiles of other files is through the "demographic overlay" process. Demographic overlay services extract information from publicly available U.S. Census average demographic data by zip code area. Sometimes catalog companies run Census Bureau tapes against rental files and mail to the "distilled" names that meet their criteria. This is an added expense, but advances in technology are providing for increasing cost-efficiencies.

3. *Recency.* The recency of a prospective customer's last mail order purchase from a given company is a relatively good indicator of overall interest in mail order offers. Recent customers are often active customers for the file's owner, and for other mail order companies as well. Almost all rental files contain "hot line" selections of customers who have purchased goods within the past three to six months. But be cautious. Don't simply assume that a purchase was made in that time period. The three- to six-

month period depends on list updates and mailing times. Always clarify this point with your broker.

4. *Frequency.* The frequency select is often available as multibuyers, meaning persons who have purchased more than one time from a particular list. However, this information should be qualified by both time period and dollar amount spent. A customer who has made only a few purchases, none recent, over a three-year period could be presented as a frequent or multibuyer. Frequency can be a valuable select, but only if you have a true understanding of what the list owner considers frequent.

5. *Monetary value.* In list rental terms, the monetary value refers to the dollar volume purchased by a selection of customers. Catalog lists are often available by average order amount. If your average order amount is, or is targeted to be, $50, it may not be profitable for you to rent a $20 select. Again, check to be sure that your understanding of average dollar order is what is being offered. Some average dollar orders represent the customer's last purchase; others are cumulative and represent a total buying history in dollars spent.

6. *Geographic.* Most list owners offer state, zip, and SCF selects. A motivating factor in choosing one of these selects is whether your merchandise appeals to certain regional customers. The primary motivation, however, is to acquire more customers from the same zip code areas that have been successful in previous mailings.

If purely statistical estimates of presort percentages are compared with actual presort percentages, it is seen that mail order customers are not spread evenly throughout all the zip code areas but tend to cluster in particular areas. Zip clustering techniques, such as Acorn® and Prizm®, have proven useful in segmenting the national zip codes into groups. Therefore, if you could determine the particular characteristics of the zip code areas in which your customers live, you could profitably select other zip code areas that have these same characteristics.

7. *Psychographic.* Another method for obtaining prospects similar in profile to your customer is called psychographics. The theory here is that people who have similar life-styles will purchase merchandise in a similar pattern. The method is to run the house list against a large file of names looking for similar characteristics that will help to determine the customer profile. Then, other names on the master list fitting that profile can be rented. For instance, if your house list, when run against the master file, shows that 70 percent bought cameras within the last year, this might prove to be an excellent market for film or developing services. We have found mixed results using psychographic techniques. The value seems to vary for different catalogs. The innovative cataloger will investigate this technique as the need arises.

8. *Source media.* Since you are prospecting by mail, you want to reach only those segments of a list owner's file that contain mail order-generated customers. Many companies have other sources for their customer names, such as lists of retail store customers and gift recipients, sales leads, warranty card registrations, and package insert respondents.

In addition, customers can be acquired from other direct response media such as space advertising, telephone marketing, and direct response television. The best match for a cataloger is the highest possible concentration of direct mail-generated customers. If, for instance, you cannot specifically select out space ad purchasers, as opposed to catalog purchasers, the list card should specify the percentage that were direct mail-generated.

9. *Method of payment.* What method of payment was used by the majority of purchasers in a given rental file? Some owners offer selects based on the type of credit card used. This can be important, as some house credit customers tend to respond less favorably than bank credit card customers. Conversely, bank credit card purchasers can prove to be a better select than those customers who paid by cash for the simple reason that credit card customers often spend more than those paying by check.

10. *CHADs.* The acronym for change of address, CHADs can signify an upgrade in housing accommodations, an increase in income, or a promotion or transfer and the purchase of goods to go with these changes. CHADs are also called COA's (change of addresses).

11. N*th name.* When testing a list on a national basis, make use of what is called the "*n*th name select." This means that for a test of 10,000 names from a list universe or select of 200,000, you would receive every twentieth name. A true *n*th select gives you a valid cross-section of the list tested.

However, in some instances, due to policy or computer operator error, you may receive a list that is not a true *n*th name select. Obtain a count by state or SCF for each rented list from the computer service house at the time of the merge/purge. Discrepancies will be evident. For example, an *n*th name test may reveal zips no higher than 70000 (zips run from 00600 to 99999). In this case, the cataloger would lose in two ways: (1) Washington, California, and Texas, all responsive mail order states, would be missing and (2) the test results would be somewhat invalid.

So insist that list orders specify true *n*th name selects. If, even after your best efforts, you discover that you did not receive an *n*th name select, try to negotiate a reduced list rental charge for future testing. Do this only for lists whose response has shown that they are worth the effort, even without proper *n*th name select.

Essential self-help steps

Selecting the right lists for prospective mailings is a challenging task. Get all the help you can from your list broker, but do your own homework, too. On an ongoing basis, read the data cards that are mailed out by owners and managers. Your broker(s) can arrange for you to get these lists. Standard Rate and Data Service Inc. (3004 Glenview Road, Wilmette, IL 60091; 312-256-6067) publishes an extensive directory of lists, which is updated six times a year. Although thorough, this service can be overwhelming to the newcomer. Purchase one to familiarize yourself with the types of lists available, then decide whether to subscribe.

Beginning with your first mailing, meticulously record all list rental activity and list selections tested. Systematically assign source codes (see Figure 7-2) to the customer identification information used in the label key-coding step of the merge/purge (see "Merge/purge," this chapter) and mail preparation processes. An easy-to-read code, established when the initial response arrives, can be used for a list's entire purchase performance history. By analyzing winning selections, you will be able to derive a marketing strategy for new audiences and for categories with proven performance.

List prospecting will always be with you. Even experienced mailers have to compensate for a drop in customer activity or the attrition of their customer file. So establish your internal systems for list selection results before your first drop in customer activity.

List testing

List testing is an almost universally accepted convention, which allows a list renter to mail a test quantity, say 5,000, 10,000, or even 20,000 names, from another marketer's file, to determine the suitability of the file. Based on the performance of the test, the cataloger decides whether to go deeper into the file for more names (a rollout), but the cataloger has no obligation to do so. Testing measures the performance of lists and/or list segments against each other to come up with a winning combination of lists and/or segments. It is not unusual for a test or mailing to be a combination of initial tests, rollouts or previously tested lists, and the cataloger's own customer list.

FIGURE 7-2
Example of source code on catalog mailing label. Courtesy Lands' End.

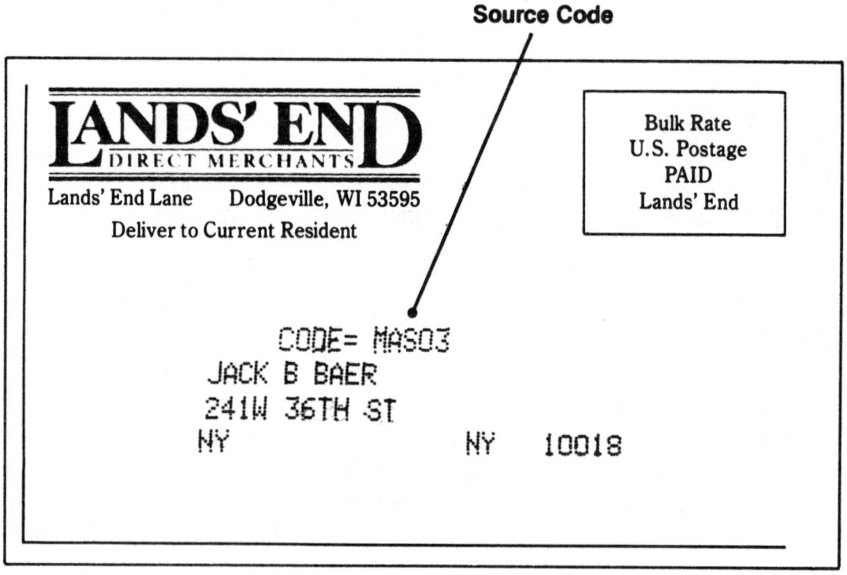

List test sample size

One of the first questions you need to answer before testing a list is "What quantity should I test per list?" The answer isn't, as some might think, "We'll just test the minimum requirement." Nor is it "This list looks like it's a really close match to our market. Let's test a large number of names." The sample size tested should be determined by a combination of these factors plus the potential universe to which you can roll out.

Because the rollout seldom performs as well as the test, statisticians have developed what is called a "confidence level"—meaning the level of confidence that the rollout will respond at the same rate as the test. A 90 percent confidence level means that 90 times out of a hundred the rollout response is expected to be within certain limits of the test response. Table 7-1 demonstrates this.

- The higher the desired confidence level, the larger the necessary sample.
- The higher the test response percent, the larger the sample necessary for the same confidence level.
- The wider the acceptable error limits on duplicating the test results, the smaller the necessary sample.

TABLE 7-1 Test sample sizes for 90%, 95%, and 99% confidence levels

	Test Response							
	1½% (.015)	2% (.02)	2½% (.025)	3% (.03)	3½% (.035)	4% (.04)	4½% (.045)	5% (.05)
	90% Confidence Level							
Error Limit ±								
.001	39,981	53,038	65,959	78,745	91,396	103,910	116,292	128,537
.002	9,995	13,260	16,489	19,686	22,849	25,977	29,072	32,134
.003	4,442	5,893	7,329	8,749	10,155	11,546	12,921	14,282
.004	2,488	3,315	4,122	4,921	5,712	6,494	7,268	8,034
.005	1,599	2,122	2,638	3,150	3,656	4,156	4,652	5,141
	95% Confidence Level							
Error Limit±								
.001	56,760	75,295	93,639	111,791	129,751	147,517	165,093	182,476
.002	14,190	18,824	23,410	27,948	32,438	36,879	41,273	45,619
.003	6,307	8,366	10,404	12,421	14,417	16,391	18,344	20,275
.004	3,547	4,706	5,852	6,987	8,109	9,220	10,318	11,405
.005	2,770	3,012	3,746	4,472	5,190	5,901	6,604	7,299
	99% Confidence Level							
Error Limit±								
.001	97,967	129,960	161,621	192,951	223,950	254,615	284,952	314,955
.002	24,492	32,490	40,405	48,238	55,987	63,654	71,238	78,739
.003	10,885	14,440	17,958	21,439	24,883	28,291	31,661	34,995
.004	6,123	8,123	10,101	12,059	13,997	15,913	17,809	19,685
.005	3,919	5,198	6,465	7,718	8,958	10,184	11,398	12,598

As an extreme example, at a 99 percent confidence level, a 5 percent test response, and a .1 percent error limit (plus or minus), a sample size of 315,000 is needed. At the other extreme, at a 90 percent confidence level, a 1½ percent test response, and a .5 percent error limit (plus or minus), a sample size of 1,600 is adequate.

The tables are valid only if the sample size is less than 1/20th of the total list size. If the test sample is more than 5 percent (or 1/20th) of the total, you must use what is known as a finite population correction factor. This formula can be found in any standard statistical text.

Although the tables are intended as a guide, rollouts generally should not exceed three or four times the initial test quantity. In some cases, test panels are prearranged; the 5,000 or 10,000 names for the test are generated from the most recent mailings, rather than the overall list. This recency factor can create an artificial test response, which will not lead to a statistically accurate rollout.

One way to avoid this situation is to test odd numbers of names, such as 6,500, rather than the more standard 5,000. Ask your list broker to recommend lists that are most likely to have accurate results on rollout.

Merge/purge

Put simply, merge/purge is the purging of duplicate names by the computerized merging of all the list tapes you have rented. This process can save you thousands of dollars and your customers the annoyance of receiving multiples of the same catalog. Here's how merge/purge works:

The procedure

1. Together with the list broker, the client develops a list rental schedule. The broker places the orders, with instructions for all tapes to be shipped to XYZ service bureau (this function is almost universally entrusted to a computer service bureau) by the predetermined date on which the merge/purge is to take place.

2. Each list owner's tapes arrive at the service bureau, where they are converted to a common format and run against those segments of your house file being used for this mailing. The duplicate names that emerge are "knocked out." Since they are in the house file, they will be mailed anyway.

3. Any "suppression tapes" are run against the duplicate-free tape. Suppressions include mailed segments of the house list, a house "bad debt" file (if one is maintained or subscribed to), unwanted zips, and the Direct Marketing Association (DMA) Mail Preference Service tapes. These tapes contain the names of consumers who have specifically asked that their names be deleted from direct mail promotions. The names are obtained by DMA through space advertisements asking consumers if they want to be taken off or added to lists. The ads are run as a self-regulatory measure designed to offset any federal regulations against the use of mailing lists in general. Be sure that the service bureau you select makes suppression of the DMA Mail Preference Service tapes a standard policy.

It is extremely important that direct marketers help to enforce this self-regulation. Most service bureaus have cooperated with this effort by not charging for the service.

4. Eventually, through a systematic passage of tape against tape, a master tape, as duplicate-free as is currently possible, is constructed from the customer file and the rented files. The names on the master tape are next sorted into zip code sequence. Then the number of names for each zip code can be counted to determine the zip codes that qualify, by density, for the USPS's presort levels (carrier route or 5/3 digit zip), which provide additional postal discounts. Those that do qualify are run against programs provided by USPS and other private sources and are arranged in presort sequence. The product is a tape or tapes, ready for printing on the label format selected or for ink-jet or laser addressing.

5. The service bureau provides a detailed report, by list, of the duplication output counts (number of duplicated names by list). The broker follows up with each list owner, reports the results of the merge/purge, specifies the payment to be remitted according to prior arrangement, and participates in any post-merge/purge negotiations.

Purging methods

The two main methods of duplicate elimination are fixed match code and mathematical equivalency algorithm. Each has its adherents. Each has its merits and problems. Both are complicated mathematical techniques. Simplified, the differences are these. (1) The fixed match code compares fixed elements of the computer-generated names and addresses as a means of identifying duplicates. This method does not identify duplicates as accurately as its counterpart. (2) The mathematical equivalency method (sometimes called a variable match code) works similarly, but picks up more elements, weighing the value of more complex duplications. However, it tends to overkill. Happily, many service bureaus offer a combination of both.

Allocation of duplicates

Since the performance of a list is based on the names it contains, the allocation of multibuyers (the duplicates) is an important consideration. For the most accurate analysis, random allocation is the most often used method. First, duplicates in the house list should always have priority. After that, duplicates should be randomly allocated among the lists being purged. This will help to ensure that each list retains its rightful proportion of multibuyers, and that the response will be valid for each list. If, for example, the list that runs first receives the lion's share of multibuyers, the test results will be skewed in its favor. (For information on the economics of merge/purge, see "Economics," Part 10.)

Your list as a profit center

The primary reason for building a house list is to have a future market for your products. But the great sums of money you have spent on list rental have also created a potential profit center. As the owner of a valuable mail order file, you retain control even if you decide to place your list on the rental market. You decide who rents your list, what portions to rent, and when. You have the final authority to approve or reject whomever you choose.

Renting the house list

To offer your list as rental property, you should have at least 5,000 current (0–12 month) names. But long before that point, you should be implementing the following guidelines.

1 Be in the continuous process of actively building your customer base. The more names you have, the greater the potential for rollout and the more attractive your names are to possible renters. See "Customer Acquisition" in Part 9 and be sure to code captured names by source.

2 From the very beginning, maintain segmentation data. Income from the rental of selects such as recency, frequency, and monetary value can substantially contribute to list rental revenues.

3 Constantly work to obtain more information about your customers. The quest for life-style or demographic data should be never-ending; this information can be collected from customer surveys, telephone contact, customer service input, fulfillment package communications, and so on. Although your main reason for this effort should always be to benefit your catalog operation, the information gained will help give your list an excellent market position and will most certainly result in more rentals.

4 Keep your list in tip-top shape. Make frequent use of the USPS address correction services and be sure that your order form encourages customers to note address changes. Incorporate this information into your files immediately. Be sure to segment/delete customer names that have opted for Mail Preference service from any names that you rent. Lists that are poorly maintained tend to respond poorly, resulting in less rollout income for their owners. Even more important, an improperly maintained list could translate into inferior sales for your own catalog.

List rental income can be extremely profitable. One well-known cataloger is rumored to make more from the rental of his list than from his highly successful catalog.

Besides the monetary value of list rental, catalogers have also found that it serves as a useful tool for the discovery of lists that may be profitable for your mailings. If your list works well for a particular mailer, there's a good chance that his or her list will work well for you. (For more information on your list as a profit center, see "Other Factors Affecting Profitability" in Part 10.)

But before you put your list on the market, talk with a couple of knowledgeable list management companies. They can help you determine the potential worth of your list over a time period. The only possible negative is that your customers will be receiving solicitations that may reduce their overall buying power. Whether this will adversely affect the bottom line of *your* catalog operation is a decision only you can make.

But remember, a smart move, if you have a large-sized list, is to rent only a portion of it, then test the rented panel versus the unrented panel to see if sales are adversely affected. And you always have the option of withdrawing the list from the marketplace.

Your list manager

If you decide to put your list on the market, you will need a list manager. You have two choices—internal or external management.

Internal management uses staff time and budget allocations for such essentials as marketing, order processing and trafficking, and invoicing and collection. An in-house manager is completely familiar with the list and can devote full attention to it. However, since good list promotion takes time, money, and expertise, in-house management is generally better left to large, established catalogers. Smaller companies usually do not have the experience or the time to do the job properly and, as a result, can lose valuable revenues.

Outside list management firms specialize in marketing list properties to the direct mail industry. Acting as the list owner's agent—for a typical commission of 10 percent of the rental fee—the outside manager prepares data cards for the list and promotes the list through direct mail promotions, space ads, in-person selling, trade shows, and more. Outside managers also handle all the processing functions, from coordinating mail date clearances to collecting rental revenues. They work closely with list brokers to familiarize them (and their clients) with the merits of your list. If you think that an outside list management firm may be right for you, find out about the firm.

- *Specialties.* Some firms specialize in certain areas. If a firm specializes, does it match your needs?
- *Performance.* How well has the firm promoted the lists it is now managing? Ask to speak directly to some of its clients.
- *Size.* Consider how well the size of your business fits in with the size of the firm's business. Will you be too small to get proper attention? Or too big for its staff to handle?

Part 8
THE BACK END

ORDER INTAKE

The back end is made up of order intake (including data entry), fulfillment, inventory control, and customer service. These areas are often taken for granted, yet getting orders in and out in a timely fashion requires planning and a good backup team. Customers who receive their orders promptly and in good condition order again and again. Statistics show that 20 percent more orders are received from customers whose initial orders are promptly filled. Those who wait and wonder often become quietly dissatisfied and just stop ordering.

Each catalog back end operation has certain qualities peculiar to it. Some are manual; others are computerized, such as the medium-size operation that will be described here. A computer is not only time-efficient but helps ensure accuracy. Even small startup ventures should invest in one.

Outline of steps

As shown in Figure 8-1, order intake is the processing of orders from the time the mail arrives to data base creation. The first step, mail opening, consists of two phases: (1) receipt of mail from the post office and (2) opening, editing (checking for complete name and address before discarding the envelope—some companies retain and attach the envelope to the order), and sorting mail by category. During the sorting process, mail is divided into four categories. Within these four categories are chains of implementation.

1 Prepaid orders with checks
   a. Post payment by amount, check number, and batch number.
   b. Batch orders and corresponding checks/money orders (usually 50 per batch).
   c. Prepare order control form.
   d. Forward to order control.

FIGURE 8-1
Flow chart of order processing procedures.

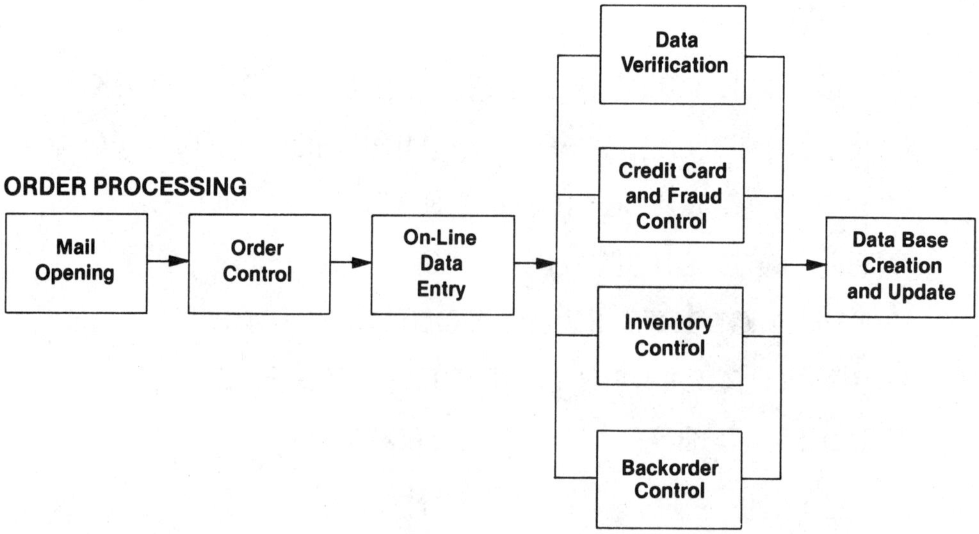

2 Credit card orders
   a. Batch orders (usually 50 per batch).
   b. Prepare order control form.
   c. Forward to order control.

3 Catalog requests
   a. Batch by source key.
   b. Forward to data entry.

4 Other
   a. Stamp with date.
   b. Forward to customer service.

In a small company, the same person who handles the initial sorting may also handle order control. Figure 8-2 outlines the order control process, which basically ensures that all batch totals match the order form totals and that both are correct.

Data entry

Now the order must actually be entered into the fulfillment system. During order entry, certain information must first be validated.

1 Does the item description match the SKU (stock keeping unit) number?

2 Is the price correct?

3 Have shipping and handling charges as well as appropriate taxes been added?

4 Is there a source or key code?

5 Are the city and state correct for the zip code?

6 For credit card orders, is the number complete and the expiration date current?

7 Has the customer provided a daytime and nighttime phone number?

Next, two questions need to be answered: (1) is the payment correct for the merchandise ordered, and (2) is the merchandise in stock or on back order? The computer will automatically update (1) customer history and (2) inventory files (by reserving each in-stock item and by updating the back-order file for out-of-stock items).

In addition, the following data should be captured.

1 Date of order, usually entered as the Julian date (see Glossary).

2 Customer name, including the title:
   a. None, Mrs., Mr., Ms.
   b. Professional titles, such as Dr., Prof., Rev.
   c. Military titles, such as Sgt., Lt.

3 Customer address.

4 Ship-to address information.

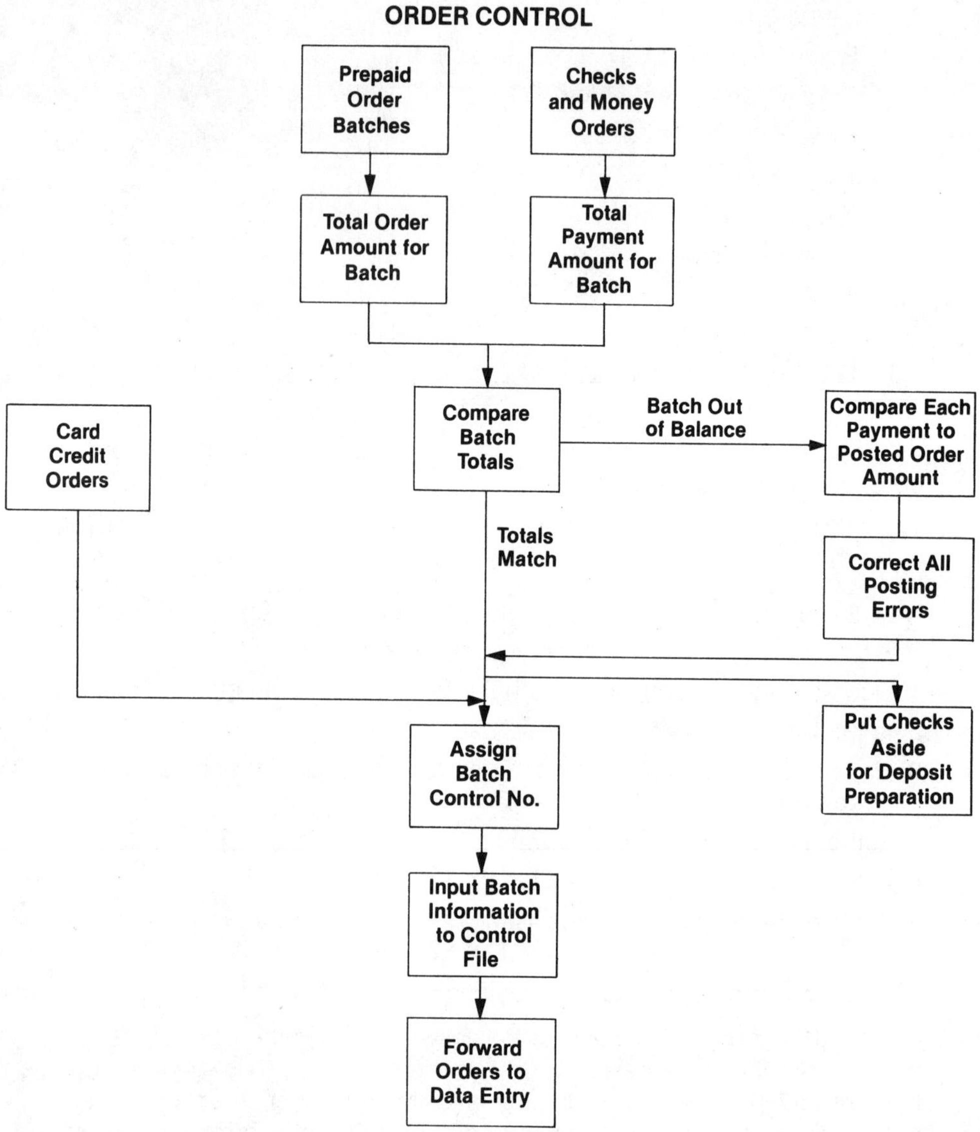

FIGURE 8-2
Flow chart of order control procedures.

5 Order number (all orders should be numbered as they are received).
6 Type of payment and amount.
7 Mail or phone order.

Credit card payment processing

The techniques currently used to process credit card charges range from simple hand processing to online computer methods. Consider waiting until shipment has been made to process the charge. This will minimize adjustments due to cancellations and will allow greater flexibility in handling back orders.

Hand processing is mainly used in startups. The charge slip (see Figure 8-3) is filled out with the credit card holder's name and address, the card number, the expiration date, and, where applicable, the interbank number. The words "mail order" or "signature on file" are written in place of the customer's signature. (When an outside telephone service is used, the service, for an extra fee, may fill in a computerized form for each order it takes.)

Depending on the volume of orders, authorization numbers can be obtained either by telephone or by using a data transmittal module. The authorizations should be obtained for all orders above the preset dollar limit established by the card company/bank, which may vary. Some catalog companies authorize all charges, believing that the additional processing costs are more than offset by reduced losses due to fraud or nonpayment.

The merchant's copy of the charge slip should be kept with the

FIGURE 8-3
Universal telephone and mail order charge forms.

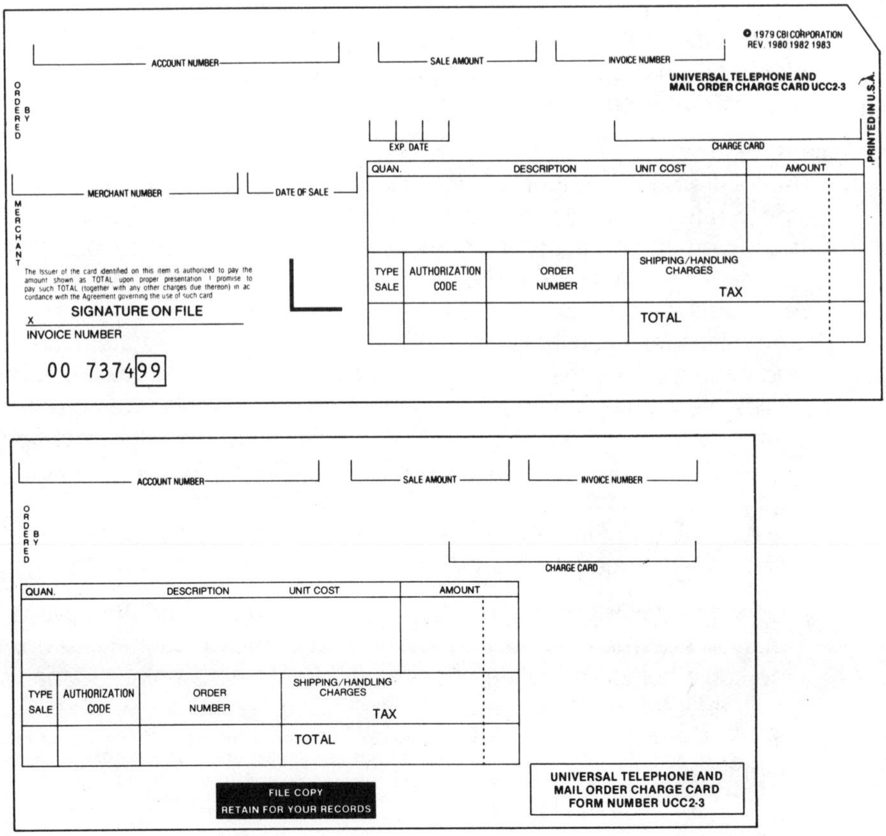
© 1979 CBI CORPORATION
REV. 1980 1982 1983
ACCOUNT NUMBER
SALE AMOUNT
INVOICE NUMBER
UNIVERSAL TELEPHONE AND MAIL ORDER CHARGE CARD UCC2-3
ORDERED BY
EXP DATE
CHARGE CARD
PRINTED IN U.S.A.
MERCHANT NUMBER
DATE OF SALE
MERCHANT

QUAN.	DESCRIPTION	UNIT COST	AMOUNT
TYPE SALE	AUTHORIZATION CODE	ORDER NUMBER	SHIPPING/HANDLING CHARGES
			TAX
			TOTAL

The Issuer of the card identified on this item is authorized to pay the amount shown as TOTAL upon proper presentation. I promise to pay such TOTAL (together with any other charges due thereon) in accordance with the Agreement governing the use of such card
X SIGNATURE ON FILE
INVOICE NUMBER
00 737499

ACCOUNT NUMBER
SALE AMOUNT
INVOICE NUMBER
ORDERED BY
CHARGE CARD

QUAN.	DESCRIPTION	UNIT COST	AMOUNT
TYPE SALE	AUTHORIZATION CODE	ORDER NUMBER	SHIPPING/HANDLING CHARGES
			TAX
			TOTAL

FILE COPY
RETAIN FOR YOUR RECORDS
UNIVERSAL TELEPHONE AND MAIL ORDER CHARGE CARD FORM NUMBER UCC2-3

order. Some catalogers keep the customer copy; others send it with the customer's order. For American Express and Diners Club, a summary slip showing total orders and dollars, signed by an authorized person within the catalog company, is mailed to the credit card company with its copy of the charge slip. For Visa and MasterCard you need the following: (1) the bank copies of each individual charge, (2) a summary slip showing the total transactions and dollars, and (3) a deposit slip showing the total amount. These are brought to the bank and deposited like any other deposit.

American Express and Diners Club automatically deduct the credit card costs from each package of slips received and send the catalog company a net check. MasterCard and Visa costs are deducted by the bank on a monthly basis, using the negotiated rate, or a figure close to that rate, which is determined by the average order that month. Because it costs the bank the same amount to process ten charge slips of $10 each as ten slips of $100 each, most banks lower the discount rate as the average order increases.

More sophisticated methods of charge card processing include: (1) online computer-to-computer authorizations; (2) immediate charge capabilities (but see FTC 30-Day Rule under "The Federal Trade Commission" in Part 12); and (3) wire transfer from data entry or phone service bureaus directly to your bank. All are similar to the manual method, but much faster. Talk with your credit representatives and your data entry and telephone answering sources to determine the most cost-effective combination for your catalog.

Credit card fraud

The toll-free 800 number is a major contributing factor to the impressive growth rate of catalogs. But it has brought problems, too. Credit card fraud is on the increase. Anyone can order merchandise by phone using the credit card number and expiration date from a carbon copy of a recent credit card transaction. Since the card hasn't been stolen, the fraud is not discovered until the cardholder receives the bill. At that time, the cardholder notifies the bank on which the card is drawn, and the bank notifies the catalog company. Although the merchandise was ordered on a legitimate card, the bank will back the cardholder, not the cataloger. And since the item has probably been shipped, the catalog company must absorb the loss.

A catalog company can take several measures to protect itself. One is to be alert to certain signals that a phone order may not be legitimate.

1 Does the caller seem nervous or hesitant? Does he or she have difficulty in answering specific questions? In a caring manner, ask for the person's home and office phone numbers. For example, "So that we may have no problems in delivering your order, could we please have the telephone numbers where you can be reached, both day and night?"

2 Is the caller having difficulty repeating specifics? If so, ask a question: "I'm sorry, but I'm not sure I got your zip code right. Could you please repeat it for me?" If the person hesitates, you may be looking at possible fraud.

3 Does the caller appear to be rushing the order? Persons attempting fraud will try to get the order completed quickly, for fear that the operator will ask a question they can't answer.

4 Is the caller a child? This may be a legitimate order, but placed without the knowledge of the parent. Be sure to get a phone number. Then at a later time call back to verify the order.

5 Does the caller sound intoxicated or under the influence of drugs? Catalog businesses that sell easily pawned items such as electronics and gold jewelry should be especially alert to these callers.

Train your operators to note unusual calls. Such calls can be handled in a number of ways.

• If the order is to be sent to a third party (a name and address different from that of the person ordering), call the person who has supposedly ordered the product. You can pretend you are calling to verify a zip code or color choice. For instance, "Mrs. Jones, this is Mary Smith at ABC Catalog Company. We just wanted to let you know that your order for the footstool will be shipped to you within four days." Whether or not the person placed the order, he or she will appreciate the call. And remember that according to FTC regulations, those who receive merchandise they have not ordered are under no obligation to return it.

• If the order is charged to American Express or Diners Club, ask the authorization center to confirm that the name and address on file is the same as the one on your order. If it is, process the order.

• If the order is charged to MasterCard or Visa, ask your bank for the name of the customer's issuing bank. The first four numbers of the credit card (called the "bin number") are the code of the issuing bank. Then call the issuing bank and ask it to check the cardholder's address against the address you have.

Don't, however, assume that a customer who exceeds the credit limit is trying to commit fraud. Hold the order for a few days and try again. The customer may not know the limit has been exceeded, or a payment may be on the way. If the order is refused a second time, use the modified form letter (Figure 8-15) to contact the customer. Some telephone ordering systems allow the operators to authorize credit card charges while the customer is still on the phone. If credit is refused in this case, make sure that operators are instructed to ask for another credit card diplomatically. For example, "I'm so sorry, but it appears that this credit card company has not yet received your last payment. Is there another one you can use, so that we can process your order without delay?"

No matter how careful you and your staff are, some attempts at fraud will succeed. Keep updated, complete records of all transactions. Compare your list of fraudulent names and addresses with those of other companies'. They are trying to fight fraud, too. Some merge/purge (list processing) service companies have a fraud file to which you can contribute names in exchange for the use of the complete file for suppressing bad names from your mailing. One of the newest approaches to fighting fraud is the Direct Marketing Guaranty Trust of Nashua, New Hampshire. Through the use of sophisticated computer techniques, it has cut losses for many catalogs. Investigate this and other services.

Bank debits

Banks are notoriously uncooperative when it comes to reversing debits. Don't let this stop you. If you have proof (such as a signed UPS receipt that the customer received the merchandise), you have a good chance of getting your money back. Don't waste time. Immediately submit a second charge slip for the amount of the sale (this is in response to the debit the bank made against your account when the customer refused payment).

The Visa or MasterCard bank representative will most likely tell you that you can submit only one charge slip per sale. This is not true. Banks allow charge slips to be resubmitted when a credit card number has been incorrectly entered, which happens frequently. Then send copies of the customer's original order and the proof that the customer did receive the item, along with an explanatory letter, to the customer, the customer's bank, and your bank. Such direct action can avoid bank interference, which could cause the transaction to take weeks to clear.

Check those checks

Even though the convenience of credit card buying has been a major contributing factor to mail order growth, many people still prefer to pay by check. The percentage paying by check depends largely on the average dollar order of the catalog. Higher ticket catalogs tend to have a higher percentage of credit card sales.

Checks have advantages in that they cost you no credit card service fee. The disadvantages are that they can bounce sky high. And, unless your bank is extraordinarily fast at clearing checks, you should ship the merchandise before the check has cleared. Remember, prompt order fulfillment is one of the major ways of keeping that valuable customer.

The good news is that most customers are honest. The majority of bad checks bounce because a customer erroneously believes there is enough money in the account. Simply redeposit the check; more often than not it will clear.

The bad news is that some dishonest people have discovered that mail order can be lucrative for them, too. Here are some basic "alert" signs for bad checks.

1. All good checks (except those issued by the federal government) are perforated. If none of the check's edges is perforated, the check is phony. Forgers may be terrific at duplicating the paper and general look of a check, but perforating the edges is more difficult.

2. Look at the numbers on the check.

- On a good check, numbers are shiny; on a bad check, they are dull. Try smearing the numbers; if you succeed, it's a bad check.
- Look at the first group of numbers with nine digits at the bottom of the check. The first two digits are the Federal Reserve district code. This code should correspond to the location of the bank on which the check is drawn (see Table 8-1). If it does not, the check will be routed to the wrong federal reserve bank. A forger may be playing for time.
- Now look at the upper right-hand corner of the check. There are two sets of numbers, one printed above the other. For example: $\frac{88\text{-}6789}{0124}$. The bottom number, in this case 0124, should correspond to the first four digits in the nine-digit number at the bottom of the check.

Table 8-1 Federal reserve bank codes

State	*Code*	*State*	*Code*
Alabama	06	Nebraska	10
Alaska	12	Nevada	12
Arizona	12 & 12	New Hampshire	01
Arkansas	08	New Jersey	02 & 03
California	12	New Mexico	11
Colorado	10	New York	02
Connecticut	01 & 02	North Carolina	05
Delaware	03	North Dakota	09
Florida	06	Ohio	04
Georgia	06	Oklahoma	10 & 11
Hawaii	12	Oregon	12
Idaho	12	Pennsylvania	03 & 04
Illinois	07 & 08	Rhode Island	01
Indiana	07 & 08	South Carolina	05
Iowa	07 & 10	South Dakota	09
Kansas	10	Tennessee	06 & 08
Kentucky	08	Texas	11
Louisiana	11	Utah	12
Maine	01	Vermont	01
Maryland	05	Virginia	05
Massachusetts	01	Washington	12
Michigan	07 & 09	Washington, D.C.	05
Minnesota	09	West Virginia	04 & 05
Mississippi	06 & 08	Wisconsin	07 & 09
Missouri	10	Wyoming	10
Montana	09		

3. Other codes you should know about.

- Some savings and loan institutions start with the digits 2 or 3.
- Some traveler's checks start with the number 8000.
- U.S. government checks have the routing number 0000-0051.
- Credit union drafts are honored by the bank on which they are drawn.

4. New accounts are dangerous. Ninety percent of "hot" checks are drawn on accounts less than a year old, so watch out for low-numbered checks. The consecutive numbers in the far right-hand corner of the check (just like the ones you record in your personal checkbook) usually start at 101. Obviously, a low-numbered check isn't always a sign of fraud, so consider other factors as well. If the order is for a high dollar amount and/or is being shipped to another address, wait until the check clears.

5. Take into consideration the appearance of the handwriting on the check (and the order form itself). Unless you've been in the mail order business for some time, this may seem a strange statement. Yet, in the same way a good buyer knows that an item will sell and an artist senses the graphics needed for a particular catalog, so can the person who processes the orders pick out a bad check. If this person feels that something is wrong with a check, even if none of the "alerts" applies, let the check clear before sending the order.

6. Be aware of checks without a preprinted name and address. This service is offered free or at minimal charge by banks to checking account holders and can indicate a reliable customer.

FULFILLMENT

Now that the "in" part of order processing has been completed, it's time to begin the "out" part. There is the picking, packing, and shipping of ordered merchandise. The intelligently equipped and arranged warehouse is important. The physical package needs attention.

And shipping choices combined with the intricacies of postage and handling round out fulfillment considerations. Figure 8-4 shows how fulfillment functions.

Pick, pack, and ship

Pick, pack, and ship is the physical movement of merchandise from its warehouse location "out-the-door." Here's how it works.

The procedure

Some fulfillment operations pick each order individually, but it is more efficient to batch orders for picking. This can be a simple procedure, if these easy steps are followed.

1 Select all orders on which there is no hold.
2 Sort the orders by type and number of line items.
   a. Drop ship orders
   b. Single-line (one product) orders (further sort these by warehouse location).
   c. Multiline (multiproduct) orders (further sort these by the warehouse location of the first item).
3 Group all orders into batches of 20 each.
4 Assign a batch number and a sequence number. For example, 1-10 = batch 1, order 10. If the "sold to" or "ship to" is different from the person ordering, issue a confirmation order (Figure 8-5).
5 Create a label file (one entry per item ordered). See Figure 8-6.
6 Sort the label file by batch number and warehouse location.
7 Print the shipping orders on your picking/packing slips. See Figure 8-7.
8 Print the picking labels. See Figure 8-6. Use latex adhesive labels so they can be peeled off easily by the picker and customer.

Pick

1 Take the first batch of picking labels to the appropriate warehouse location.
2 Pull the item indicated on the first picking label from the shelf on which it is located and attach the pressure-sensitive label.
3 Place the item, with its label, on the picking cart.
4 Repeat the preceding steps until the entire batch has been picked.
5 Move the cart to the staging rack and unload. (A staging rack is an open rack divided into various shelves, each of which is numbered.) Each item from a multiline order is placed on the correct shelf of the staging rack. In this way, a number of people can work on the same order simultaneously (pulling products from different locations in the warehouse).

Pack

1 Remove all the items for the first order from the staging rack.
2 Place the items on the packing table.
3 Match to corresponding shipping document.
4 Check off verification slip (Figure 8-7) as each item is wrapped and packed.
5 Apply shipping label to each carton. Enclose packing slip and bounce-back material.
6 Post number of cartons and packer's initials on verification slip.
7 Attach verification slip to first carton and place on conveyor.

Ship

1 Remove verification slip from lead carton.
2 Weigh each carton and post weights on verification slip.
3 Put package aside for UPS or USPS pickup.
4 Forward verification slip to data entry.

Shipping verification

Whether working with a computer or manually, double-check orders. Verification helps inventory control, avoids FTC violations, keeps customer service files updated, and much more. So, after receipt of the verification slips from the shipping department, key in the order number to verify the name and address of the customer. Make sure to back order any unshipped items and update the credit card billing file, the customer order/inquiry file, and the inventory/sales file. The number of cartons, the weight of each, and the packer identification should also be keyed for UPS records.

The warehouse

Every warehouse must be tailored to meet the requirements of the individual catalog operation. Even catalogers who've been in business for years

FIGURE 8-4
Flow chart showing fulfillment functions.

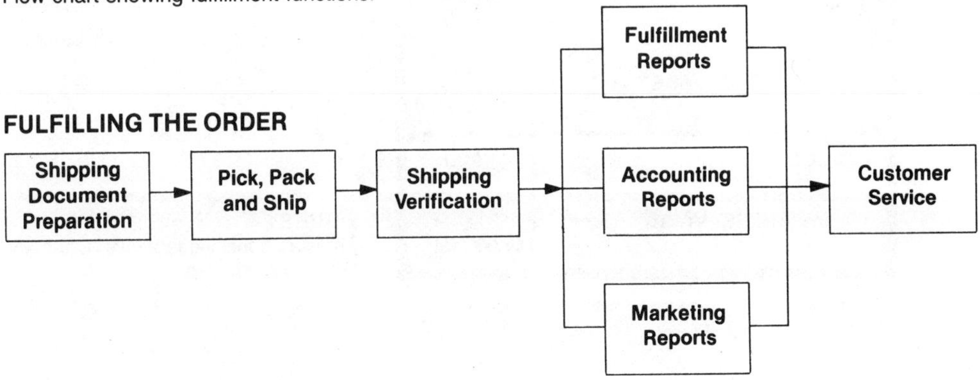

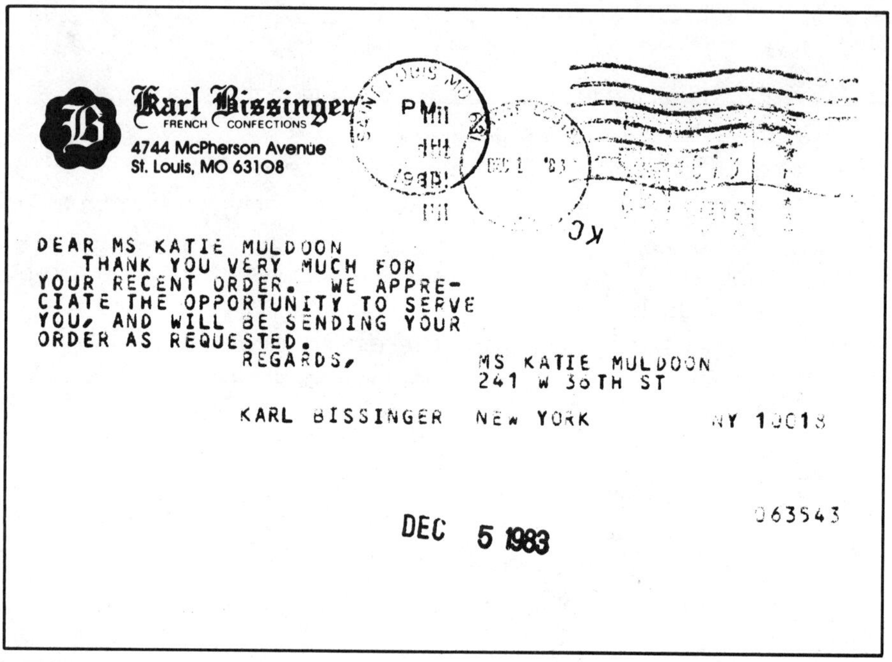

Karl Bissinger
FRENCH CONFECTIONS
4744 McPherson Avenue
St. Louis, MO 63108

DEAR MS KATIE MULDOON
THANK YOU VERY MUCH FOR
YOUR RECENT ORDER. WE APPRE-
CIATE THE OPPORTUNITY TO SERVE
YOU, AND WILL BE SENDING YOUR
ORDER AS REQUESTED.
REGARDS,

KARL BISSINGER

MS KATIE MULDOON
241 W 36TH ST
NEW YORK NY 10018

DEC 5 1983

063543

FIGURE 8-5
Confirmation order.

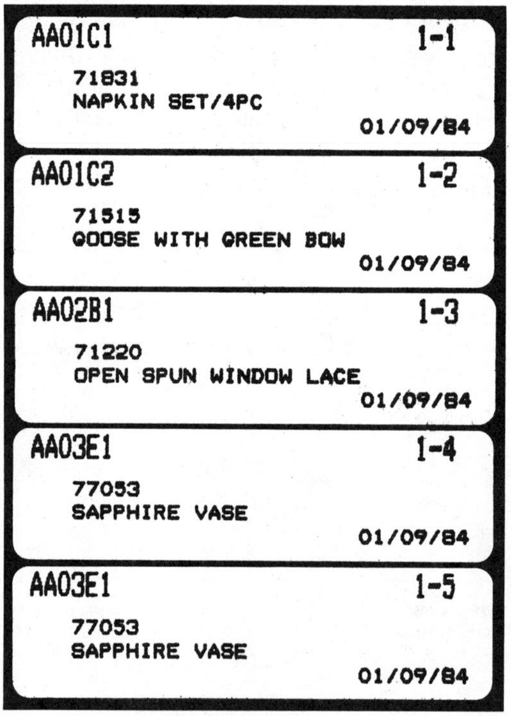

AA01C1 1-1
71831
NAPKIN SET/4PC
01/09/84

AA01C2 1-2
71515
GOOSE WITH GREEN BOW
01/09/84

AA02B1 1-3
71220
OPEN SPUN WINDOW LACE
01/09/84

AA03E1 1-4
77053
SAPPHIRE VASE
01/09/84

AA03E1 1-5
77053
SAPPHIRE VASE
01/09/84

FIGURE 8-6
Pressure-sensitive label file. Courtesy Lifestyle Marketing.

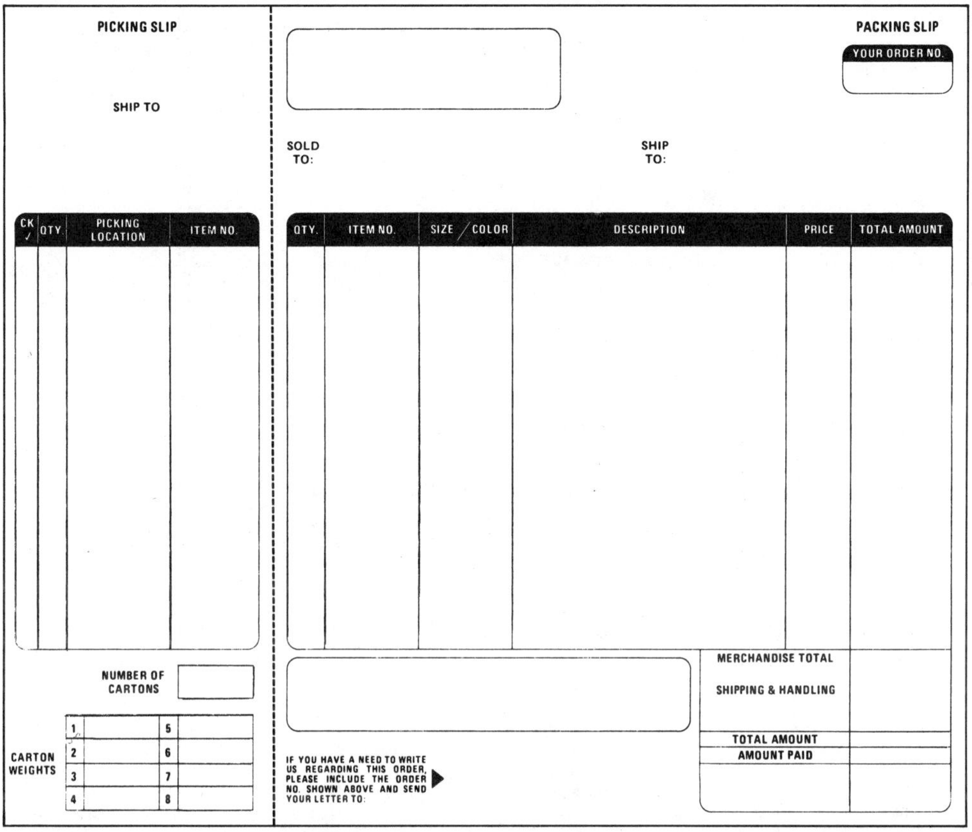

PICKING SLIP

SHIP TO

CK ✓	QTY.	PICKING LOCATION	ITEM NO.

NUMBER OF CARTONS

CARTON WEIGHTS

1		5	
2		6	
3		7	
4		8	

PACKING SLIP

YOUR ORDER NO.

SOLD TO:

SHIP TO:

QTY.	ITEM NO.	SIZE / COLOR	DESCRIPTION	PRICE	TOTAL AMOUNT

IF YOU HAVE A NEED TO WRITE US REGARDING THIS ORDER, PLEASE INCLUDE THE ORDER NO. SHOWN ABOVE AND SEND YOUR LETTER TO:

MERCHANDISE TOTAL

SHIPPING & HANDLING

TOTAL AMOUNT

AMOUNT PAID

FIGURE 8-7
Combination picking slip and packing slip, with package verification section on bottom of picking slip. Courtesy Lifestyle Marketing.

periodically change the setup to meet new needs or accommodate new equipment. (See the floor plan in Figure 8-8 as an example.) Here's a list of considerations for an efficiently run and well-organized mid-size operation:

- Keep working aisles wide enough to allow easy movement of people and picking carts. A minimum of eight feet is generally recommended.
- Startups should probably locate materials by size and weight, keeping smaller items closest to the packing stations. For established catalogers with a sales history, it makes more sense to keep high-volume products closest to the packing stations. In both cases, keep items within a picking area in numerical sequence. A blackboard poster can be kept at the end of each aisle to indicate the SKU (stock keeping unit) numbers in that aisle (similar to the way a library marks book locations). Because many warehouses make use of part-time help, taping a picture of an item from the catalog to the corresponding bin or shelf can be helpful, especially if one shelf contains two items that look similar.

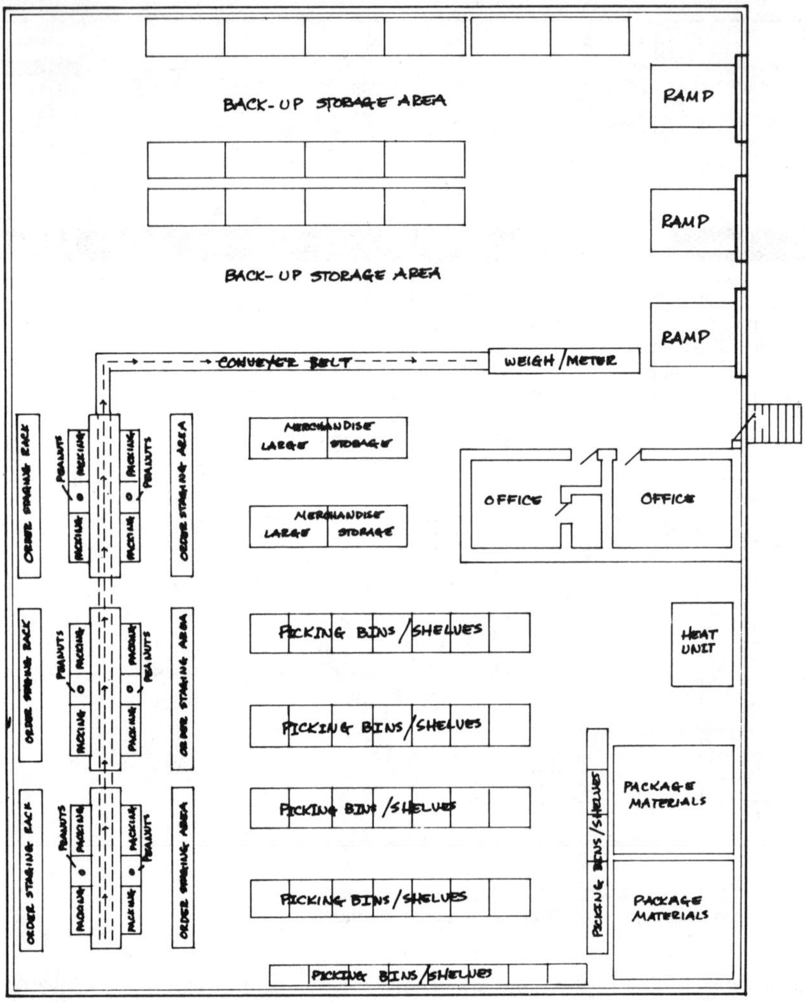

FIGURE 8-8
Warehouse floor plan for mid-size fulfillment operation.

- Label all picking bins with bold Magic Marker.
- Keep heavy, prepacked items on the pallets on which they come. Store these in a separate area (see Merchandise—Large Storage in Figure 8-8).
- If you're not on computer, use brightly colored cards or a blackboard at the end of each aisle to keep track of low stock levels. One person should be responsible for checking stock levels at regularly scheduled intervals.
- Keep easily pilferable items away from doors and on the highest tiers. Don't hesitate to let employees know that you will prosecute anyone who is caught stealing. Keep trash cans away from areas containing highly pilferable items and don't let trash be collected near the warehouse area.

- Use rubber mats on concrete floors in areas of the greatest activity or where employees must stand for long periods (especially packing table and metering areas). They'll more than pay for themselves by reducing employee fatigue and increasing working time.
- Keep a section of the warehouse for stock backup, apart from the everyday pick-pack flow. Some catalogers use a grid system to locate merchandise quickly. The floor in the backup storage area is visually divided into numbered sections. A computerized or manual card system indicates the location of the merchandise by manufacturer. Be sure to keep this log up to date as merchandise is moved.

No matter what warehouse design you choose, don't be locked into it. Experiment and adjust to your changing needs.

If this is your first catalog, don't feel that major equipment investments are necessary. Create your own equipment. For instance, one cataloger realized that a conveyor belt was not yet a necessary expense. To avoid having to stack and then physically move packed merchandise, he raised the legs on one end of a standard table with bricks and attached a board to the other end to stop packages from falling off. Packages placed on the high end of the table moved continuously to the metering station. Another cataloger simply used grocery-style carts and baskets to move items from one location to another.

Receiving merchandise

Every cataloger must find the right merchandise-receiving system. Here's a checklist of points to consider.

- Retain the original photographic sample to check against the merchandise as it arrives.
- Consider prepacking merchandise as it is received. Items most likely to be shipped in their own cartons can be totally packed. Other items can at least be wrapped in foam. This will save time during pick-pack operations and protect products from damage while on the shelves.
- Instruct vendors to label outside packages with the item number, total unit quantity, and your purchase order number. Your P.O. number should also appear on invoices and packing slips, whether the order is complete or partial, to reduce paperwork for both your staff and your accountant.
- Instruct vendors to assign only one SKU number item per master carton. This may not be possible at the beginning, when you are ordering small quantities. However, ask vendors to do this whenever feasible.
- For security reasons, don't leave cartons on the loading dock. Count them immediately. Shortages or damages must be noted on the freight bill at the time of delivery to expedite a claim settlement.
- Check all merchandise against the vendor's packing slip. Numerous errors occur in packing and the accompanying paperwork. Merchan-

COUNTRY NOTEBOOK
MERCHANDISE RECEIPTS REPORT
FOR THE MONTH ENDING 05/05/84

PAGE 1

ITEM NO	DESCRIPTION	RECEIPT DATE	POSTING DATE	VENDOR	PO NUMBER	RECEIPT NO	QUANTITY RECEIVED	UNIT COST	EXTENDED AMOUNT
70042000000	STEIN & GOLDSTEIN HORSE	04/11/84	04/11/84	108	11372	9	20	15.00	300.00
70043000000	DENTZEL RABBIT	05/02/84	05/02/84	108	11534	3	21	15.00	315.00
70044000000	DENTZEL LION	05/02/84	05/02/84	108	11534	3	17	15.00	255.00
70045000000	CARMÈL JUMPER	04/26/84	04/26/84	108	11663	1	8	15.00	120.00
70046000000	DENTZEL CAT	04/18/84	04/18/84	108	11372	10	50	15.00	750.00
		05/02/84	05/02/84	108	11534	3	4	15.00	60.00
				**** PRODUCT SUBTOTALS ****			54		810.00
70047000000	ILLIONS HORSE	04/11/84	04/11/84	108	11372	9	10	15.00	150.00
		04/18/84	04/18/84	108	11372	10	3	15.00	45.00
				**** PRODUCT SUBTOTALS ****			13		195.00
70062000000	CEDAR COW	04/12/84	04/12/84	164		1	5	18.00	90.00
70072000000	BUGLER	04/05/84	04/05/84	160	11640	1	7	17.00	119.00
		04/05/84	04/05/84	160	11532	4	8	17.00	136.00
		04/26/84	04/26/84	160	11640	2	20	17.00	340.00
				**** PRODUCT SUBTOTALS ****			35		595.00

COUNTRY NOTEBOOK
Nº 1253 RECEIVING REPORT

# OF CARTONS	PIECES PER CARTON	VENDOR ITEM NUMBER	DESCRIPTION	TOTAL PIECES	OUR ITEM #	LOCATION
4	12	CH-2	Candle Holders—Glass	48	47-100	CA12A
6	6	CD-1	Candy Dishes	36	47-102	CA12B

DATE RECEIVED: 3/24/84
VENDOR NAME: Jones Glass Co.
CARRIER: UPS
CLIENT: Country Notebook
RECEIVED BY: [illegible]
☑ PREPAID ☐ COLLECT
PURCHASE ORDER # 10302
PARTIAL ☐ COMPLETE ☑
DATE ENTERED: 3/24/84
ENTERED BY: [illegible]

WAREHOUSE: ATTACH ALL SHIPPING DOCUMENTS - TRUCK SLIPS - PACKING SLIPS - ETC.
WHITE COPY — PURCHASING YELLOW COPY — ACCOUNTS PAYABLE PINK COPY — PERMANENT RECORDS

FIGURE 8-9
Computerized and manual receiving reports. Courtesy Lifestyle Marketing.

dise should be counted, inspected, and posted to a receiving report (Figure 8-9), which should then be compared with the purchase order by someone other than the receiving person. A receiving person who has a purchase order in hand is easily convinced that what should have been received is what is received and, too often, this is not true.

- Keep a manual or computerized receiving log (see Figure 8-9). Include date, carrier, pro number (bill of lading number), shipper, number of cartons received, and the initials of the person who received them. This will help to resolve disputes later.

The packing station

1 The most sensible packing table for general merchandise is 6 feet wide, 3 feet deep, and 30 inches high, enough room to hold orders, supplies, and equipment. It should be fitted with a superstructure to hold shipping cartons. Do not provide chairs or stools; packers who stand tend to be more productive than those who sit.

2 Try not to use more than 5 to 12 carton or bag (soft pack) sizes. If more sizes are necessary, keep low-volume sizes farthest from the packing station. Avoid the use of UPS oversized cartons. (UPS maximum size is a total of 108 inches. Measure the five "surface" sides—length and width and width and height and height—and add them up.) Also, no single package should weigh more than UPS's 70-pound maximum.
3 Pack high-value or easily pilferable items at a separate packing station, preferably one with added security.
4 Always insert a bounceback (catalog, order form, flyer, and so on) in outgoing packages.
5 Include how-to-return information (see "Customer Service" later in Part 8).
6 Be sure that someone other than the picker double-checks outgoing orders before sealing packages. Check that product(s) match the order and that sales material, return instructions, notice of partial shipment, and so on, are all included.
7 Regularly check your scale for accuracy, especially if it's electronic. UPS and USPS provide valuable services, but there's no reason to overpay them.
8 Keep an amiable relationship with UPS and USPS personnel. It's to your benefit to develop a smooth relationship with the individual responsible for seeing that packages are picked up in time and delivered in good order.
9 Although UPS is supposed to do the loading of parcels on outbound trailers, mutual cooperation is always to everyone's advantage.
10 When arranging parcels for pickup, position heavier items to the front to be loaded first. This means that they will wind up on the bottom, allowing lighter items to rest on top.

The package

When a package arrives in a customer's home, the catalog's image comes with it. Compare it to a store: if the clothing is hanging straight on the racks, the aisles are clean, and the store looks generally inviting, you'll probably want to shop there again. The same is true of a mail order package. Here are some pointers on how to project a good image.

- Keep it neat and tidy looking. This is the major physical contact your customer is likely to have with your company.
- Keep the label centered; avoid a torn or crinkled look.
- Packing materials should be adequate to protect the item, but not overdone. Too much packing is not cost-efficient, and can be annoying to the customer. To ensure that the packing material will do the job, send test packages to friends in various parts of the country. Breakable items generally should be wrapped in white foam sheets, securely taped, then put in the outer carton, which is filled with plastic pellets or chips. Avoid using shredded newspapers. They often leave the con-

sumer's hands blackened by ink, which could come off on the product. Guess who will get the soiled item returned?

- Use plain paper labels and apply with cellophane tape. Pressure-sensitive labels increase cost, can fall off, and, if preprinted separately, require additional labor to match with packing slips.
- Don't cut down cartons. This reduces the structural strength and can result in excessive damage and high returns.
- Whenever possible, put small items inside large items or tape them to the inside top flap of the box. Be sure that the packing slip clearly indicates the number of items in the package to ensure that the customer does not throw the merchandise away with the packing material.
- Make up a stamp that says "This is a partial shipment. Other item(s) will be arriving in a separate shipment." When shipping partials, stamp the packing slip and any inner cartons. Also, multiple-carton shipments should be boldly marked "1 of 2," "2 of 2," and so on, in case a shipment is separated in transit. Both procedures will save a great deal of customer service time.
- Check with vendors to see if items can be purchased individually boxed in reshippable cartons. Many times the incremental cost to the manufacturer is cheaper than packing the item yourself. But be sure that the manufacturer's name is not on the outside of the carton; there is no need to give away your sources or confuse your customers.

Shipping

You can pack and ship from your own fulfillment center or have your vendors do drop shipping. Read on to find why, in general, catalogers do most of their own packing and shipping, what it really costs, and how to charge for postage and handling.

UPS versus USPS

The common belief is that the United Parcel Service is the only way to deliver orders. But a highly economical alternative is the "pound rate" the U.S. Postal Service offers for bulk third-class mail. This may be the best method for similar-size, "machinable" packages weighing under one pound.

For instance, a 12-ounce item can be sent anywhere (there's no cost difference based on zone, as with UPS) for only 34 cents. Bulk rate third-class is computed at 45 cents per pound for all packages mailed at one time. Packages weighing less than 3.8 ounces are charged the minimum per piece rate, which is 11 cents. Conversely, UPS rates are based on the next highest pound. For instance, a one-half pound package would have to be sent at the pound rate.

Parcels need not be the exact same weight for bulk rate third class, but at least 200 pieces, or a total weight of 50 pounds, are required at any given time. If, for example, you have 100 packages of 2 ounces each and 100 packages of 6 ounces each, all would be mailed at the minimum rate of 11 cents each.

Post office rules were recently changed to benefit third-class mailers, so schedule a meeting with your USPS customer service representative, even if you are a small mailer, to determine whether this cost-saving service is right for your company. The meeting costs nothing. Also, obtain a copy of the *USPS Domestic Mail Manual* (even before you meet with your USPS representative). It clearly outlines all the rules and regulations regarding third-class mail. No mail order company should be without a copy of this publication.

Keep up to date by subscribing to Postal Manual supplements to the *USPS Domestic Mail Manual.* If you decide that the economics of the USPS service are too good to pass up and that your fulfillment center will have no problem conforming to its regulations and requirements, consider a few other points.

- How much longer will it take the package to arrive if sent via bulk rate than by UPS? Is the time difference substantial enough to cause customer dissatisfaction? Large shippers using this method have experienced only two- to three-day delays over UPS, but this can vary based on volume, location, and destination.
- How valuable are the products you plan to send via USPS? Third-class shipments cannot be insured (UPS packages are insured) or traced. Avoid shipping high-value merchandise via USPS.

Mailers who use a combination of UPS and USPS have had no significant problems with delivery of unsigned-for packages. But monitor USPS deliveries carefully. If customers receiving packages through this method are ordering less, it could be a sign that they are unhappy with the time it takes for delivery. Have customer service calls increased on the USPS parcels? This could be another sign that a problem exists. At all times, balance cost savings with customer satisfaction.

Postage and handling

Despite the common belief that most consumers object to paying postage and handling, tests show that, when given a choice, the consumer will pick a lower price plus postage and handling over a higher price without postage and handling. Most consumers understand that the cataloger spends money to send a product, and that their own time and the cost of gasoline, parking, babysitters, and so on, add up to more than they are paying in postage and handling charges. Smart catalogers diplomatically state these facts on their order form, preferably near the shipping and handling information. Nevertheless, since consumer attitudes change, and testing on any policy should be an ongoing process, this current truth should be reevaluated at timely intervals.

A manifest system

A manifest system allows a company to ship products without a label showing the actual cost of shipping. (The normal meter used for UPS charges generates a label showing actual costs.) The manifest system allows the company to pass on its real costs, without alienating customers. If, for example, the postage charge is $1.25 and the customer has paid $2.50 for postage and handling, the customer could feel cheated—temporarily forgetting about the cataloger's costs for manpower and shipping materials. This potential problem can be circumvented by keeping a manifest, or log, of daily UPS charges. Figure 8-10 shows a computerized shipping manifest. If you are not using the manifest system, simply keep a daily log of the information shown in Figure 8-10.

Real costs

Be sure to weigh every product in the carton and the packing material in which it is to be sent. Use the UPS charge for Zone 5 (the farthest you can send the product; unless you are receiving orders from Alaska, Puerto Rico, Hawaii, or Canada) to determine shipping cost.

Adjust your figures later, after you know which zone constitutes the average shipping point. For cartons and soft-side envelopes, figuring the cost of each piece is relatively easy. Only through experience will you learn how much packing material to allocate per package. Carefully watch costs of shipments outside the continental United States. Most likely, you will need to ask customers to pay a set surcharge.

Determine how long it takes warehouse personnel to put the product

FIGURE 8-10
Computerized manifest system.

PKG. . . . D	UPS ZNE	CUSTOMER NAME. .	CUSTOMER ADDRESS.	CITY.	ST	ZIP. .	NO. PKG	CTN WGT	O S	BASIC CHRGE	ADDED INSRE	COD CHRGE	TOTA CHRG
112171*1	2	DEBRA WALKER	1435 LEXINGTON ST	ARLINGTON	VA	22205	1	1		1.29			1.29
112166*1	2	RACHEL VIAS	RT 1 BOX 1059	MAURERTOWN	VA	22644	1	2		1.37			1.37
112138*1	2	CECILIA MUNOZ	501 MARINE RD	MOUNT HOLLY	NJ	08060	1	4		1.54			1.54
112150*1	2	LEILA SAFATLE	1472 FIRESTONE LANE	SILVER SPRING	MD	20904	1	4		1.54			1.54
112157*1	2	LOIS ROTHSTEIN	8419 CASTLE RD	FAIRFAX STATION	VA	22039	1	3		1.46			1.46
112163*1	2	ISABEL STUARDO	RT 80 BOX 341	MECHANICSVILLE	VA	23111	1	4		1.54			1.54
112168*1	2	YOLANDA ROMAN	1019 LONGWOOD RD	BALTIMORE	MD	21210	1	5		1.63			1.63
112170*1	2	M R SOLLOSQUI	890 MAPLE LANE	PALMYRA	PA	17078	1	1		1.29			1.29
112170*2	2	M R SOLLOSQUI	890 MAPLE LANE	PALMYRA	PA	17078	1	2		1.37			1.37
112173*1	2	LESLIE DEGAP	6940 BOOTHVILLE	EASTON	PA	18042	1	1		1.29			1.29
TOTAL ZNE	2						10	27		14.32	0.00		14.32
112213*1	3	TED DEWITT	6 RIVERSIDE AVE.	PAWCATUCK	CT	06379	1	8		2.13			2.13
112156*1	3	ROBERT CRESPO	920 WOODLAWN DR	NORTH TONAWANDA	NY	14120	1	2		1.44			1.44
112155*1	3	D. VILA	4183 FOREST PARK	MEDINA	OH	44246	1	6		1.90			1.90
112179*1	3	C. DENES	52 TRAVER RD	HARTSDALE	NY	10530	1	2		1.44			1.44
112111*1	3	TANYA BASINI	67 NASSAU DRIVE	NEW YORK	NY	10162	1	9*		4.10			4.10
112191*1	3	MARILYN HOUPT	268 UNION RD	STORRS	CT	06268	1	5		1.78			1.78
112095*1	3	LAUREL PLOTKIN	HONEYCOMB RD	SOMERS	NY	10589	1	2		1.44			1.44
112204*1	3	WILLIAM ALBRECHT	9 ANPELL DRIVE	DANIELS	WV	25832	1	5		1.78			1.78
112139*1	3	M Q RUBIN	RD 5 BOX 5099	CANONSBURG	PA	15317	1	1		1.32			1.32
112169*1	3	ANDREW STRANGE	6615 WETHEROLE ST	DUDLEY	MA	01570	1	1		1.32			1.32
112197*1	3	OLGA SCHORR	936 WESTBURY DR	ERIE	PA	16505	1	8		2.13			2.13
112199*1	3	GILDA HOLZER	17528 IVORY RD	BYRON	NY	14422	1	4		1.67			1.67
112201*1	3	BELLA SCHESSEL	7381 BIRCHWOOD DR	MENTOR	OH	44060	1	7		2.02			2.02
112206*1	3	RUTH GOLDMAN	21 DOWN ST	PETERBROUGH	NH	03458	1	3		1.55			1.55
112208*1	3	MARINA CORDOVA	GLENDALE ROAD	RUTLAND	MA	01543	1	1		1.32			1.32
112225*1	3	RACHEL SZERENA	8 CLOCK ST	STONINGTON	CT	06378	1	1		1.32			1.32
TOTAL ZNE	3						16	65		28.66	0.00		28.66
112123*1	4	ROBERT MILLER	28562 YELLOWSTONE	LIVONIA	MI	48152	1	9*		5.03			5.03
112122*1	4	S ALFSTAD		INDIANAPOLIS	IN	46208	1	9*		5.03			5.03
112192*1	4	N UBILES	17 SAUNDERS	BRUNSWICK	ME	04011	1	4		1.51			1.51
112105*1	4	MABEL SOLER	RT 75	EVANSVILLE	IN	47712	1	1		1.82			1.82
112165*1	4	SAMUEL COX	2794 OZORA CHURCH RD RT 2	LOGANVILLE	GA	30249	1	1		1.36			1.36
112120*1	4	WILLIAM LYNN	175 ORCHARD ST	COHASSET	MA	02025	1	9*		5.03			5.03
112114*1	4	EDWARD ORTON	1044 COLLEVE AVE	FORT CAMPBELL	KY	42223	1	9*		5.03			5.03
112147*1	4	GINA TORRISI	1509 DELANCEY ST	PORTAGE	MI	49002	1	7		2.28			2.28
112214*1	4	L COLON	5281 JACKSON LANE	DOWNERS GROVE	IL	60515	1	4		1.82			1.82
112203*1	4	FALANA ACOSTA	55805 DAWSON ST	UTICA	MI	48087	1	4		1.82			1.82
112207*1	4	HANS DREICHLER	P O BOX 1901	LITTLETON	MA	01460	1	10		2.73			2.73
112129*1	4	ROSEMARY GOLDMAN	1244 GRAVESEND ST	TROY	MI	48098	1	4		1.82			1.82
112134*1	4	RICHARD BEAUDET	109 SUGAR HILL RD	AUBURN	NH	03032	1	1		1.36			1.36
112146*1	4	RITA CALDERON	819 MADISON ROAD	WILMETTE	IL	60091	1	11		2.89			2.89
112148*1	4	LINDA NAKOVICS	251 OLD COUNTRY RD	GLENWOOD	IL	60425	1	1		1.36			1.36
112162*1	4	RUTH SCHWARTZ	1509 WILSON RD	MILFORD	MI	48042	1	2		1.51			1.51
112164*1	4	MELISSA CAMHY	380 UNION ST	NATICK	MA	01760	1	2		1.51			1.51
112177*1	4	M PORTALATIN	BOX 78-C RTE 1	HAMPTON	SC	29924	1	2		1.51			1.51
112185*1	4	L JOHNSON	580 PROSPECT	MARSHALL	MI	49068	1	1		1.36			1.36

in stock, locate it in response to orders, pack the box, and load it onto the UPS truck. Multiply this time by the packers' rate (include the dollars you allocated for overhead, insurance, and so on). The hourly rate varies, but let's assume the allocated rate is $5 per hour, and the worker spends one-half hour on the fulfillment. The formula is:

Hours × Hourly rate = Labor cost
(.5 hours × $5/hour = $2.50)

The formula to determine the total cost of shipping and handling for UPS mailings is:

Labor cost + Materials + UPS = Total cost of shipping and handling
($2.50 + .20 + .83 = $3.53)

The same formula applies to costs of shipping by USPS.

How to charge

The three most common ways of charging a customer for postage and handling are:

1. No charge (the cost is absorbed by the company or in the selling price of the item).
2. The cost of postage and handling is shown after the retail price of each item in the catalog.
3. A postage and handling chart is provided on the order form.

L. L. Bean currently charges no postage and handling, The Sharper Image displays the charge in brackets after the retail price, and all Hanover House catalogs use a chart. Each method has its merits.

Not charging for postage and handling must be financially evaluated by individual companies. Can the cataloger afford to absorb the cost or increase the retail price of the merchandise to cover this expense?

The disadvantage of the shipping charge after the item is that a customer can be subconsciously discouraged from buying a product. What's more, if the customer has decided to purchase many products, this method of allocating separate postage and handling charges for each product can add up to many dollars, and may even persuade the customer to order less.

A postal chart is less likely to deter a customer from buying, because it comes after the decision to buy. Figure 8-11 shows postage and handling charges used successfully by a sampling of catalogers. To determine the best chart for your merchandise mix, follow the steps outlined under "Real costs," earlier in this chapter. You will also need to segment merchandise by the price point categories listed in the chart (Figure 8-11). Then see if the average fulfillment cost per price point category is adequately covered by the chart.

View your shipping charges as a totally separate area. It is an accepted, and smart, practice for postage and handling to become a profit

FIGURE 8-11 Sample postage and handling chart

If Order Totals	Please Add
$20.00 and under	$2.95
$20.01-$30.00	$3.95
$30.01-$40.00	$4.95
$40.01-$55.00	$5.95
$55.01-$75.00	$6.95
$75.01-$100.00	$7.95
$100.01 and over	$8.95

center in itself. Test different pricing structures to find one with which both you *and* your customers will be comfortable.

Drop Shipping

The term "drop ship" is used when the product is actually shipped from the supplier's warehouse. Orders are sent directly to the supplier for filling.

Advantages of drop shipping

Inventory costs are reduced. Because you do not take inventory on products that are drop shipped, your inventory costs are reduced and you do not have overstock problems. If sales are weaker than projected, you needn't worry about how to dispose of leftovers.

Convenience to you on certain kinds of merchandise. Oversized and monogrammed items are ideal for drop shipping, as are extremely expensive items. Because it takes up so much space and weighs so much, an oversized item, such as the cabinet safe American Express has sold, is too cumbersome for efficient warehouse handling. It is also relatively expensive. You'd be wise to let the vendors fulfill such oversized items.

Monogrammed items can be personalized in a great many ways. When monogramming is left to the supplier, the cataloger is saved the expense of purchasing the equipment necessary to meet the wide variety of monogramming needs.

Disadvantages

Drop shipping is costly. The manufacturer charges a drop ship fee to cover the time spent filling the order and passes on the UPS charge. These charges are almost always more than they would be if the cataloger filled the order. And they are often too high to pass on to the customer. Therefore, the additional amount is often added to the cost of goods, resulting in reduced sales. Alternately, it can be absorbed by the cataloger, but this can result in a less-than-ideal markup.

You lose time. Not only is there the additional step of sending the order to the drop shipper, but there's the time spent following up on individual orders. And the customer can get the order later than if you had stocked the item in your own efficient fulfillment center.

You can't use bouncebacks. It is unlikely that the drop shipper will be willing to include advertising material in outgoing orders. Therefore, you lose a valuable profit center. Even if the drop shipper agrees, you can't be sure (unless flat bounceback sales tell you so) whether or not the materials were actually inserted.

You give away your merchandise sources. Since drop shippers sometimes use their own cartons or shipping labels, smart competitors can order an item to discover its source.

In all cases, evaluate what it would cost you to perform the fulfillment in-house against what it costs to have it done by individual vendors. Don't choose drop shipping because it appears easier. Look carefully at the cost-efficiencies involved, remember how valuable prompt service is to your customer, and determine the pluses and minuses for each possible drop ship product.

INVENTORY CONTROL

Determining how much of a particular item to stock is one of the greatest challenges direct marketers face. A cataloger must balance the cost of too much inventory against the possibility of losing customers due to sold-out merchandise. For catalogs with a sales history, past response lays the groundwork for inventory estimates, but for first-timers, it's strictly guesswork.

Forecasting

Everyone has different estimating methods. One startup cataloger used the unorthodox method of ordering exactly the number of items, per space allocated per product, that he needed to make a small profit. His method worked, but he is one of the luckier individuals ever to walk the face of this earth. His method is not recommended. Of those that are, let's take the easiest first.

Pre-mailing forecasting

Past sellers

Sales history is a great starting point, but don't forget to consider other determining factors.

- *Seasonality.* Is the item great for cold weather, but not suitable year round? Gift items are strongest in the fall, but are surpassed in sales by "me-oriented" products in January.
- *Recent sales trend.* Has the item shown a downward sales trend? If so, there are three choices: withdraw the item from the catalog for a few editions, discontinue it completely, or allocate less display space to it.
- *Placement.* Did the product move to a more or less prominent sales position within the catalog?

Similar items

Even though merchandise is new, its similarity to past sellers gives an estimating edge over a totally new product. Use the same criteria as for past sellers.

New products

For new products, you must use common sense and any sales information you can garner from vendors and other catalogers. A look at profit and sales projections for the catalog can also help.

First, project the average order and response rate of the catalog. Multiply these two figures to determine your gross sales. Next, determine the in-mail cost of your catalog and the cost of merchandise. Now look at your sales projections. Do they seem reasonable based on promotional costs? It is helpful to divide your promotional costs by the number of pages in the catalog. This will show the gross sales needed to pay for each page. Further, divide the per page number by the number of items on that page to get a rough estimate of gross dollars required to pay for a particular item. (This is not to be confused with square-inch analysis, which is discussed in "Catalog Analysis," Part 9.) On the basis of your

TABLE 8-2 Example of weekly sales projection

Week	Percent Sales Completion
1	6
2	18
3	27
4	35
5	55
6	69
7	76
8	79
9	84
10	88
11	92
12	96
13	100

rough estimate, you can make necessary adjustments to items that may be over- or underprojected.

Post-mailing forecasting

Here's your chance to make up for any inventory commitment errors. You can begin to plot a response curve, which will give you a more accurate assessment of your inventory needs.

Let's assume a 500,000 mailing, a 2 percent response expectation, and an average order size expectation of $70. That's 10,000 orders, equaling $700,000 in gross sales, which can be projected over a 13-week period as in Table 8-2. (The percentages in the table, of course, are only examples and are based on historical curves used by the direct marketing industry; each catalog responds differently.)

If orders continue to come in at the rate shown in Table 8-3, the response will be considerably higher than the 10,000 originally projected and inventory will need to be adjusted (see "Economics," Part 10, for additional information on order curves). The formula used to calculate the anticipated total demand in Table 8-3 is: cumulative orders divided by percent of anticipated completed sales equal anticipated demand. For example, for week 1:

650 ÷ .06 (6% expressed as a decimal) = 10,833

TABLE 8-3 Example of anticipated demand based on cumulative orders and anticipated percent completion of sales

Week	Cumulative Orders	Anticipated Completion of Sales (%)	Anticipated Total Demand
1	650	6	10,833
2	2,150	18	11,944
3	3,500	27	12,963
4	4,750	35	13,571

Inventory needs per item can be projected using the same formula on a per item basis. Projections should be updated to keep up with product demand.

When to order?

Another consideration is how long it actually takes to place orders and receive merchandise. (The individual elements that must be considered are covered in "Merchandising," Part 3). To determine when to place an order, you first need to know:

1 The number of units in stock.

2 The number of units currently on order.

3 The anticipated total number of units that will be sold (per Table 8-3).

4 The anticipated amount of time that will elapse between order placement and order receipt.

Using the same formula that was used in Table 8-3, project the demand week by week. For instance, assuming that 250 pieces are in stock and actual sales are 95 units by week 3,

$95 \div .27 =$ Anticipated total demand of 352 pieces.

To determine the week you can expect merchandise to be depleted, divide the in-stock quantity, in this case 250 pieces, by the anticipated demand, in this case 352:

$250 \div 352 = .71$ or 71%

According to Table 8-2, merchandise would be completely gone during the seventh week.

Now determine how much time is needed between placing the order and actual receipt. Factor in this time, allowing a few days leeway. Also, remember to update projections weekly. Even your own historical charts change with such buyer influences as weather and economic trends.

How much to buy

To determine the quantity to buy, answer the following questions.

1 How much storage room is available?

2 How much can you afford to spend, both initially and taking cash flow into consideration?

3 How much insurance coverage do you have?

4 What arrangements have you made with the vendor regarding ordering quantity and product availability?

5 What is the cost in employee time and paperwork to cut multiple orders?

Each case must be considered individually. But always remember that the long-term cost of losing a customer due to product unavailability can mean much more to a bottom line than minimum overbuying.

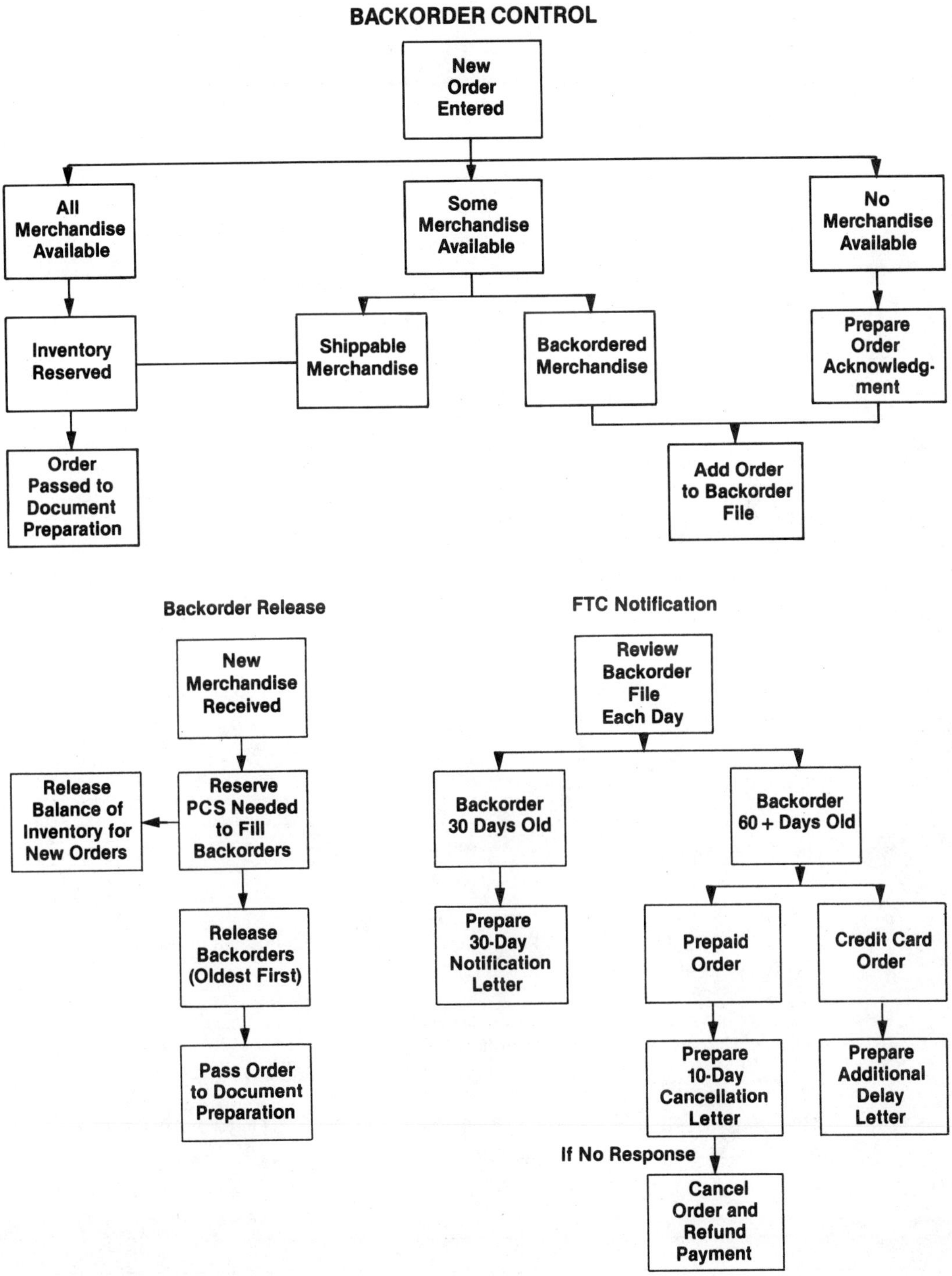

FIGURE 8-12
Flow chart of steps in backorder control.

FIGURE 8-13
Sample first-delay letter

ABC Catalog Company
123 Main Street
Anywhere, USA 00000
000-000-0000

Date

Customer's Name
Address

Order Number

Dear Customer:

Thank you for your order for ________________________

Due to unforeseen circumstances, shipment of your order will be delayed ______ days. Please be assured that we will not deposit your check (or process your credit card payment) until shipment can be made.

Thank you for your understanding and patience.

Sincerely,

P.S. We have included our latest catalog in the hope that we may continue to serve you in the convenience of your own home.

If you wish to cancel your order, please check the appropriate boxes and return to us in the enclosed postage-paid envelope:

______ Sorry, I can't wait. Please cancel my order and:
☐ Send me my check or a refund.
☐ Hold my payment as a credit toward my next order.

IF I WISH TO WAIT, I UNDERSTAND I NEED NOT RETURN THIS FORM and that my order will be sent as soon as possible (maximum of 30 days).

________________ ________________________________
Date Signature

FIGURE 8-14
Sample second-delay letter

ABC Catalog Company
123 Main Street
Anywhere, USA 00000
000-000-0000

Date

Customer's Name
Address

Order Number

Dear Customer:

We are sorry to inform you that your order for ________________ has been unavoidably delayed for longer than our original 30-day delay.

We estimate shipment time to be between ____________ and ____________. Please forgive us for this disappointing development.

We wish to continue to serve you and hope you understand that we are doing everything possible to speed your order. If you have paid by check and we do not hear from you within 30 days, a prompt refund will be sent. If you requested we charge your order, be assured that no charge will be made.

Thank you for your understanding and patience.

Sincerely,

____

Please check all the appropriate boxes and return in the enclosed postage-paid envelope.

- ☐ I am willing to wait—please don't cancel my order.
- ☐ I paid by check—please send me my refund.
- ☐ I paid by credit card—simply cancel my order.
- ☐ I paid by check, but wish the amount credited to my next order.

____________ ____________________
Date Signature

Back orders

It is impossible for every item to be in stock all the time. Figure 8-12 includes information on how back orders "flow" through the system. Basically, this chart breaks at the first level after order entry into three sections:

1 Merchandise is available and shipped.

2 Merchandise is in a back-order situation. As soon as new merchandise is received, it is released to inventory and orders are filled.

3 Merchandise is not expected to be available at any time in the future. The order cannot be filled.

If the merchandise is not expected to be available, inform the customer by letter and refund the customer's money immediately. If merchandise is in a back-order situation, read on.

FTC rules

The FTC (Federal Trade Commission) takes its job seriously and so should you. Not knowing the rules and regulations will not be an acceptable excuse if you inadvertently break them. Penalties can run as high as $10,000 per infraction, so read under "The mail order merchandise rule" in "The Federal Trade Commission" in Part 12, and remember two major points.

1. If an item will not be available for delivery within 30 days and this has not been noted in the catalog, a first-delay letter must be sent to the consumer who has ordered it—within 30 days of the time of order. This letter must include a postage-paid, pre-addressed postcard/envelope with which the consumer can cancel the order (see Figure 8-13).

2. A second-delay letter must be sent within the second 30-day period. If the customer fails to respond within 14 days, the order must be canceled and a refund (if payment was by check) must be processed (see Figure 8-14). Each company should modify the basic form letters shown in Figures 8-13 and 8-14 to reflect its own personality.

The importance of abiding by the FTC 30-day rule cannot be stressed strongly enough. Abide by the FTC rulings to the letter to keep out of trouble and have the added benefit of improved customer relations.

CUSTOMER SERVICE

Customers are the lifeblood of your catalog. Although they may be expensive to obtain, they constitute the heart of your profit. If they decide to order from a competitor, their loyalties may shift forever. Take care of your customers as you would your most prized possession.

Handling complaints and inquiries

Each customer complaint or inquiry should be acted on promptly. Make one person responsible for the first reading of every letter received to decide to whom it should be forwarded for proper action. Most customer service inquiries break down into five categories.

1 a need for more information on a particular product
2 the status of an order
3 cancellations and changes
4 returns
5 refunds and credits

For customer service representatives to act promptly, they must, of course, have access to up-to-date information. Even small companies should investigate the benefits of computerized customer service records. Some microcomputers can handle a surprising amount of information. If cash outlay is a problem, look into renting. Computerization can make a big difference in the speed and accuracy with which you handle customer inquiries.

Another advantage of a computerized system is that it virtually eliminates the cold, impersonal printed letter often sent in response to a customer's problem. Although form letters can be a necessity, those that answer customers' complaints with the appropriate box checked are unfriendly and convey a lack of interest in the customer's problem. With a computer, you can capture every detail of a customer's order and recall it as needed. Then, when Mrs. Smith calls to find out where her order is, you can immediately tell her the exact date the order was received and filled. If she writes, either the computer can generate a letter addressing her problem or you can make the form letter more personal by adding the specific information from the computer.

Informed customer service representatives

Customer service people can do their job well only if they have the right answers when customers call. Put those in charge of answering questions about products in a room that contains a sample of every product in your catalog. Then, if a question or problem arises regarding a product, service staff will have easy access to the product. Arrange a time with the staff to explain intricacies or details of the products that may be important to customers.

Be sure to capture every detail of a customer complaint or correspondence for each and every occurrence. Keeping good customer service records will alert you to customers who have made more than one complaint in a short period of time. This may call for a personal letter to let the customer know that you are monitoring the problems and will act on them immediately. Or, if a customer constantly returns items or repeat-

FIGURE 8-15
Sample incorrect information/payment letter

ABC Catalog Company
123 Main Street
Anywhere, USA 00000
000-000-0000

Date

Customer's Name
Address

Order Number

Dear Customer:

Thank you for your recent order for ____________________. However, we are unable to process your order for the reason(s) checked below:

☐ Payment not enclosed
☐ Order not enclosed
☐ Incorrect amount of money enclosed:
$__________enclosed
$__________correct amount
$__________amount due
☐ Did not specify size
☐ Did not specify color
☐ Invalid credit card
Please verify your credit card number. Charge cannot be validated with number as shown. Please write corrected number on the line below.
Correct Credit Card Number: ______________________________
☐ Expiration date on credit card is needed before we can process your order.
☐ Card is declined. Please contact your credit card company if clarification is necessary, or submit an alternative credit card.
☐ Other

Please make the necessary corrections and return this letter in the enclosed envelope.

Thank you for your order. We look forward to serving you again.

Sincerely,

edly claims nondelivery, strongly consider deleting the name from your mailing list. Most people are honest, but some take advantage of the fact that a catalog may be operating from a distance.

Figures 8-15, 8-16, and 8-17 provide the information you need for several types of customer service letters. Use them as content guides only; revise them to meet your company's needs and add a more personal touch.

FIGURE 8-16
Sample out-of-stock refund letter

ABC Catalog Company
123 Main Street
Anywhere, USA 00000
000-000-0000

Date

Customer's Name
Address

Order Number

Dear Customer:

Thank you for your order of our item ______________________. Unfortunately, we no longer have that item available.

☐ A refund check in the amount of $__________ is enclosed.
☐ Be assured that the credit card charges you authorized will *not* appear on your next statement.

Thank you for shopping with us. We hope we may have the opportunity to serve you in the future. We have included our most recent catalog so that, should you desire, you may make an alternate selection from the convenience of your home.

Sincerely,

The how-to-return form

No matter how large or small your catalog company, in all outgoing packages be certain to include explicit instructions outlining how to return enclosed merchandise. This does not increase returns, as might be expected, and does substantially cut down on customer service phone calls.

Generally speaking, returns are an insignificant problem in cataloging, ranging from 1 percent (exceptional cases have been even less) to a high of 20 percent (higher percentages have been known to happen, but they are totally unacceptable). The percentage of returns is directly related to the type of merchandise offered. The higher percentages occur mostly in the clothing industry, where incorrect size or fit lead to exchanges.

An easy-to-understand "how-to-return" form accomplishes several goals at once: (1) it makes it quick and easy for customers to solve a problem with merchandise; (2) for customers who do not have a problem, it reconfirms the company's willingness to stand by its guarantee to ser-

FIGURE 8-17
Sample refund-to-dissatisfied-customer letter

ABC Catalog Company
123 Main Street
Anywhere, USA 00000
000-000-0000

Date

Customer's Name
Address

Order Number

Dear Customer:

Thank you for promptly returning the ______________________. We are sorry you were not satisfied.

☐ A refund check in the amount of $__________ is enclosed.
☐ A credit card refund voucher in the amount of $__________ is enclosed.

Please feel free to make an alternate selection from our latest catalog, which we are sending along for your convenience.

Thank you for shopping with us and we hope to serve you again in the future.

Sincerely,

---

vice any complaint they may have; and (3) it helps keep the cost of customer service down.

If buyers can readily understand the how-to-return form provided, it will save them time and eliminate the perceived aggravation they fear may result out of a direct confrontation via the phone. Instead, they can simply fill out the form, return the merchandise, and wait for the company to resolve the problem.

Figure 8-18 shows a clear example of a how-to-return form. Depending on the size and economics of your company, this information can be displayed on the back of a computer-generated packing slip or merely photocopied and inserted in the package. Regardless of the format, no package should leave the fulfillment center without one.

Customer service policies

Every cataloger needs to determine the best customer service policies for his or her catalog. Here are some general guidelines to help get you started in writing your own policy.

OUR GUARANTEE

If for any reason you are not completely satisfied with any product you buy from us, simply return it within 30 days of receiving it, and we will promptly refund the purchase price -- or; if you desire, replace the product free of charge.

When returning any part of your order, please fill in the information below and enclose this form in the package. Send the package to the address shown in the upper left-hand corner on the front of this form. Please insure it for full value and retain all your postal and insurance receipts.

RETURNED MERCHANDISE:

Qty.	Item No.	Description	Reason For Return (Circle Reason)
			1 2 3 4 5
			1 2 3 4 5
			1 2 3 4 5

REASON CODES

1 – Defective
2 – Damaged in Shipment
3 – Wrong Merchandise Sent
4 – Wrong Merchandise Ordered
5 – Other ____________

ACTION REQUESTED

☐ Replace ☐ Credit

☐ Exchange (Complete section below) ☐ Refund

☐ Other ____________

PLEASE COMPLETE THIS SECTION FOR EXCHANGES OR TO ORDER ADDITIONAL MERCHANDISE

Qty.	Item No.	Description	Price

PAYMENT FOR ADDITIONAL ITEMS OR DIFFERENCE ON EXCHANGED ITEMS

☐ BY CHECK ENCLOSED ☐ CREDIT CARD (COMPLETE INFORMATION BELOW) ☐ OTHER ____________

☐ MASTER CHARGE ☐ AMERICAN EXPRESS

☐ VISA BAC

CARD NO ____________ MASTER CHARGE INTERBANK NO ____________ EXPIRATION DATE ____________

SIGNATURE X ____________

FIGURE 8-18
How-to-return form (printed on back of packing slip, Figure 8-7). Courtesy Lifestyle Marketing.

CUSTOMER SERVICE CHECKLIST

- ✔ Whenever possible, process and send all orders within one week. The conversion rate of customers who receive orders promptly is over 20 percent higher than for those who receive less efficient fulfillment. Also, customers who must wait too long for orders lose interest, too often resulting in returned merchandise.
- ✔ Submit credit charges for payment only after shipment has been made.
- ✔ No merchandise substitutions are allowed by law unless clearly explained within your catalog. Customers often keep the substituted item only because it is too much of a hassle to return it. However, the next time they order by mail

they may choose to order from a competitor who didn't substitute merchandise.

- When some items are back ordered, partial orders should be shipped with a note indicating that the package contains a partial order.
- The customer should pay return postage, unless the shipment is damaged or incorrect, in which case you pay.
- Do not make replacements or exchanges until the original item has been returned.
- Shipments should be made to those underpaying by up to $5* by check. The underpayed amount is billed with the shipment. Credit card orders are adjusted and billed the correct amount.
- For underpayments of $5* or more, shipments should be held and the customer notified.
- "No collect calls" should be displayed on your order form; however, collect calls should be accepted.
- Credit card overpayments should be submitted to the credit card company in the correct amount.
- For check overpayments of $5.01* or more, a refund should be sent to the customer. For overpayments under $5.01*, a credit memo can be sent with the shipment, which the customer can apply to the next order or sign and return for a refund.
- Refunds for out-of-stock items that are not expected to be available should be issued within four days.
- If a customer claims nondelivery for items with a total value of $25* or less: (a) reship, (b) file a tracer, and (c) keep open charge (do not credit customer's charge) on the customer's account until the tracer results are known. Claims for items with a total value of more than $25.01* should be handled individually.
- If a customer claims to have returned an item, which you have not received, a new item or refund should be sent only if the customer agrees to file a tracer naming the cataloger as beneficiary.

*Dollar amounts must be individually determined based on the catalog's average dollar order, margin of profit, and processing costs.

True-to-life vignette

To service a customer properly, you must first clearly understand the request. An example of what can happen if customer service representatives misunderstand the complainant's wishes occurred not too long ago to a major, well-known cataloger.

A male customer, on receipt of the slacks he ordered, found them too short. So he pinned up the pants and enclosed a note saying that the amount he had pinned up the pants showed the *additional length* he needed. The customer service people, however, misunderstood the instructions and *shortened* the pants up to where they were pinned. The man, now slightly frustrated, sent the erroneously shortened pants back and included a pair of his own pants. His note indicated that the old pants he was sending were the length he wanted in the new pants.

The customer service people promptly shortened the customer's own pants and sent them both back to him! Here's a case where customer service people truly believed they were servicing the customer above and beyond the call of duty. In truth, they were guilty of not following the customer's instructions not once, but twice! So be sure your people take the time to carefully read customers' requests and really understand them.

KEEPING CONTROL

To run an efficient organization of any size, establish a workable system of control reports. Daily reports show the status of work in progress and identify daily problems. Weekly reports evaluate the productivity and efficiency of a particular area. Monthly or work cycle reports make use of all the previous information to highlight problem areas and spot trends.

Types of reports

The first step is to decide which areas to address within your own company. Some suggestions are

1 order counts
2 inventory levels by item
3 unit costs
4 productivity levels
5 number of customer complaints by type

A mailroom report, for instance, would most likely show the quantity of mail received, how much mail still awaits attention, and how many hours per person were spent performing tasks. Monthly reports should be issued to check one month against another.

A data-entry report would closely follow the mail report in content. It would include a breakdown of work by type of data processed, the number of orders processed, the number of orders rejected, and why they were rejected.

Inventory control reports would show quantity of out-of-stock products by item, the date an item went out of stock, anticipated arrival date of new merchandise, and the date orders were placed. Reports should also include total inventory levels by category.

Quality control requires physical inspection of merchandise at regular intervals. Reports should state how many of a particular item were checked, the percentage of good versus bad quality by manufacturer, and the time spent.

Returns control reports would keep track of product returns caused by delivery problems or customer dissatisfaction, including the number of customer-returned packages that had been opened and the number that came back unopened. Monthly reports help speed up discovery of defective or unacceptable products and/or delivery problems.

A customer service report would include a breakdown of complaints by type; source (customer, governmental agency, and so on) and seriousness of complaint; required research; simple form answer, and so on. Weekly customer service reports are essential. Customers are a cataloger's most valuable commodity, and trends must be spotted as soon as possible.

Reports more than pay for the time spent preparing them by helping a cataloger to run his organization knowledgeably. No successful business can be without them; structure yours to fit the individual needs and personalities they will serve. Keep all reports simple, to the point, and on time—a report received too late for timely action is worthless.

Data-entry productivity

Accurate data entry is of critical importance to the cataloger. Yet employee productivity should not be forgotten. After all, "time is money," and an efficiently run center makes everyone, employees and employers alike, happier. The following checklist for data-entry productivity is applicable to any size catalog operation from startup to established giant.

- ✓ Is the information to be entered presented to the operator in an orderly manner? Are the data on the order form in the same order as they are to be entered? Is enough space allowed on the order form for customers to fill in information legibly? Is the customer specifically asked to print?
- ✓ Do such common elements as the date order was received automatically appear in other records once they've been entered?
- ✓ Is the operator's work station laid out so that work can be processed in an organized manner?
- ✓ Are the equipment and programming cost-efficient? Or, by trying to save money, are you actually reducing employee productivity?
- ✓ Do you keep accurate records on time spent versus work performed?

Productivity and quality of surroundings/equipment should never be taken for granted, but monitored and carefully controlled from the outset.

Fulfillment productivity

Several areas important to data-entry productivity, such as up-to-date equipment and well-organized surroundings, can also effectively increase fulfillment productivity. But some other guidelines also apply.

- Establish definite standards by which to evaluate employees, for example, a certain number of pieces (to be sorted or picked) per hour.
- Keep a weekly record of the work done by each employee (actually maintained by the employee or by a supervisor).
- Reward employees who exceed the set standards.
- Follow up on a regular basis, making sure that the program is working for both the catalog company and the employees. These guidelines can also be applied to increase the productivity of office personnel.

Part 9
GETTING AND KEEPING CUSTOMERS

CUSTOMER ACQUISITION

Whether you're a first-time cataloger or an old-timer, the acquisition of new customers should be a top priority. Without new customers, your company cannot grow. Traditional acquisition methods—mailing lists, space ads, and inserts—still seem to pull best. New ones are being tried, some showing more promise than others.

Mailing lists

Those first entering direct marketing may wonder how they could ever need more names than appear on mailing lists. But catalog buyer lists, with their high duplication factor, represent fewer names than it seems. Second, only a certain portion of available lists meets the profile needed by your catalog. Third, many other catalogs use the same lists, resulting in increased competition. Fourth, some lists are available only on an exchange basis.

Catalog mailing lists are an essential part of your customer acquisition program, but definitely not the whole story. There are some other methods you should consider.

Space ads

The main purpose of most space ads is to generate new customer names—customers who will purchase products from the catalogs you send them.

Your first decision is whether to run a product in the ad or merely advertise your catalog. Many catalogers believe that customers who respond to an ad featuring a product are responding to that product only and will not convert to catalog buyers. Others believe that by showing a product, you will not only help offset advertising costs, but will also give the respondent a better indication of the kind of merchandise your catalog carries, resulting in a better catalog customer. Omaha Steaks, for instance, found that single-product ads worked ten times better than catalog-only space ads. Bob Bernardi, vice-president of marketing for Omaha Steaks, believes this is because the company image is important; in this case, a juicy, mouth-watering steak.

Before running a space ad, consider the image you want your catalog to project. For example, The Company Store offers "factory direct prices" on down comforters and pillows. Since low cost is one of the major selling features of the catalog, they choose to display the product and the low selling price (see Figure 9-1). On the other hand, a catalog like Piaffe targets such a specific market—petite women who wear sizes 0 to 6—that it has chosen not to limit itself to a particular product, but to offer a catalog that meets a real need for its market. Talbots relies on the credibility of having been in business since 1942 to sell its catalog and also chooses not to limit itself by showing only one product. Pier 1 Imports uses the general advertising already being used to generate store traffic. The ads show related products, generally in a room setting, but they help reinforce Pier 1's image and are economically advantageous to the overall program.

Product ads vary tremendously in size and content, all of which have advantages and disadvantages. Let's look at some.

A single-item, small space ad presents the problem of fitting enough information into the ad to do a good selling job. The coupon, toll-free

SAVE 50% AND MORE OFF NORMAL RETAIL
Scandinavian
Spring Down Comforters
& DOWN PILLOWS
FACTORY DIRECT PRICES
A down comforter for warmer seasons and milder climates! The Scandinavian Spring Down comforter has uniquely crafted narrow vertical channels and less down. Perfect for any environment— consider where you live, your home heating habits or whether you sleep warm or sleep cold. The fabric is poly/cotton, double stitched at the edges and filled with the finest white European Down. A Scandinavian tradition crafted with elegance and comfort in mind. Our down pillows are the perfect complement for total sleep comfort.
We're the factory outlet for Gillette Industries (founded in 1911), the national manufacturer of Bill Blass women's down coats. We're America's Down Experts manufacturing down comforters, down pillows, designer down robes, and other quality down products in Wisconsin. Call or write for your free 1984 color down catalog.
The Company Store TM
1-800-356-9367
Scandinavian Spring Down Comforters
Colors
☐Twin (60"x86") $59
☐Queen/Full (86"x86") $89
☐King (102"x86") $119
☐Dusty Rose
☐Dusty Blue
☐Silver
Down Pillows
Colors
☐Standard (20"x26") $30
☐Queen (20"x30") $40
☐King (20"x36") $55
☐Lt. Blue
☐Beige
ORDER BY PHONE 1-800-356-9367 TOLL-FREE: Use your credit card when ordering by phone.
OR ORDER BY MAIL: ☐M.C. ☐VISA ☐Am. Exp. ☐Check
Acct. No.: Exp. Dt.
Comforters:$ +$ =$
Pillows:$ +$ =$
Ship. & Hdlg. -$5.00 per item:$
TOTAL:$
Signature:
Address:
City, State, Zip
Send to:
The Company Store, Dept. 451, 1205 S. 7th St., La Crosse, WI 54601. Guarantee: If for any reason you are not completely satisfied, please return for a full refund. Delivery: Immediate.

FIGURE 9-1
In a comparatively small space ad The Company Store displays a quality image, product, low price, and free catalog request. © 1984 by The Company Store TM, and used with permission.

information, guarantee, and so on leave little space for photograph and copy. Also, because it's small, the ad may get lost or buried in the magazine and not be easily seen by potential customers.

It's difficult to choose just the right products, so you'll need multiple ads, each with a product keyed to the audience of a specific publication. Selecting that "just-right" product can be difficult. One experienced direct marketer, who makes a most comfortable living by selling products through space advertisements, reports that he is pleased if two out of ten products perform well. And this is after years of experience.

The single-item, larger space ad affords the cataloger opportunity to incorporate more "sell" into the ad and reinforce the company's image. It will also often receive a better position within the publication. But it costs more, so be sure that the product is a terrific seller and/or that the publications selected provide outstanding results.

The product/catalog request combination allows consumers the option of buying the product or sending for a catalog with more product choices. The potential customer feels more comfortable buying from a magazine advertiser who has the financial stability necessary to produce a catalog. The catalog and product shown together can graphically attract the customer's interest more strongly than a single-product or catalog-only ad, and give the feeling that this is a "real" company, not an individual with only one product to sell. The sales of the product also help cover the cost of the ad.

A multiproduct ad gives consumers a better "feel" for the kind and variety of merchandise your catalog offers, and gives the company a more credible image because several products are offered. The multiproduct ad doesn't rely as heavily on the selection of that just-right product. But because it needs more space, it costs more, so consider using it only in publications that have demonstrated good response to smaller ads.

The right approach to generating customer names through space advertising depends on budget and catalog type. In the beginning, test as many publications as possible. To do this economically, keep initial ads as small as possible, but not so small as to greatly affect response. Then increase ad size in the most responsive publications. If it is important to realize an immediate return on your investment, run a product in the ad, but always include a check-off box that allows the customer to request the catalog only. Even when the ad does not indicate that a catalog is available, the customer often requests one. Therefore, to increase your catalog request response and the number of potential customer names, make sure to incorporate a catalog request line into all your ads.

Catalog collections

An increasingly popular method of acquiring new customer names is through the catalog collections offered by some major publications (see Figure 9-2). All you need do is send the publication a black-and-white photograph of your catalog (or logo if no photo is available) and limited copy that describes your catalog. The cost of insertion is generally less than if you run the ad alone, and you realize the added impact afforded by a section devoted entirely to catalogs. Each publication has its own method of presentation and of handling catalog inquiries.

For instance, *Town and Country* charges nothing for the production of the ad (you supply the photo and copy). They list the subscribing cata-

FIGURE 9-2
The first page of a six-page catalog collection in *Savvy* magazine for March 1984. © 1984 by Savvy Company and reprinted with permission.

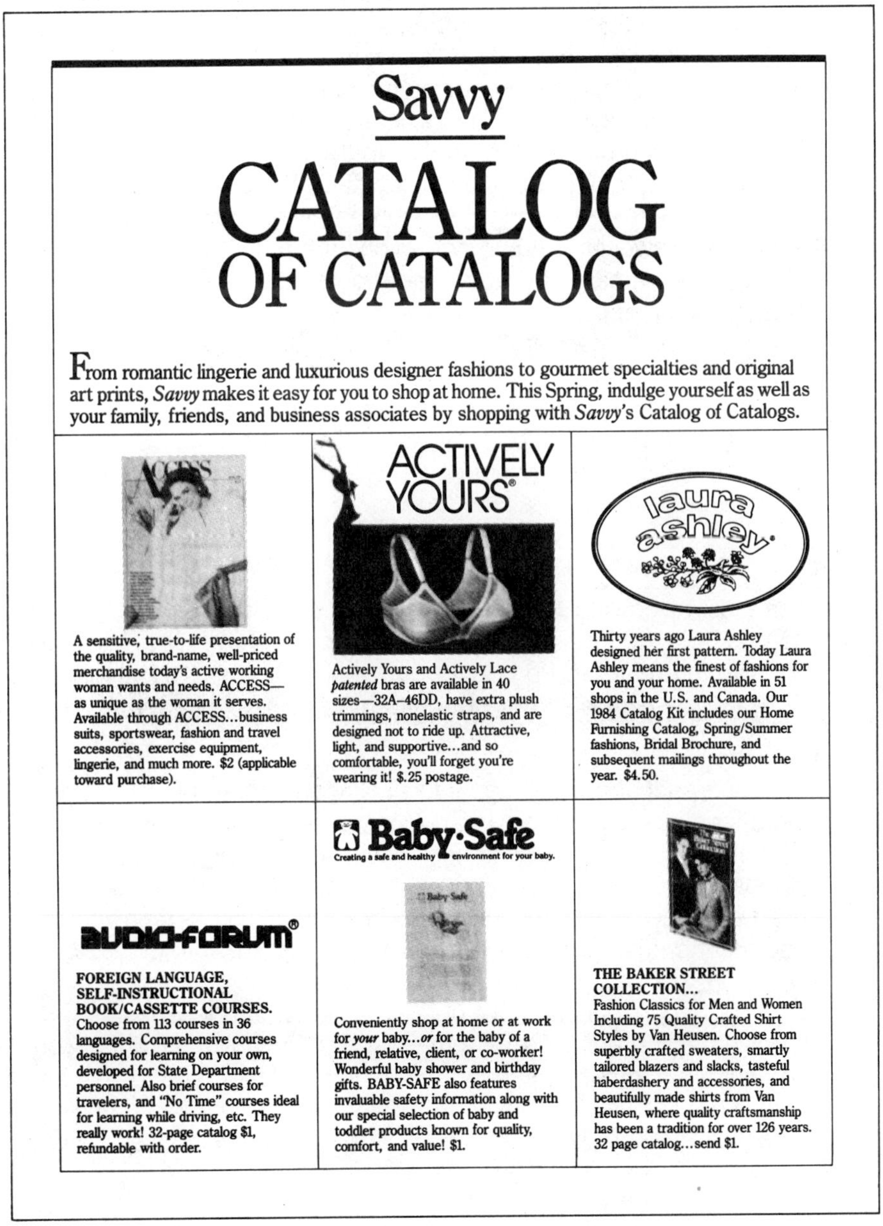

Savvy

CATALOG
OF CATALOGS

From romantic lingerie and luxurious designer fashions to gourmet specialties and original art prints, *Savvy* makes it easy for you to shop at home. This Spring, indulge yourself as well as your family, friends, and business associates by shopping with *Savvy*'s Catalog of Catalogs.

A sensitive, true-to-life presentation of the quality, brand-name, well-priced merchandise today's active working woman wants and needs. ACCESS— as unique as the woman it serves. Available through ACCESS...business suits, sportswear, fashion and travel accessories, exercise equipment, lingerie, and much more. $2 (applicable toward purchase).

ACTIVELY YOURS®

Actively Yours and Actively Lace *patented* bras are available in 40 sizes—32A–46DD, have extra plush trimmings, nonelastic straps, and are designed not to ride up. Attractive, light, and supportive...and so comfortable, you'll forget you're wearing it! $.25 postage.

laura ashley

Thirty years ago Laura Ashley designed her first pattern. Today Laura Ashley means the finest of fashions for you and your home. Available in 51 shops in the U.S. and Canada. Our 1984 Catalog Kit includes our Home Furnishing Catalog, Spring/Summer fashions, Bridal Brochure, and subsequent mailings throughout the year. $4.50.

AUDIO-FORUM®

FOREIGN LANGUAGE, SELF-INSTRUCTIONAL BOOK/CASSETTE COURSES. Choose from 113 courses in 36 languages. Comprehensive courses designed for learning on your own, developed for State Department personnel. Also brief courses for travelers, and "No Time" courses ideal for learning while driving, etc. They really work! 32-page catalog $1, refundable with order.

Baby·Safe
Creating a safe and healthy environment for your baby.

Conveniently shop at home or at work for *your* baby...*or* for the baby of a friend, relative, client, or co-worker! Wonderful baby shower and birthday gifts. BABY-SAFE also features invaluable safety information along with our special selection of baby and toddler products known for quality, comfort, and value! $1.

THE BAKER STREET COLLECTION...
Fashion Classics for Men and Women Including 75 Quality Crafted Shirt Styles by Van Heusen. Choose from superbly crafted sweaters, smartly tailored blazers and slacks, tasteful haberdashery and accessories, and beautifully made shirts from Van Heusen, where quality craftsmanship has been a tradition for over 126 years. 32 page catalog...send $1.

logs in alphabetical order and insert a postcard (often called a "bingo" card) for easy response. The postcards are addressed to *Town and Country,* which processes them. Advertisers receive gummed addressed labels or Cheshire labels for immediate catalog mailings, plus a duplicate set for future use. The cost of insertion into two catalog collections (March and May 1984) plus 1/12 page black-and-white ad (you supply the art) in any issue from January through June 1984 was $2,895. In addition, there is a service charge of 20 percent on any monies collected for catalogs on which there is a charge, or 5 cents per inquiry on free catalogs.

When asked how responsive readers are to catalog collections, publications invariably produce impressive statistics. But remember that the response statistics quoted are a summation of all the advertisers listed in a particular issue or for a specific time period. Ethically speaking, publications cannot reveal the number of responses generated by individual catalogs. Nor do they have access to the percentage of catalog requesters who convert to customers. Statistics on the long-term value of customers obtained through this comparatively new service are not yet available. However, catalog collections are a cost-efficient method of obtaining new names, and acceptable percentages of respondents do convert to customers.

Both newcomers and experienced catalogers should test catalog collections as a customer acquisition method. Telephone the publications that best fit your customer or targeted market's profile to determine if they now have or plan to offer a catalog collection service. Stay in touch even with publications that do not now offer such a service. New catalog collections are appearing all the time.

Inserts

The most appealing feature and primary common denominator of inserts, co-ops, and stuffers is that they require no postage. They are also inexpensive to create and produce. But along with these pluses come some minuses. Let's look at the advantages and disadvantages of each.

Package inserts

Because package inserts go into packages containing recently ordered merchandise, you're reaching not only someone who has purchased by mail, but also someone who has purchased recently. Also, the package contains merchandise desired by the recipient, giving the insert the implied endorsement of the shipper. If the merchandise received is as expected, the customer will be pleased and receptive to other mail order offers.

But because inserts are placed in outgoing packages as orders are received and processed by a mail order company over which you have no control, you must rely on the projected number of outgoing packages supplied to you by that company. These projections, of course, are based on anticipated sales and can be different from actual sales—meaning that the real number inserted may not be the number anticipated. Additionally, you simply must trust that the insertions were not misplaced or lost and are actually going into the packages as promised. To a degree, the second problem can be circumvented by working with only the most reputable mail order companies and following up on the status of the inserts. Another smart approach is to work with list brokers who specialize in inserts; they have the contacts to ensure that your program is being implemented. And they can advise you on the most reliable insert programs.

Actual response can vary significantly (depending on the offer and presentation), but package inserts almost always produce fewer immediate sales than do offers mailed to a list with similar demographics.

Because the inserts do not physically go into the package until the order is received and processed, it may take longer than anticipated for the insert to actually go out. Even then, time must be allowed for the package to be delivered to the recipient's home and action to be taken on the offer.

Another disadvantage is that inserts cannot be specified for such selects as average dollar order, sex, and zip code.

Weight and size restrictions imposed on your sales promotion for economic reasons by the company into whose packages the promotion is inserted can limit the presentation of your offer. This is not a major problem, but be sure to determine exactly what these specifications are before proceeding with development and production.

The cost of insertion is inexpensive, running from $35 to $45 per thousand, exclusive of the cost of producing the insert. Some think that the more inserts per package, the greater the possibility that the recipient will read them. Others think that too many inserts mean too much competition. In reality, it isn't the number of inserts that matters as much as it is the strength of your offer.

Co-ops

Co-op packages allow noncompetitors to combine the benefits of an "in-mail" offer with the cost savings of shared postal expense. If co-ops do work for you, the potential audience is extensive.

But many co-op offers are savings-oriented, so you share space with cents-off coupons and similarly distracting offers, and you don't choose the mailing date; the co-op does. This may or may not be to the benefit of your product. Co-op packages are also subject to the same weight and size restrictions as package inserts.

Co-op card decks

Made up of loose or bound-in cards the size of a postcard, co-op card decks allow noncompetitors to share postal and production costs. The targeted market shares a common life-style or occupation (see Figure 9-3). The postage-paid format allows for quick and simple response, but the postcard format (usually 3½″ × 5½″) limits copy and art.

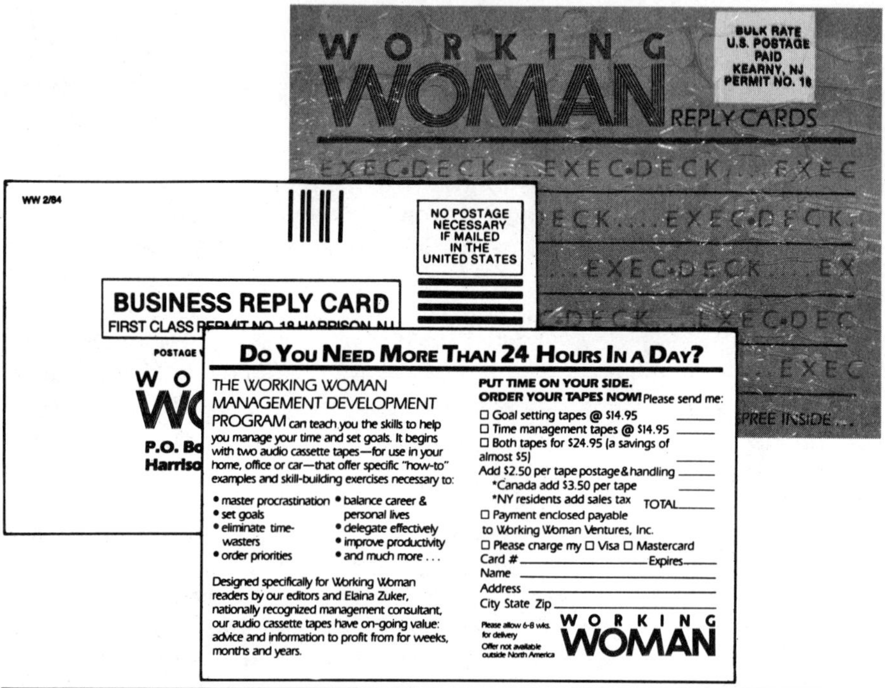

FIGURE 9-3
Outside wrap of *Working Woman*'s Exec-Deck card deck and sample deck card. Courtesy Working Woman Ventures.

Statement Stuffers

Since statement stuffers are mailed with bills or statements regularly sent to consumers by department stores, charge card organizations, oil companies, and so on, there is no postage expense. However, they share the same weight and size limitations common to package inserts and co-ops. Rental costs run from $25 to $50 per thousand.

Statement stuffers are available for general audiences as well as more tightly targeted markets. The offer arrives in an envelope showing the billing company's name, usually such an impressive one as MasterCard, BankAmericard, or a well-known publication. As they are mailed first class, stuffers have a more predictable date of arrival than promotions mailed via bulk rate.

Since some statement stuffers tie into the credit offered by the host company, customers have the dominantly displayed option of buying now and paying later.

Tell-a-friend

Some of your best prospects are friends of current customers. Give customers every opportunity to provide their friends with your catalog. Include tell-a-friend information on your order form or your packing slip, or enclose separate postage-paid postcards in outgoing packages or in your catalog. By and large, tell-a-friends have an impressive conversion rate and cost almost nothing.

Cable/videotex

The new electronic media are exciting and complicated. The options range from PIs (per inquiry; you pay the station or network a percentage of the sales of your product, which it advertises, and you provide the commercial) to interactive communications (Viewtron is up and running in Florida). Although the future seems extremely bright for this medium, the current cost makes it advisable only for established catalogs. For more information on this timely subject, read *Cable/Videotex: A Compendium for Direct Marketers;* Monograph Volume 6, published by the Direct Marketing Association, and "New Technology and Catalog Marketing," Part 11 of this book.

Publicity

Don't overlook the value of "free" publicity. It can be especially valuable for a new catalog, as, in effect, the catalog receives an editorial recommendation from the publication in which it appears.

Send copies of your catalog, or photos of particularly outstanding products, along with a press release to publications that may have an interest in your product mix. If the publication should choose to write about your company, the results can be amazing. One of our clients, who received coverage in a well-known gourmet food magazine, received hundreds of orders for the item featured and thousands of requests for his catalog.

Many books can teach you the "ins and outs" of preparing a publicity release. A good choice is *The Publicity Manual,* published by Visibility Enterprises, 11 West 81st Street, New York, NY 10024.

New approaches

Innovative direct marketers have been exploring new approaches to customer acquisition. For the most part, these efforts have not proved to be as effective as the more traditional methods of space advertising and insert programs. However, since direct marketing's big advantage is the ability to test a new idea and really know how effective it is, you should be aware of alternative sales vehicles.

Take-ones

Take-ones allow you to reach large numbers of prospective customers at a low cost. Display racks, set up in such high-traffic locations as supermarkets, are often part of community bulletin boards, helping draw attention to the take-ones. Promotion pieces are usually similar in size and design to those used in insert programs, and a number of different companies' pieces are often displayed together—another attention-getter. Rates are on a per store basis and range from $4 to $8 per month, per store, depending on the length of distribution time and the number of stores selected. Take-ones are available on a city, neighborhood, or individual store basis. The cost per thousand is low, the potential audience high.

Alternate delivery

Private delivery services physically deliver sales materials to individual dwellings for fees ranging from $35 to $400 per thousand. Most commonly, multiple inserts are placed in a clear plastic wrapper and hung from the doorknob of the resident's home. Fees depend on weight and saturation or targeted local delivery. The highest fees are for books or Spiegel-type "big book" catalogs taken to specific addresses; the lowest fees are for promotional pieces inserted into the plastic bag (usually with two or three other pieces) used to saturate a specific area, but not specific addresses.

Free-standing inserts

Distributed through Sunday newspapers across the country, free-standing inserts are the four-color fliers that contain cents-off coupons and mail order ads. Direct marketers can purchase remnant space at a special low rate, substantially less than that offered to national advertisers. The minimum is usually one million, and although you can specify particular markets, there is no guarantee that you will receive them. Likewise, since available space consists of "leftovers," circulation may vary somewhat. For a test of one million, the actual test quantity could be 800,000, or 1,100,000, or any close variance. Cost for insertion ranges from $1 per thousand for a dollar-bill-size panel to about $6.50 per thousand for a full page, depending on the size of the circulation tested. Obviously, the higher the circulation, the lower the cost per thousand. You must supply the artwork.

Testing this method of customer acquisition is inexpensive and provides a potential market of many millions. Some catalogers choose to offer products but others offer only their catalogs (see Figure 9-4). In either case, the middle-income demographics of this type of vehicle must be considered before deciding whether it is right for your catalog.

Evaluating new-customer acquisition costs

Most customers shop with a catalog for only a certain time period, and during this time period they spend a certain amount of money. How long they "stay" and how much they spend determines their value as customers. Unfortunately, when evaluating the profitability of different media, too many catalogers tend to look only at the immediate value of a customer—and not the long-term value. This is understandable in a startup venture, where immediate recouping of funds can be critical, but is inexcusable for catalogers who intend to stay in business for a long time. They should keep meticulous records of customers' buying habits by ac-

FIGURE 9-4
Wisconsin Cheeseman makes excellent use of very little space in this free-standing insert ad. © 1983 by The Wisconsin Cheeseman Inc., and used with permission.

quisition source to be able to evaluate the long-term value of their customers.

1 How many years have they continued to purchase?
2 How many times did you mail them catalogs?
3 How much did each mailing cost?
4 What was their rate of response?
5 How much did they spend?
6 How much did you actually make (deducting cost of goods, and so on)?
7 What is their real worth as customers?

One cataloger discovered that lists showed the best immediate return, but space advertisements generated the best customers—those who continued to buy and spend. The cataloger cut back on list rentals and expanded the space program. A superior customer evolved—one who spent more over a longer period.

CATALOG ANALYSIS

The key to catalog success is continuing analysis, no matter how small or large the program. This is the only way to monitor the progress of the business, determine its weak and strong points, and improve or maintain profits. It is central to keeping customers.

Many established catalogers have arrangements with service bureaus to do the computer runs for their analysis. Others, with in-house computers, do their own. (A brief discussion of more detailed methods and some of the mathematical techniques involved are presented at the end of this chapter.) The analysis that follows could easily be handled on a microcomputer, even by those unfamiliar with catalog analysis.

List analysis

For each list, determine (1) the total number of catalogs mailed, (2) the total number of orders received, and (3) the dollar amount of sales generated. To determine the *response rate* for each list, divide the number of orders for each list by the number of catalogs mailed to that list, times 100.

Response % = (Number of orders ÷ Number of catalogs mailed) × 100

Then determine the *average order.* Divide the total dollar value of the orders from a list by the number of orders from that list:

Average order = Total dollars ÷ Number of orders

Catalogers have developed a formula that combines the preceding two measurements into a third criterion, the *amount of sales in dollars per thousand catalogs mailed,* which facilitates the comparison of many lists with different average orders and response rates. Multiply the response percent by the amount of the average order times ten.

An electronic spreadsheet

The preceding calculations can be done on a microcomputer or on paper. The computer just makes it easier. Set up an electronic spreadsheet, such as Visicalc, to consist of columns and rows. Then to it, add actual list data.

AN ELECTRONIC SPREADSHEET

	A	B	C	D
1	List name			
2	List code			
3				
4	No. of catalogs mailed			
5	No. of orders			
6	Total dollars			
7				
8	% response			
9	Average order			
10	$/M catalogs mailed			
11				

A SPREADSHEET WITH DATA

	A	B	C
1	List name	ABBA	
2	List code	101	
3			
4	No. of catalogs mailed	9,873	
5	No. of orders	221	
6	Total dollars	$12,155	
7			
8	% response	2.24 [(B5 ÷ B4) × 100]	
9	Average order	$55 (B6 ÷ B5)	
10	$/M catalogs mailed	$1,232 (10 × B8 × B9)	
11			

Unknown orders

Unknown orders can result either from errors in data entry or, more likely, from the failure of telephone personnel to capture the list code when taking the order. Some catalogers refer to these as "white mail" (even though most are phone orders).

If orders from unknown sources are a high percentage of the total, then the validity of the analysis and the accuracy of the rollout potential are impaired. In order to improve validity, methods have been developed to allocate these unknowns to the various lists used. One method of distributing unknowns is simply to allocate them to each list in the known-list orders to total orders ratio (i.e., if a list has 10 percent of the known orders, it will receive 10 percent of the unknown). The same technique is used to allocate sales dollars.

First, subtract total unknown orders (or sales) from the total number of orders (or sales). Then divide the total number of orders (and the total dollars) for each list by the difference.

For orders:

Total orders from all lists ÷ (Total orders from all lists − unknown orders) = Order factor

For total dollars:

Total dollar sales from all lists ÷ (Total dollar sales from all lists − unknown sales) = Dollar factor

Let's assume the catalog received 12,000 orders, with 1,800 unknowns, and the total sales were $400,000, $63,000 of which were from orders where the list is unknown. (Since phone orders are credit card charges, the average order generally is higher than orders received by mail.) The order factor would be:

$$12{,}000 \div 10{,}200 = 1.1765$$

The dollar factor would be:

$400,000 ÷ $337,000 = 1.187

This would change the analysis as shown in the revised spreadsheet.

THE REVISED SPREADSHEET

	A	B	C
1 List name	ABBA		
2 List code	101		
3			
4 No. of catalogs mailed	9,873		
5 No. of orders	221		
6 Total dollars	$12,155		
7			
8 % response	2.24 [(B5 ÷ B4) × 100]		
9 Average order	$55 (B6 ÷ B5)		
10 $/M catalogs mailed	$1,232 (10 × B8 × B9)		
11			
12 Including unknown allocation			
13			
14 No. of orders	260 (B5 × 1.1765)		
15 Total dollars	$14,428 (B6 × 1.187)		
16			
17 % response	2.63 [(B14 ÷ B4) × 100]		
18 Average order	$55.49 (B15 ÷ B14)		
19 $/M catalogs mailed	$1,459 (10 × B17 × B18)		

By using the computer's replication command, you can apply the formulas to each list, then compare the performance of the various lists to decide whether a list should be dropped, retested, or rolled out. To do the calculations manually, use the same format, but be prepared to spend more time.

Square-inch and page/spread analysis

Square-inch analysis determines profit or loss for each product. The basic format used in square-inch analysis (see Figure 9-5) is also used in page/spread analysis, so to simplify matters, we'll treat them together. Let's make some assumptions:

1 The total cost of the catalog in the mail is $200,000.

2 The fulfillment charge for shipping and handling equals the fulfillment costs (see "The Back End," Part 8).

Product space allocation

The number of square inches per product is obtained by simply measuring the space occupied by the product and its copy. Work with a ruler

FIGURE 9-5
Product profit/loss based on square-inch analysis

A	B Measured Sq. In. per Product	C No. of Sq. In. per Product Incl. White Space (Factor = 1.2)	D Cost of Space at 66.84/Sq. In.	E No. of Orders	F Net $/Order	G Total Net $	H P/L
1. Pages 2&3							
2.							
3. SKU 1234		1.2 × B3	66.84 × C3			E3×F3	G3−D3
4. 1235		1.2 × B4	66.84 × C4			E4×F4	G4-D4
5. 1236		1.2 × B5	66.84 × C5				
6. 1237		1.2 × B6	66.84 × C6				
7. 1238							
8. Pg. 2 Total		sum of C3 to C7	sum of D3 to D7			sum G3 to G7	G8−D8
9. SKU 1239							
10. 1240							
11. 1242							
12. 1243							
13. 1244							
14. 1245							
15. Pg. 3 Total		sum of C9 to C14	sum of D9 to D14			sum G9 to G14	G15−D15
16. Spread Total		C8 + C15	D8 + D15			G8 + G15	G16−D16

NOTE: The order form and its space can be considered separately, but it is preferable to treat it as pages in the catalog. The number of pages would depend on the size of the order form.

that shows tenths of an inch and use some judgment. If the photo is an easily measured rectangle, the result is obvious. But what if it's a silhouetted product? Measure the space that seems to be devoted to that product. And don't worry if you're off a fraction of an inch; it won't affect the result.

White space allocation

Because photos and copy don't completely cover a spread, some white space is left after all the measurements are added. For example, if your catalog is 8½ × 11″, each page is 93.5 square inches, and each spread is 187 square inches. Calculating to one decimal place is adequate for estimates. If all the space allocations on a spread add up to 160.8 square inches, 26.2 square inches of white space remain.

If your catalog's front cover has been designed to show an image rather than to sell particular merchandise, it still has a cost. That space and cost must be allocated over the whole catalog. To determine this space allocation per page, divide the total number of square inches per page by the number of pages in the catalog (less the cover). For a 32-page catalog (31 pages and image cover), the formula is

93.5 sq. in. ÷ 31 pages = 3.0 sq. in. per page, or 6.0 sq. in. per spread.

The 6.0 square inches per spread are added to the 187 square inches for each hypothetical spread, giving a total of 193 square inches for the spread. If the cover is used to sell a product or products, it should be treated as any other page selling products and its space should not be allocated to the other pages.

White space formula

To allocate the white space between products, a common factor is derived for the spread (usually different for each spread) by dividing the total space by the product space.

Total space ÷ Product space = Factor
193 ÷ 160.8 = 1.2

In the example, each product's allocated space is equal to 1.2 times its measured space. A product that has 10 square inches of measured space actually has 12 square inches of allocated space.

Cost of space

The next consideration is space cost. First, you must know the total in-mail cost of the catalog, including postage. Divide the total cost by the number of spreads, pages, and square inches in the catalog to determine the cost per spread, cost per page, and cost per square inch. For example, assume the in-mail cost to be $200,000. For an 8½″ × 11″, 32-page catalog, the cost per spread is $12,500 ($200,000 ÷ 16), the cost per page is $6,250 ($200,000 ÷ 32), and the cost per square inch is $66.84 ($200,000 ÷ 2,992 sq. in.). On the basis of the cost per square inch, profit or loss can then be determined (see Figure 9-5). In this example, we divide the cost by the 32 pages rather than 31. By allocating the cover space we have automatically allocated the cost.

Category analysis

Knowing the profit and loss for each product in a catalog is not enough. The items should be listed by categories and an analysis performed for each category of merchandise (see Figure 3-4). This is done because merchandising tends to be sourced by category rather than by individual item. Buyers should be directed to increase or decrease particular categories based on profits.

Category analysis is made somewhat easier by having already done the square-inch analysis for items. Simply add up the space cost of all the items within a category and compare the result to the total net sales from that category.

CATEGORY ANALYSIS FORMAT
CATEGORY #02, TABLE ACCESSORIES—USEFUL

	Item	Space Cost	Net Sales
SKU No.	———	———	———
SKU No.	———	———	———
SKU No.	———	———	———
	Total # of Items	Total Space Cost for Category	Total Net Sales

To compare categories, set up a chart as shown.

A COMPARISON CHART

Category or Price Range	Total Allocated Space	Space Cost	% Space Cost	Net Sales	% Net Sales	Total P/L	Performance Index
A			11.6		4.88		.4
B			7.43		8.6		1.2
C			11.8		14.6		1.2
D			3.58		2.1		.6
E			5.7		9.2		1.6
			5.7		6.4		1.1
			4.1		4.4		1.1
			15.4		13.8		.9
			12.6		11.3		.9
			22.2		24.8		1.1

The performance index is the ratio of net sales percentage divided by space cost percentage.

Price range analysis

Similar calculations should be performed by using a price range of merchandise as a type of category. Add up all the space costs for items in each price range and their net sales. Price ranges could be set as under $10, $10.01–$20.00, $20.01–$30.00, and so on. Set up a similar chart to analyze the results. In this case, the performance index is the ratio of net sales percentage (in a particular price range) to space cost percentage (for that same price range).

Some catalogers find a simple histogram useful for price range analysis once they decide the desirable mix of price ranges (see Figure 9-6). For first-time catalogers, this histogram is the only way of analyzing price ranges (or categories).

By combining price ranges into more useful segments, the two histograms in Figure 9-7 evolve. One shows the actual, the other the preferred range.

Use of the price range histogram can alert catalogers to errors in their pricing strategy. In this example, the cataloger has not determined the market and is attempting to appeal to both high- and low-end buyers.

Other analyses

The methodology outlined in the preceding section was selected to give a basic understanding of catalog analysis techniques. But there are many possible variations on these methods. For example:

FIGURE 9-6
Price range histogram showing lack of price range targeting

$0–$10.00	|***************
$10.01–$20.00	|***
$20.01–$30.00	|********************
$30.01–$40.00	|**********
$40.01–$50.00	|*****
$50.01–$60.00	|***
$60.01–$70.00	|*****
$70.01–$80.00	|*****
$80.01–$90.00	|**
$90.01–$100.00	|*
$100.01–$110.00	|***
$110.01–$125.00	|***
$125.01–$150.00	|****
$150.01–$175.00	|*****
$175.01–$200.00	|***
$200.01–$250.00	|**
$250.01–$300.00	|*
$300.01–$500.00	|*
$500+	|*

FIGURE 9-7
Ideal and actual price-range histograms

Price ranges as they should be (approximately)	
Under $20.00	*************
$20.01–$40.00	*************************
$40.01–$60.00	***
$60.01–$100.00	*************************
$100.01+	**************
Price points as they are in Figure 9-6	
Under $20.00	**
$20.01–$40.00	************************
$40.01–$60.00	********
$60.01–$100.00	***************
$100.01+	**********************

1 Variable list costs can be used in list analysis.
2 Net sales rather than gross sales can be used in list analysis.
3 Category sales can be analyzed as a function of lists.
4 Retailers can separately track exclusive-to-catalog versus common-to-store merchandise.
5 Rate of response, customer conversion rates, and customer value versus cost of acquisition can be tracked for different customer acquisition methods.
6 Mail order data can be used for retail store site selection.
7 Merge/purge results can be used to predict mailing response.
8 Market research data can be combined with psycho/demographic data to target the audience more tightly.
9 Customer profiles can be developed based on frequency distribution rather than customer profile averages.

The desired result of any analysis is an improvement in the bottom line of the catalog. A perfect analysis would also result in totally individualized catalogs, received on the date specified for each person. From a list of 5,000 names, possibly only 200 catalogs would be mailed, and all of the recipients would purchase the exact same merchandise from the catalog, giving a 100 percent response rate and an extremely high average order. This choice is never likely to be either available or economically feasible. Nor is no analysis a viable choice, leaving the catalog's growth to luck. There is, however, a middle ground in which the results of the analysis far outweigh the costs.

Mathematical methods

In any well-run catalog business today, much useful data are compiled. Mathematical techniques can help identify the most important data and define relationships between the variables. Often these factors are not evident merely by compiling the data, but can be represented only by complicated mathematical functional relationships. Although these specialized methods require a high level of mathematical knowledge, the cataloger should at least have an understanding of their potential applications for analysis of catalog data.

Regression techniques

In its simplest form, regression analysis is used to determine the relationship between two variables, say height and weight. If the height versus weight of a randomly selected group of people were plotted on a graph, most of the points would appear to cluster along an imaginary straight line. A regression analysis gives the equation of this line and indicates how well it fits (matches) the data.

For catalogs, we might use the number of orders received and the time since mailing (or since the first order was received) to predict total results of the mailing. This is more complicated, since a straight line would not represent the most accurate equation. As seen in the curves in Figures 10-1 to 10-3, "Economics," Part 10, this function might have a complex shape. We would write $y = f(X)$, where y is the number of orders received at some given time, and X is that time. Again, we would use regression to determine the final form of the equation (curve) and how well it fits. If, in fact, it fits well, the equation can be used to predict order quantities at some future time in the mailing. However, as more data (orders) are received, the regression should be updated to refine predictions.

Multivariate regression is used to determine the most and least important variable in an equation. The equation might have the functional form $y = f(X_0, X_1, X_2 \ldots X_n)$, with the Xs representing variables and their interactions. Suppose we let y equal the probability that the customer orders. The Xs might be characteristics of the catalog's customers, such as income, age, zip code, and so on. If we set up a regression equation and systematically remove one or more variables from the equation at a time, the changes in the equation caused by our removals would identify the important factors, as well as the interactions between variables that are important. We could then attempt to maximize our mailings to the type of person with the important characteristics.

Pattern recognition techniques

Many of the clustering or classification techniques now being used by direct marketers are offshoots of earlier work performed under government contracts. This work concerned itself with artificial intelligence, pattern recognition, and decision and information theory. The reasons direct marketers have adopted these techniques are clear; picking a radio or radar signal out of a set of noise pulses is no different from picking a likely catalog customer from the large set of people who have not previously purchased. As the need for new names becomes more important to catalogers, so do these techniques.

Clustering techniques are used to categorize potential purchasers into geo/demographic segments, in particular, to maximize the intergroup distances and minimize the intragroup distances in a mathematically described *n*-dimensional space having the same number of dimensions as there are independent variables (such as income, age, and so on). As a new data point (possible buyer) appears, it is assigned to one of the clusters. The decision as to which cluster this data point is assigned (buyer/nonbuyer) can be aided by discriminant or measurement functions. Clustering techniques are often combined with discriminant functions to help decide whether the new data point represents a likely buyer or nonbuyer.

Analysis and profit

Whether you are a newcomer or an experienced cataloger, the most important element of any analysis is accurate data. From the first mailing on, collect and retain all the data outlined in "The Back End," Part 8. Without this essential information, none of these sophisticated, and effective, methods can be implemented.

After the analysis, use the results to compare the projected P&L (profit and loss) statement prepared before the implementation of your first catalog to the actual P&L. Continue to compare P&Ls for each succeeding catalog. A P&L should be evaluated as one of a series, not in isolation. This will allow you to better understand the causes of increased profits or losses. For example, are losses due to postage increases? Or are your suppliers getting too high priced? Or is it simply that sales are down? Maybe it's time for a new creative approach or a change of merchandise mix. A good cataloger constantly analyzes results and overall economics. Analysis must be used, but no amount of analysis is helpful unless the results are used by the cataloger to improve the return on the next catalog.

Part 10
ECONOMICS

THE BUSINESS PLAN

Before preparing a business plan, you'll need to write an overview, outlining the economics of your prospective mail order business. All of the characteristics in the lists that follow are desirable, but seldom does every condition exist in a startup venture. Obviously, the more the better.

Overview

Your overview should cover the following.

1 Reason for existence

- Product line has attributes that can be better explained/shown than in a store.
- No other catalog is currently serving this particular consumer need.
- The targeted market is large enough to be profitable.
- The market is relatively easy to reach.
- The targeted customer has long-term buying potential.
- The product line has the potential for diversification.
- The product line is not seriously affected by seasonality.

2 Finances

- Enough capital is available to sustain the venture over a reasonable startup period.
- The product line will provide a satisfactory return on investment.
- Sales will not be greatly affected by the loss of any one supplier.
- The anticipated average order will be higher than the norm.
- The necessary facilities (warehouse, office space, and so on) are available at a reasonable cost.

3 Management

- Key people have previous mail order experience.
- There is previous experience running a business.
- Management is knowledgeable about strategy and long-range planning.

Once you've written the overview, it's time to do a business plan. A business plan is just as important for a catalog as for any other company. Although a business plan can be prepared manually, the low cost of microcomputers and the availability of electronic spreadsheet programs, such as Visicalc and Lotus 1-2-3, make profit and loss statements (P&Ls), cash flow reports, and so on, simpler to do by machine.

To determine the economics of the proposed catalog operation, you need to project *profit and loss* and *cash flow.* But before you do that, you need (1) *cost estimates for the catalog,* (2) *operating expenses for the company,* (3) *inventory costs and turnover,* and (4) *sales and profit margin figures.* Let's consider them one at a time.

Catalog cost estimates

Make cost estimates as accurate as possible by getting actual quotes from prospective suppliers. Here's a checklist.

COST ESTIMATES—CATALOG

- ✓ Design/layout
- ✓ Copy
- ✓ Type
- ✓ Type specifications
- ✓ Mechanicals
- ✓ Photography (including assistants and film and processing)
- ✓ Props/rentals
- ✓ Van rental
- ✓ Location fee
- ✓ Models
- ✓ Stylist (hair/makeup)
- ✓ Stylist—stills
- ✓ Photostats
- ✓ Illustrations
- ✓ Retouching
- ✓ Dupes
- ✓ Assemblies
- ✓ Separations
- ✓ Stripping
- ✓ Printing
- ✓ Paper
- ✓ List rental costs
- ✓ Computer costs
- ✓ Merge/purge
- ✓ House file update
- ✓ Order forms
- ✓ Mailing labels or ink-jet tape
- ✓ Lettershop
- ✓ Freight
- ✓ Inserting
- ✓ Postage
- ✓ Miscellaneous expenses (long-distance phone calls, messengers, air express, photocopies, taxis, and so on)

Be sure also to ask suppliers for their terms of payment. Payment terms will affect your cash flow.

Operating expenses

Catalogs do not exist in a vacuum. A company structure supports them, and the costs associated with this structure must be considered. Even if you are using existing space for your office and/or warehouse, direct overhead costs must be allocated to the catalog.

OPERATING EXPENSES

- ✓ Rent (office and warehouse)
- ✓ Utilities
- ✓ Telephone costs
- ✓ Office supplies

- Insurance
- Accounting services
- Equipment for office and warehouse (cost of purchase or lease)
- Salaries
- Travel and entertainment
- Attorney's/accountant's fees
- Miscellaneous (e.g., dues & subscriptions, maintenance & depreciation)

Inventory costs

No cataloger wants to run out of merchandise or to be left with unsold merchandise that (unless there is an outlet store) must be liquidated at a fraction of its cost. In an ideal world, the cataloger purchases exactly the correct amounts of products for the catalog. As the last order is filled, all the items have been sold and there are no outstanding back orders. This doesn't happen. However, the closer one comes to the ideal, the better for the bottom line, and for sleeping at night.

When to order is a function of predicted need for merchandise and the lead time from order to receipt of order. How much to order is a function of purchase cost, warehouse costs, and order demand. These will vary for each catalog and vendor and must be calculated by the cataloger for each situation. (For how to minimize inventory problems, see the chapter "Inventory Control" in Part 8.)

Figure 10-6 shows how inventory costs might look over a certain time period and under certain conditions. The actual numbers, of course, depend on the merchandise mix and the payment structure negotiated with vendors. A rule of thumb used by some catalogers is that 50 percent of the inventory should be on hand the first month the catalog is in the mail, 30 percent the second month, and 10 percent the third and fourth months. An established cataloger controls inventory through a system that combines order backup vendors with historical catalog sales curves and an analysis that predicts well ahead of time whether an item will be oversold.

Projecting total orders

The percentage of completion (number of orders received in a certain time) can be used to project the number of orders for an item. Historical order curves are modified by the current order curve to get the percentage complete. Then, the quantity of an item that will be sold is determined by using the following formula:

$$\text{Total orders expected} = \frac{\text{Number sold to date}}{\text{Percentage of completion (expressed as a decimal)}}$$

For more about when to order additional merchandise, see the discussion of inventory forecasting in the chapter "Inventory Control" in Part 8.

In reality, inventory control is complicated by such factors as minimum purchase requirements, large-order discounts, and delivery times.

The cataloger must sometimes choose between overstocking and unhappy customers.

Order curves

Order curves are regression lines that show orders as a function of time, beginning when the first order arrives. Time is calculated from the receipt of the first order, because of variation in the in-mail and the in-home receipt of the catalog dates.

For many seasons, an order curve of 13 weeks gave the completion percentages shown in Table 10-1.

Recently, however, there have been considerable variations from this curve. For some catalogs, the order curve was completed in four weeks and never reached more than 70 percent of the otherwise expected orders (see Figure 10-1).

Another catalog did much better the same season, but again the curve was different (see Figure 10-2). Each week's modification of the curve showed that sales were better than anticipated.

For the curve shown in Figure 10-2, the best equation is:

$$\log(y) = a_1 + a_2 (\log x) + a_3 (\log x)^2.$$

In the equation, x is the number of days since first order, y is the number of orders on the xth day. The values of coefficients a_1, a_2, and a_3 are generated by the computer using a regression program that fits the catalog order data to the best curve so that future order projections can be made. As more data points are available, the error factor in the equation will decrease. Another useful curve to obtain the total orders for a catalog or a product is:

$$y = a_1 + a_2 (a_3^x).$$

In this curve, y is the total orders received by day or week x. The shape of the curve is shown in Figure 10-3.

TABLE 10-1
Example of completion percentages of historical order curve

Week	%
1	6
2	18
3	27
4	35
5	55
6	69
7	76
8	80
9	84
10	88
11	92
12	96
13	100

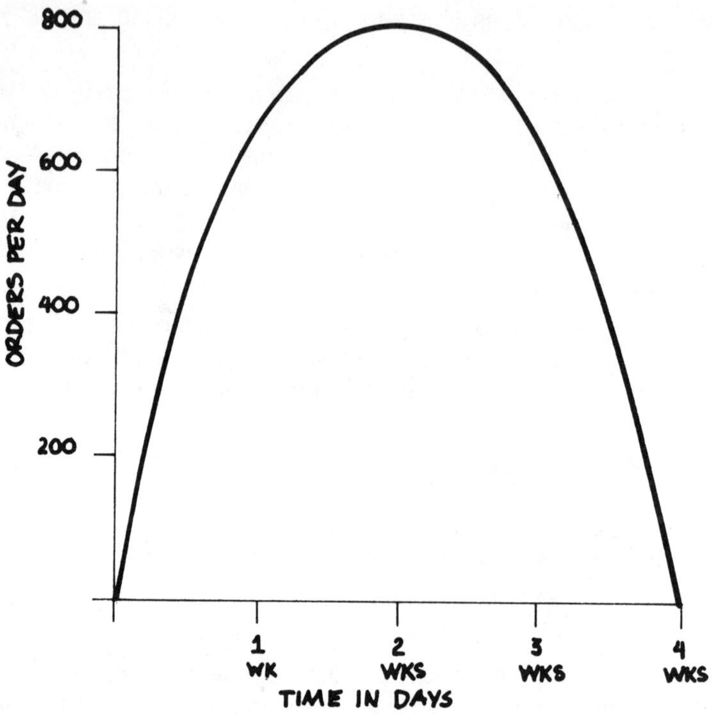

FIGURE 10-1
Example of a four-week order curve.

Affordable programs available for most microcomputers allow quick determination of these curves and give not only the coefficients and the order predictions but also the probable error limits on the results. With such a program, results can be updated daily or at least weekly to provide the data needed for inventory control.

Gross and net sales

In developing P&L projections and cash flows, most expense items can be determined quite accurately. But sales projections must be estimated. For established catalogs, response rates and average order sizes from previous editions can be used as a basis for estimating gross sales, including seasonal variations.

Unless they are pretested offshoots of established operations, new or proposed catalogs do not have this advantage. Their sales projections must be based on estimates.

Projecting gross sales

Gross sales projections include (1) the number of catalogs to be mailed, (2) the response rate, and (3) the average order. The accuracy of these projections is influenced by many factors, some of which may not be fixed until actual results of a mailing are known.

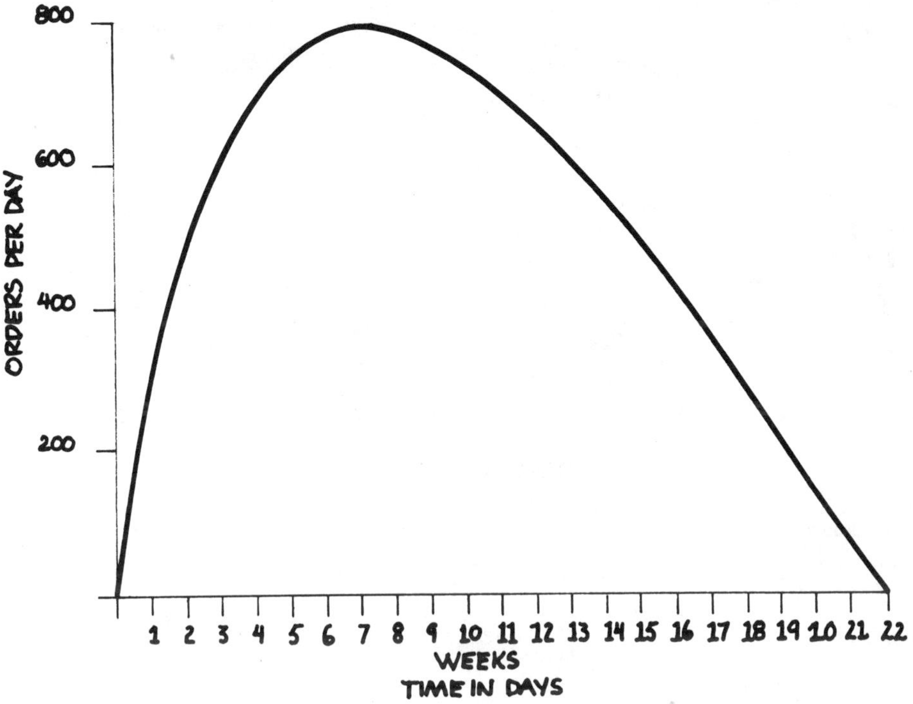

FIGURE 10-2
Example of an order curve for catalog with 22-week life.

• *Number of catalogs mailed.* Catalogs should never be mailed simply to bring the mailing to some preset total. The number mailed should be based on the number of perceived profitable names available. You may set up a projection based on a certain mailing quantity, but this should be updated continually, as the number of available names becomes more apparent.

• *Response rates and average orders.* Estimates of response rates and average orders are subject to such influences as politics, weather, macroeconomics, and mail delivery. Again, the estimates should be updated based on such information as published sales trends, conversations with other catalogers, or the changes in the economy.

Calculating net sales

The gross sales figure is simply the total dollar amount of goods sold, in other words, the sum total of all the orders received through the catalog. To arrive at a net sales figure, you must make certain deductions from the gross sales amount. These deductions are not uniform in the industry. Some catalogers treat such factors as telephone sales cost as part of overhead, rather than as a deduction from gross sales. This is particularly true of catalogs with an in-house phone staff instead of an outside service. The formats used in this section are not meant to be all-inclusive or arbitrary, but simply to serve as guides.

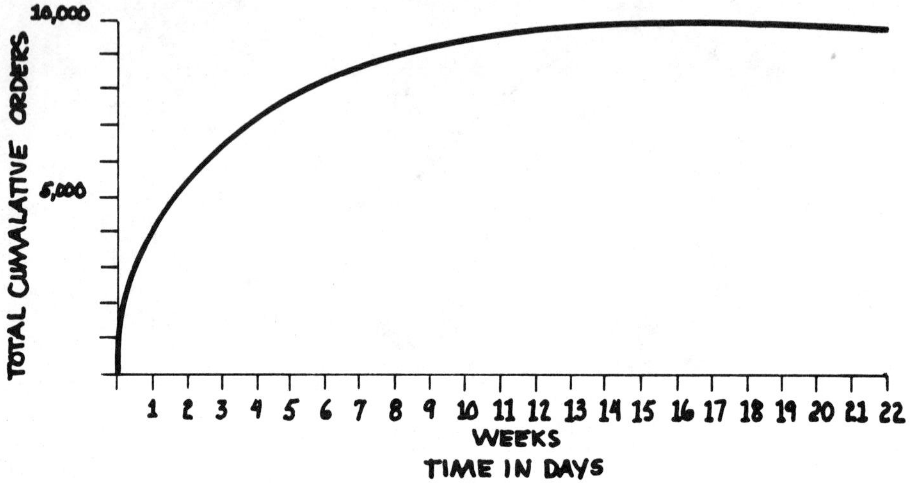

FIGURE 10-3
Example of a cumulative order curve.

Deductions

From gross sales make the following deductions:

1 Cancellations of orders.

2 Returned merchandise costs. This amount depends on whether merchandise can be refurbished and resold from stock or sold through an owned retail outlet, or must be disposed of through a liquidator at a substantial loss. For fashion catalogs, the cost of returned merchandise can be a significant figure. Returns must be kept to a minimum to ensure profitability (see "Merchandising," Part 3).

3 Credit card charges. MasterCard/Visa charges vary, depending on your average order and banking relationship. Some fulfillment or phone services offer low discount rates for credit cards. These should be explored by new catalogers or established ones dissatisfied with their current rates.

   To determine these costs, assume that a certain percentage of orders will be paid by credit card as opposed to checks. Although the percentage varies from one catalog to another, the higher the average order, the stronger the tendency for credit card use. For now, assume the following.

   a. Credit card orders will be 50 percent of all orders.
   b. Two-thirds of credit card orders will be paid by MasterCard or Visa. Assume a discount rate of 3 percent for both.
   c. The remaining one-third will be paid with travel and entertainment cards, such as American Express, with the higher discount rate of 4 percent.

4 Telephone order costs. Many catalogers use telephone answering service bureaus to take telephone orders. This is recommended for new catalogers because of the high startup costs and time demands of in-house service. Let's assume a telephone cost of $2.50 per order. The percentage of orders received by telephone is assumed to be 30 percent.

The calculation

Gross sales − Adjustments (cancellations, returned merchandise costs, credit card charges, and telephone order costs) = Net sales

Cash flow

Even though a catalog operation is profitable, it may have periods of negative cash flow. A simple explanation is that catalog production and inventory costs must often be paid for before the money starts coming in from orders. To help prevent poor cash flow management, catalogers must keep up-to-date cash flow records and projections.

In many cases, cash flows are done weekly as a combination of detailed sales and expense projections. In addition, when receipts are being received from more than one catalog, individual cash flows must be done for each catalog as well as an overall cash flow to determine the company's total cash needs and surpluses.

Cash flow projections should be as detailed as possible, and the assumptions should be included in the financial notes to the projections. A number of "what if" studies should be done to determine cash needs and surpluses under a variety of circumstances, responses, and so on.

The effect of credit

To minimize cash requirements and increase return on investment, advantageous credit terms should be sought by every cataloger. Although this is easier to accomplish for established catalogs or large corporations, all should attempt to negotiate credit in two important areas: catalog production and merchandise inventory.

Depending on bank references, many manufacturers will give credit even on initial orders. This will not be true in all cases, but with each credit received or delivery deferred, which is also a form of credit, your cash flow improves.

Similarly, catalogers should attempt to obtain credit from catalog production suppliers, printers, separators, typographers, and photographers; many give credit under the right circumstances. Explore this with them openly, then be sure to meet the terms to which you have agreed. The more reliable you are with promised payments, the better your chances of increased credit for future catalogs.

The newcomer will find it much harder to obtain credit on list rentals. However, with good references, it is sometimes possible. For an established catalog, the majority of list rentals will be on credit. Since list rentals are a significant factor in catalog costs, start working on credit with your list broker as soon as possible.

Unfortunately, there is one area where no credit can be obtained. Postage must be paid at the time of mailing. Don't be tempted to stagger a mailing over a longer period of time in order to spread costs. List results can be skewed and overall response could be negatively affected.

Return on investment

This figure, called ROI, is defined as the annual profit divided by the equity investment in the company (expressed as a percent). In recent years, with corporations more oriented to managing for cash flow and longer-term planning, the ROI of any given year has become less meaningful.

FINANCIAL PROJECTIONS

A series of financial reports/projections in the form of financial statements comprises this chapter. These have been developed to demonstrate how to set up reports and projections. While the numbers used are internally consistent, they are meant *only as a guide.* The financial profile of each cataloger will be different, depending on the individual characteristics of the catalog and other factors, such as location.

FIGURE 10-4
Spreadsheet of catalog cost estimate (figures in dollars).

CATALOG #	001	002	003	004
CATALOG DESCRIPTION	FOUR COLOR, 24 PP. 60LB 8&1/2X11 120 PHOTOS 24 FASHION 20 PHOTOS	SAME BUT 32 PP. 160 PHOTOS 32 FASHION	SAME AS 001	SAME AS 002
PRESS RUN	300M	500M	500M	1MM
PRE-PRESS COSTS				
DESIGN/LAYOUT	$4200	$5600	$4200	$5600
COPY	3600	4800	3600	4800
TYPE & PHOTOSTATS	3200	4300	3200	4300
TYPE SPEC/PASTE-UP	3000	4000	3000	4000
PHOTOGRAPHY	14000	18000	14000	18000
LOCATION IF ANY	----	----	----	----
PROP RENTALS	500	500	500	500
MODELS	4000	6000	4000	6000
STYLIST	1000	1200	1000	1200
DUPES	3000	4000	3000	4000
ASSEMBLIES	2400	4000	2400	3000
SEPARATIONS	12000	16000	12000	16000
PRINTING COSTS				
STRIPPING	1500	1500	1500	1500
PRINTING, INCL. PAPER	27000	53000	44000	96000
ORDER FORM COSTS				
PRE-PRESS	2450	2450	2450	2450
PRINTING	4800	7200	7200	12500
OTHER COSTS				
LETTERSHOP	4800	7900	7900	12500
LIST RENTAL	30000	53000	51000	110000
COMPUTER COSTS	2600	4600	4600	8400
POSTAGE	30000	48000	48000	93000
HOUSE LIST UPDATE		500	1000	1000
TOTAL COST PER EDITION	$154050	$245550	$218550	$404750
COST PER CATALOG	0.51	0.49	0.44	0.40

FIGURE 10-5
Spreadsheet of catalog cost payments (figures in dollars).

EXPENSE ITEM	FIRST YEAR MONTH-1	2	3	4	5	6	7	8	9	10	11	12
PRE-PRESS		$53350					$69850					
PRINTING/LETTERSHOP			$19100	$19000				$34800	$34800			
LIST RENTAL			15000	15000					53000			
POSTAGE			30000					48000				
COMPUTER COSTS				2600					5100			
TOTAL MONTHLY COST		$53350	$64100	$36600	0	0	$69850	$82800	$92900	0	0	0

EXPENSE ITEM	SECOND YEAR MONTH-13	14	15	16	17	18	19	20	21	22	23	24
PRE-PRESS		$53350					$69850					
PRINTING/LETTERSHOP			$30300	$30300				$61250	$61250			
LIST RENTAL				51000					110000			
POSTAGE			48000					93000				
COMPUTER COSTS				5600					9400			
TOTAL MONTHLY COST	0	$53350	$78300	$86900	0	0	$69850	$154250	$180650	0	0	0

TOTAL INVENTORY COSTS
XXXXXXXXXXXXXXXXXXXX

CATALOG 1	$ 90000
CATALOG 2	$230000
CATALOG 3	$220000
CATALOG 4	$600000

FIRST YEAR

MONTH 1	2	3	4	5	6	7	8	9	10	11	12
	$45000	$27000	$18000			$115000	$69000	$23000	$23000		

XXXXXXXXXXXXXXXXXXXXXXXXXXXXXXXXXXXXXXXXXXXXXXXXXXXXXXXXXXXXXXXXXXXXXXXXXXXXXXXXXXXXXXXXXXXXXXXXXX

SECOND YEAR

MONTH 13	14	15	16	17	18	19	20	21	22	23	24
	$110000	$66000	$44000			$300000	$180000	$60000	$60000		

FIGURE 10-6
Spreadsheet of inventory cost projections (figures in dollars).

FIGURE 10-7
Spreadsheet of overhead expense projections (figures in dollars).

MONTH	1	2	3	4	5	6	7	8	9	10	11	12
OVERHEAD COSTS												
RENT-OFFICE	$ 750	$ 750	$ 750	$ 750	$ 750	$ 750	$ 750	$ 750	$ 750	$ 750	$ 750	$ 750
RENT-WAREHOUSE	1333	1333	1333	1333	1333	1333	1333	1333	1333	1333	1333	1333
UTILITIES	300	300	300	300	300	300	300	300	300	300	300	300
TELEPHONE	1500	1000	1000	1000	1000	1000	1000	1000	1000	1000	1000	1000
OFFICE SUPPLIES	2000	300	300	300	300	300	300	300	300	300	300	300
DUES/SUBSCRIPTIONS	400	400	400	400	400	400	400	400	400	400	400	400
TRAVEL	3600			3600			3600			3600		
LEGAL	2000	100	100	100	100	100	100	100	100	100	100	100
ACCOUNTING	1500	100	100	100	100	100	100	100	100	100	100	100
SALARIES & BENEFITS	5060	5060	5980	7360	7360	7360	7360	7360	7360	7360	7360	7360
EQUIPMENT (PURCHASE)	15000											
EQUIPMENT (LEASE)	250	250	250	250	250	250	250	250	250	250	250	250
INSURANCE	1000	1000	1000	1000	1000	1000	1000	1000	1000	1000	1000	1000
TOTAL MONTHLY OVERHEAD	$34693	$10593	$11513	$16493	$12893	$12893	$16493	$12893	$12893	$16493	$12893	$12893

XXXXXXXXXXXXXXXXXXXXXXXXXXXXXXXXXXXXXXXXXXXXXXXXXXXXXXXXXXXXXXXXXXXXXXXXXXXXXXXXXXXXXXXXXXXXXXXXXX

MONTH	13	14	15	16	17	18	19	20	21	22	23	24
OVERHEAD COSTS												
RENT-OFFICE	$ 750	$ 750	$ 750	$ 750	$ 750	$ 750	$ 750	$ 750	$ 750	$ 750	$ 750	$ 750
RENT-WAREHOUSE	1333	1333	1333	1333	1333	1333	1333	1333	1333	1333	1333	1333
UTILITIES	300	300	300	300	300	300	300	300	300	300	300	300
TELEPHONE	1000	1000	1000	1000	1000	1000	1000	1000	1000	1000	1000	1000
OFFICE SUPPLIES	300	300	300	300	300	300	300	300	300	300	300	300
DUES/SUBSCRIPTIONS	500	500	500	500	500	500	500	500	500	500	500	500
TRAVEL	3600			3600			3600			3600		
LEGAL	100	100	100	100	100	100	100	100	100	100	100	100
ACCOUNTING	500	100	100	100	100	100	100	100	100	100	100	100
SALARIES & BENEFITS	8855	9085	9545	9545	9545	9545	9545	9545	9545	9545	9545	9545
EQUIPMENT (PURCHASE)												
EQUIPMENT (LEASE)	250	250	250	250	250	250	250	250	250	250	250	250
INSURANCE	1000	1000	1000	1000	1000	1000	1000	1000	1000	1000	1000	1000
TOTAL MONTHLY OVERHEAD	$18483	$4718	$15178	$18778	$15178	$15178	$18778	$15178	$15178	$18778	$15178	$15178

FIGURE 10-8
Spreadsheet of catalog net sales projections (figures in dollars).

CATALOG NET SALES FIRST YEAR

	SPRING	FALL
GROSS SALES	$225000	$575000
CANCELLATIONS	-1125	-2875
RETURNS (NET COST)	-2250	-5750
CREDIT CARD CHARGES	-3751	-9585
TEL. ORDER COSTS	-3375	-7475
NET SALES	$214499	$549315

CATALOG NET SALES SECOND YEAR

	SPRING	FALL
GROSS SALES	$550000	$1500000
CANCELLATIONS	-2750	-7500
RETURNS (NET COST)	-5500	-15000
CREDIT CARD CHARGES	-9169	-25005
TEL. ORDER COSTS	-8250	-19500
NET SALES	$524332	$1432995

NET SALES IN DOLLARS	
CATALOG-1	214499
CATALOG-2	549315
CATALOG-3	524332
CATALOG-4	1432995

FIRST YEAR

MONTH 1	2	3	4	5	6	7	8	9	10	11	12
			$96525	$85800	$32175			$192260	$219726	$109863	$27466
MONTH 13	**14**	**15**	**16**	**17**	**18**	**19**	**20**	**21**	**22**	**23**	**24**
			$235949	$209733	$78650			$501548	$573198	$286599	$71650

FIGURE 10-9
Spreadsheet of sales projections (figures in dollars).

FIGURE 10-10
Spreadsheet of cash flow projections (figures in dollars).

CASH FLOW

	MONTH 1	2	3	4	5	6	7	8	9	10	11	12
CASH AT START		$-88043	$-207736	$-282849	$-220817	$-147910	$-128628	$-329971	$-494664	$-431197	$-250964	$-15399
NET SALES				96525	85800	32175			192260	219726	109863	27466
CATALOG COSTS	53350	64100	36600				69850	82800	92900			
INVENTORY COSTS		45000	27000	18000			115000	69000	23000	23000		
OVERHEAD COSTS	34693	10593	11513	16493	12893	12893	16493	12893	12893	16493	12893	12893
TOTAL EXPENSES	$88043	$119693	$75113	$34493	$12893	$12893	$201343	$164693	$128793	$39493	$12893	$12893
CASH AT END	$-88043	$-207736	$-282849	$-220817	$-147910	$-128628	$-329971	$-494664	$-431197	$-250964	$-153994	$-139421
	MONTH 13	**14**	**15**	**16**	**17**	**18**	**19**	**20**	**21**	**22**	**23**	**24**
CASH AT START	$-139421	$-157909	$-335977	$-495455	$-409184	$-214629	$-151157	$1539785	$-889213	$-643493	$-149073	$ 122348
NET SALES				235949	209733	78650			501548	573198	286599	71650
CATALOG COSTS		53350	78300	86900			69850	154250	180650			
INVENTORY COSTS		110000	66000	44000			300000	180000	60000	60000		
OVERHEAD COSTS	18488	14718	15178	18778	15178	15178	18778	15178	15178	18778	15178	15178
TOTAL EXPENSES	18488	178068	159478	149678	15178	15178	388628	349428	255828	78778	15178	15178
CASH AT END	$-157909	$-335977	$-495455	$-409184	$-214629	$-151157	$-539785	$-889213	$-643493	$-149073	$ 122348	$ 178820

FIGURE 10-11
Spreadsheet of profit and loss projections (figures in dollars).

	YEAR 1	YEAR 2
NET SALES	$763815	$1957327
CATALOG COSTS	$-399600	$-623300
INVENTORY COSTS	-320000	-820000
OVERHEAD COSTS	-183636	-195786
PROFIT/LOSS (PRE-TAX)	$-139421	$318241

Assumptions

The financial statements shown in Figures 10-4 through 10-11 are for four different, hypothetical catalogs produced and mailed in a 24-month period. The figures are based on *assumptions* about costs, sales, inventory, and credit arrangements. Remember, these are only assumptions—not necessarily true-to-life figures.

1 Number of catalogs/timing. Two catalogs will be mailed each year: one the last week of April, the other the last week of August. The first spring mailing is 300,000 catalogs, the fall mailing is 500,000 catalogs. The second spring mailing is 500,000, the second fall mailing is 1,000,000.

2 Computer costs for first year's catalogs.

Merge/purge in:	333M × $3/M	= $999 Spring	587M × $3/M	= $1761 Fall
Merge/purge out:	300M × $4.50/M	= $1350 Spring	500M × $4.50/M	= $2250 Fall
Presort	150M × $1.50/M	= $225 Spring	300M × $1.50/M	= $450 Fall
Total		$2574		$4461

3 Catalog costs. Prepress paid in month before mailing; printer/lettershop paid ½ at mailing, ½ within 30 days; postage paid at mailing; computer costs paid 30 days after mailing; list rental costs for the first catalog ½ in month of mailing, ½ in month following mailing. All other list costs are 100 percent in month following mailing.

4 Inventory costs. Inventory deliveries are distributed as follows:

For spring: 50 percent one month before; 30 percent at first order date; 20 percent one month after. *For fall:* 50 percent one month before; 30 percent at first order date; 10 percent one month after; 10 percent two months after. No credit assumptions have been made. All deliveries are paid for in the month before receipt. This is a conservative approach. Some credit would probably be available even for the first catalog's merchandise and more for succeeding mailings.

5 Sales.

Spring order cycle of 2½ months: 45 percent of orders in month 1; 40 percent of orders in month 2; 15 percent of orders in month 3.

Fall order cycle of 4 months: 35 percent of the orders in month 1; 40 percent of the orders in month 2; 20 percent of the orders in month 3; 5 percent of the orders in month 4.

6 Sales responses and average orders.

Catalog 1:	Sales response 1.5%	Average order $50.00
2:	2%	$57.50
3:	2%	$55.00
4:	2.5%	$60.00

Although the house list would be expected to perform better than rented lists, in the interests of keeping examples as simple yet as meaningful as possible, house list results have been averaged into the response figures.

7 List rental income. None is included nor are costs lowered by list exchanges.

8 Space ads. At some point most catalogers develop a space ad program to acquire names of potential customers. This program can range in scope from ⅙-page ads to two-page spreads. Because the results of a space ad program are evaluated by the number of respondents, the conversion rate, and the long-term value of the customer, the cost and results of such a program have not been included in the financials.

OTHER FACTORS AFFECTING PROFITABILITY

Your economic calculations and projections need to include several categories of expenses not yet detailed. Postage is a place where you can significantly reduce costs. Merge/purge of lists is another; zip code correction is part of merge/purge savings. The renting and exchange of your mailing list are opportunities to increase revenues. Finally, taxes have to be accounted for in figuring profit.

Postage

Almost all catalogers take advantage of the savings achieved by using bulk third-class mail. To mail bulk rate third class, a yearly permit is required at a current annual fee of $40. The minimum for a bulk rate third-class mailing is 50 pounds or 200 pieces. The minimum per piece rate is 11 cents for up to 3.91111 ounces and goes up incrementally to 45 cents for 15.99 ounces.

For catalogers, the most common way to pay bulk rate postage is by using an indicia. (The other options are using a meter or precanceled stamps.) Indicia are defined by the post office as imprinted designations consisting of city and state and a permit number, used on mail pieces to denote payment of postage (see Figure 10-12 top). An indicia allows mailing only from the particular city, state, and post office shown. In order to use an indicia, there is a one-time permit fee of $40. The indicia number is permanent so long as the permit holder mails at least once in each 12-month period.

The city, state, and permit number may be omitted from the indicia (see Figure 10–12 bottom) if the permit holder has permits at two or more post offices, provided the exact name of the company or individual holding the permits is shown in the permit imprint. When this style of company permit is used, the mailing piece must bear a complete return address. The permit holder must maintain for a three-year period, and make available for inspection and audit on request of post office officials, records showing the post office at which any particular mailing was made, date of mailing, weight of a single piece, and the amount of postage paid. A sample piece from the mailing must also be available.

Since postal requirements can change overnight, keep informed by subscribing to such publications as the *Domestic Mail Manual* and *Postal Bulletin,* which can be ordered care of Superintendent of Documents, U.S. Government Printing Office, Washington, DC 20036.

Presort savings

If you presort your mailings to five-digit zip codes or carrier routes, the post office will allow you a discount on the bulk third-class rate. The cur-

BULK RATE
U.S. POSTAGE
.00 PAID
Chicago, Ill. 60607
Permit No. 1

BULK RATE
US POSTAGE PAID
John Doe Company

FIGURE 10-12
Two types of postal indicia.

TABLE 10-2
Third-class mail prices and requirements

Type of Mail	Price	Requirements
Residual third-class bulk rate	11 cents	Per mailing: 50 lbs. or 200 pieces in zip sequence. Pieces can weigh up to 3.91111 oz. Pieces weighing more must go at a rate of up to 45 cents per 15.99 oz. You cannot mail one-pound packages at bulk rate.
5/3-digit	9.3 cents	50 pieces per 1–5 digit zip or 3-digit multizip post office. Pieces must be bagged and tagged for that particular zip code.
Carrier route	7.4 cents	10 or more pieces for the individual letter carrier's route.

rent residual bulk third-class 11 cent per piece minimum, when presorted, goes down to 9.3 cents per piece for 5/3-digit presort and 7.4 cents per piece for carrier route presort. There must be a minimum of 10 pieces for each carrier route and 50 pieces per 5/3-digit zip or zip group (based on sacking needs) to obtain the discount. (For a comparison of requirements and prices, see Table 10-2.)

Postal presorts are usually done by your computer house at the time of the merge/purge. The output list is sorted into zip sequence and then run against a presort tape. Typically, charges are based on the number of names qualifying for the presort discount and include the mail bag tags the post office requires. Table 10-3 gives approximate postage costs based on presorted mailings of 300,000, 500,000, and 1 million catalogs. Some typical charges are: (1) for carrier route qualified names, $2.50 per thousand names and (2) for 5-digit and residual (basic bulk names), $1 per thousand names.

Now consider the costs and savings. Charts that give presumed presort qualifying percentages for various mailing sizes tend to give low presort discount figures. For example, one chart indicated that for a 250,000 mailing (national), 14 to 16 percent would qualify for 5-digit presort rates. In a recent mailing of 195,000, however, 104,000 (or 53 percent) qualified for 5/3-digit presort. Such results indicate that geographically mail order customers tend to cluster together, making presort discounts more likely.

In the case just cited, the cost of the computer run was $195. The presorting of 104,000 pieces at the discount rate of .017 cents per piece saved $1,768 in postage alone. The net savings to the mailer on a computer run was $1,573. On larger mailings, even more savings can be achieved by carrier route presort, where the presort savings are $36 per thousand with a computer cost of $2.50 per thousand.

TABLE 10-3
Approximate postage costs based on presort

Percentage per category		No. of Pieces	Rate	$
Postage on 300M				
5-digit	60	180,000	.093	$16,740
Residual	40	120,000	.11	13,200
				$29,940
Postage on 500M				
Carrier route	10	50,000	.074	$ 3,700
5/3-digit	60	300,000	.093	27,900
Residual	30	150,000	.11	16,500
				$48,100
Postage on 1MM				
Carrier route	20	200,000	.074	$14,800
5/3-digit	60	600,000	.093	55,800
Residual	20	200,000	.11	22,000
				$92,600

Postal rate increases

In November 1983, USPS filed with the Postal Rate Commission for proposed increases in all categories. At the time of this writing, the case is still before the Postal Rate Commission and the actual amount of the increases that will be allowed and their effective date are still unknown. The changes shown in Table 10-4 of most concern to catalogers apply to the bulk third-class postal categories.

The minimum per piece weight also would be changed from 3.91111 ounces to 4 ounces.

Merge/purge cost and savings

The cost of the merge/purge varies depending on the computer service bureau. A typical cost would be $3 per thousand inputted names and $2 to $4.50 per thousand outputted names, depending on the form of output; tape or Cheshire labels cost less than pressure-sensitive labels. If we assume a mailing of 500,000 names and a duplicate rate of 15 percent, the input of approximately 588,000 names at $3 per thousand would cost $1,764. The output cost for the 500,000 names on tape, at $2 per thou-

TABLE 10-4
Present and proposed third-class rates

Category	Rate/Piece ($)	Proposed Rate/Piece ($)
Carrier route presort	.074	.095
5-digit presort	.093	.111
Residual bulk third-class	.11	.132

sand, would be $1,000. In some cases, there may be additional charges depending on the number of lists tested, or for zip string creation.

In this example, one would save the in-the-mail cost of some 88,000 catalogs. A comparison of this amount with the cost of merge/purge shows why almost all catalogers use merge/purge. If the mailer is on a net-name basis for list rentals (discussed in "The rental transaction," Part 7), further savings of up to 15 percent could be realized on rental costs. In addition, a potential customer is not alienated by receiving a deluge of identical catalogs.

Zip code correction

If a response to a mailing is 2 or 3 percent, then 97 or 98 percent of prospective customers do not buy. One reason is that a certain number never receive catalogs because of incorrect zip codes. Today, most computer service bureaus will check for incorrect zip codes as part of their merge/purge operation, then match and correct them. In most cases you pay only for the corrections, not the valid deliverable matches, so this procedure is cost-effective.

Although the numbers vary from list to list, assume that 3 to 5 percent of a list does not have the correct zip/state combination. The catalog would arrive at the wrong post office and either be forwarded to the correct one (unlikely) or not delivered. Considering the lost orders on a large mailing and the cost of each catalog thrown away, the zip code correction clearly enhances results.

Your list as a source of revenue

Renting your customer list can be a major source of revenue, especially if your list is well maintained and offers such selects as recency and dollar amount.

Some segments of your house list will be rented more often than others, and overall list rental income will be a function of how well your list performs during testing by others. An estimate of net annual rental income is $1 per name, but the figure can be considerably higher for a desirable list used regularly by many catalogs.

Assume a list rents for $80 per thousand names and has a $50-plus (average order) select at $10 per thousand additional and a 0–6 month hot-line at $5 per thousand additional. If both selects were taken, the gross revenue would be $95 per thousand names rented. Against this revenue, costs would include $24 in commissions for the broker and list manager based on 30 percent of the base rate ($80 per thousand). Computer costs for a tape or Cheshire labels would be $2–$3 per thousand depending on quantity run. The cost of pressure-sensitive labels would be passed on to the renter. Tape reels are provided at no charge, if returned, and the renter pays the freight charges. List maintenance and update costs are not considered here, because these functions should be performed even if the list were not available for rental. This gives a net figure, for this example, of $68 per thousand names (or $53 per thousand names if no selects are taken).

The annual net profit from list rentals can be shown as an asset amount (value of list) on your balance sheet at the end of the year. Some catalogers also add the net yearly merchandise sales profit generated by the house list to the balance sheet as an asset. (The balance sheet should not be confused with the income/P&L statements, on which these items always appear.)

Exchanging lists

Another way to obtain revenue from the house list is through list exchanges. Some lists can be obtained only on exchange; others can either be exchanged or rented. Exchanges diminish list rental income, but may be of more overall profit than rental.

Assume the same prices noted in the previous section for the house list and the list you obtain in the exchange, and a cost of exchange of $6 per thousand in commissions plus a $3 per thousand running charge. There is a loss of income on the house list rental of $68 per thousand and a cost of $9 per thousand for the exchange. This then means that you are paying only $77 per thousand for a list that would have cost $95 per thousand to rent, a savings of $18 per thousand. This can change a marginal list into a profitable one.

Don't assume, either, that every time you exchange lists you forgo rental income. Your list may not always be as desirable for rental as it is for exchange and, by exchanging, you may be cutting your costs without losing rental revenue.

House list maintenance

Of increasing importance to catalogers, list maintenance refers to periodic updating and cleaning of the house list. If, as is usual, the catalog's own customers outperform those from rented lists, then customers must not be lost because of carelessness or indifference.

Periodically, the mailing labels for the house file (or the area on the cover adjacent to the label) should contain the words "Address Correction Requested." Americans, as a group, are highly mobile and up to 15 percent of the house list may have changes in address (CHADs) each year. The U.S. Postal Service imposes an additional charge for address corrections, but because people tend to purchase more in the first year after moving to a new home, it is important to reach customers at that time.

"Address Correction Requested" should not be used on rented lists. Why go to the expense of cleaning someone else's list? But be sure to include the words "Postmaster: If addressee has moved, please leave with current resident" on the mailing label or adjacent to it. A new tenant in the house of a former respondent has some probability of being a respondent.

At the time of update, any change-of-address notifications received from customers (for instance, change-of-address postcards) are inputted to your data files, together with information on new customers, including the codes that will be used to track them during their lifetime as customers. Also, the order data will be entered for old customers who purchased from the last mailing. Such data are used to determine customer value and for list segmentation.

The time period between updates usually depends on how often you mail. The more often you mail, the more often you should update your list.

Most house lists are maintained by computer service bureaus who own large-scale, mainframe computers. The best and least expensive method is to furnish them with the order tapes generated by the in-house or data-entry service computers. The least desirable method is a printout or list of names, addresses, and order data, because it has to be entered by hand and checked at considerable expense.

Usually, the computer service bureau also generates the tapes for those who are renting test or rollout segments of the customer file. The house list is set up to segment not only by *n*th name, but also by such other selects the cataloger may offer, as dollar and hot line. Again, the list's desirability for rental depends on how often it is updated and cleaned.

Taxes

Three types of taxes are of concern to catalogers.

1 Employee-related taxes, such as Social Security and withholding tax.

2 Taxes on the overall income of the business.

3 Sales taxes on the merchandise sold through the catalog.

The first two should be discussed with your accountant or attorney before the actual start of business operations. You should also consult the section, "Sales and use taxes," in Part 12.

State and local sales taxes are currently of concern to catalogers, as they are in a condition of change. The U.S. Supreme Court has ruled that if your only contact with a state is through the mails, advertisements, and/or common carriers (such as UPS), you do not have to collect taxes for that state. If, however, you have a "business presence" in a state, you must collect sales taxes for that state.

As states find the need to raise more money, they are attempting to create new definitions for a business presence to increase the state sales taxes collected. Because underpayment now can be quite costly at some future time, all catalogers, whether new or established, should periodically consult their tax attorney to be sure they are in compliance with the complex and ever-changing sales tax laws.

Part 11
NEW TECHNOLOGY AND CATALOG MARKETING

DATA BASE MARKETING

A data base is a collection of facts set up in a systematic manner and retrievable in many ways. A simple example might be a telephone directory. Here the facts are the names, addresses, and telephone numbers of people in an area. The system is alphabetical. In another case, the telephone numbers might be for a government agency and the system set up by departments.

Catalogers, too, use data bases. They have found that the more closely you can define your potential audience and maximize catalog delivery to those who fit the definition, the better the profits. Data base marketing is also cost-effective.

Data bases in catalog marketing are usually of three types.

1 The in-house customer list, indicating not only names and addresses, but all the data on purchase patterns, source, and so forth.
2 The output data of the analysis of prior mailings, such as list or house-file segment performance, geographic analysis, and so forth.
3 Outside data banks, such as demographic overlays, life-style overlays, market mapping programs, ethnic data, and so forth.

At its simplest, the data base might be used to segment the house list by recency purchase, or dollar unit of last order. Or, to set up an initial mailing of a new specialty catalog, a cataloger might segregate the names of all those who had purchased merchandise in particular categories.

A more complex example is the matching of the cataloger's own data base of names and addresses against a geographic/demographic census data base. From this matching might be obtained not only a demographic profile of the catalog customer, but also the geographic regions in which new customers are most likely to be found.

Market research data can be added to your data base to enhance its value. For example, learning the occupations of customers allows a cataloger to target some of the next issue's merchandise, resulting in increased sales.

Data base marketing has been made possible by the surge in availability and the lowered costs of today's computer systems. The ability to store, sort, and analyze large amounts of data exists today even with so-called personal computers. In addition, their use interactively with mainframe computers allows the cataloger virtually unlimited computing power. The types of analysis that can be performed, such as multivariate regression, can indicate to the cataloger the nature of profit-producing customers; this knowledge can be combined with other data bases to efficiently find new customers.

In effect, catalogers have done this for many years. The difference today is in the larger amounts of data that can be processed and the lowered cost of such processing.

PERSONALIZED PRINTING

During the past few years you've undoubtedly witnessed a steady increase in personalized solicitations: sweepstakes offers showing your name as a possible winner, sales letters that repeat your name throughout the body of the letter, and order forms that already have your name and address filled in. New computerized printing capabilities, teamed with impressive responses to personalized mailings, indicate that this trend has only begun. New applications are constantly becoming available and are being warmly welcomed by the catalog industry.

Impact and nonimpact printing

Personalized printing is usually either impact or nonimpact. Impact printing transfers ink onto paper by mechanically "impacting" the paper as a typewriter does. Of course, industrial impact printers are much faster and less costly. Impact printing is most often used to personalize individual elements within a solo mailing package. Catalogers use it primarily to individualize sales messages on cover wraps.

Nonimpact printing is of two types, laser and ink-jet. Computer-driven laser imprinting is faster than impact printing and affords greater font selectivity. Currently, however, it is used by catalogers only for such prebindery applications as cover wraps. Ink-jetting, on the other hand, offers bindery flexibilities and many applications that are most appealing to catalogers.

Ink-jet printing

All of the several kinds of ink-jet printers propel pressurized ink through a small orifice and onto a printing surface. Commands from a computer-driven, electrically charged field determine which ink droplets strike the paper and in what pattern. The equipment itself is located in the bindery.

The capability of ink-jet stations varies by printer. R. R. Donnelley & Sons, for instance, has two different ink-jet stations, each able to personalize 6 lines of 50 characters, plus a 30-character field for name and address information. Catalogers most commonly use ink-jetting to address the back cover and fill in the order form with the recipient's name and address simultaneously. The order form is also ink-jetted with the list code, eliminating the need for the customer to peel a label from the back cover, and effectively increasing trackable codes. Because part of the order form is already completed, it is even easier for the customer to order.

But there's much more to ink-jetting than simply printing names and addresses. If your data base contains segmentable buying history, you may wish to add a specific message addressed to a particular segment. For instance, suppose a certain segment of a garden catalog list buys many roses, and that the cataloger plans to introduce a new rose, which in all probability will be of interest to this segment. Through the magic of ink-jetting, it is a simple matter to provide only this segment to the mailing with a message that informs them of the newest rose, even providing the page number of the catalog on which the new rose appears.

Spring Hill Nurseries does a variation of this by offering a sale on roses. It cleverly includes the prospect's address and state or town within the back cover sales message. And it doesn't stop there. The order form has a similar "special message," this time with the prospect's name,

FIGURE 11-1
Covers of the same Eddie Bauer® catalog with two labels produced by R. R. Donnelley's Selectronic® Stickers system. © 1983 Eddie Bauer® and used with permission.

specific product suggestions, the time to order, and the name of the recipient's town. If this weren't enough to induce the prospect to buy, Spring Hill shows a facsimile of a credit card bearing the customer's name and address and enticingly announcing "instant credit" for "the gardener named."

Another application, for a cataloger with retail stores, might be to list the addresses and phone numbers of the individual stores by geographic select. Because some printers have the capability to stack their ink-jetting stations, the lines of personalized information can be utilized in a variety of ways. For example, a retail cataloger may choose to use all of the personalized lines available to list store locations on the back cover, rather than dividing up the lines by personalizing the order form.

Ink-jetting is one of the best things ever to happen to the catalog industry. Investigate the cost for your mailing size and the features offered by different printers. Remember, although ink-jetting has many pluses, it should not be the major reason for choosing a printer. Also, it is a rapidly growing service, so keep up to date on new applications that may serve you even better than those already in existence.

Selectronic® Gathering

Selectronic® Gathering (computer controlled binding) is a technique used by R. R. Donnelley that has the capability to custom-make catalogs by binding different covers or including different pages. It uses the same magnetic tape as for ink-jetting. Selectronic® Gathering enables the cataloger to develop catalogs based upon information known about potential customers. The obvious advantage is the ability to test variations on a basic catalog with cost-efficiency.

Because all catalogs, no matter what their individual differences, can be bound at the same time, postage discounts are maximized. One cataloger saved $50,000 in postage on a 2,500,000 mailing by producing one catalog electronically.

Selectronic® Gathering can also be employed to bind in postcards selectively. For instance, you may wish to bind in a tell-a-friend postcard to only the best-response segment of your house list. Or, suppose a gardening cataloger wants to bind in a postcard offering a subscription to a horticulture magazine. An overlay of the subscription file against house customers would eliminate those already subscribing, effectively cutting paper costs and maximizing profit potential.

One more example of electronic wizardry is Selectronic® Stickers. Tied into the same tape that drives the ink-jet imaging, these preprinted stickers can be applied to the front of the catalog to announce a particular offer or warn a certain segment of your list that, unless they order now, this could be their last catalog. (See Figure 11-1.)

ELECTRONIC MEDIA

There's been extensive press coverage on both cable and videotex. Depending on which publications you read, they're either the hottest new technology or a total bust. Actually, they are a combination of both, but before explaining why, let's begin with an explanation of the two media.

Cable is a nonbroadcast electronic signal, usually television, transmitted over hard wires from a central location, which may be originating the signal or retransmitting a signal received from another origination point. In simple terms, these are the TV programs for which you pay a monthly fee. To channel the signal to the TV, you need a converter.

Videotex, on the other hand, requires a two-way interaction between you and some form of visual communication. For this, a terminal is needed. The most common variety has a keyboard and a modem attached to the TV set or a monitor and a telephone. Newer versions, however, are free-standing keyboards and require no modem or phone. The major application for videotex has been to provide access to information in a host computer. Once you access the computer, a menu appears, offering such options as news, weather, airline flight times, dining information, and stock reports.

Cable

For catalogers, cable seems to hold little appeal. One of the major problems is that there are hundreds of cable companies, which do not interconnect. This fragmentation makes it difficult to reach any large market with consistency.

One cataloger who has demonstrated his belief in the value of cable is Richard Thalheimer, president of The Sharper Image. On his catalog's order form, he has advertised "Now. See your catalog come to life on cable." The copy listing the stations on which the Living Catalog™ can be viewed gives some indication of the problems caused by the existence of so many different cable companies. The copy reads: "Watch us on Satellite Program Network (SPN), Thursday evenings at 8:30 Eastern, 7:30 Central, and 5:30 Pacific. Also on Modern Satellite Network (MSN) at noon Eastern, 9:00 AM Pacific. Frequently local cable operators run the Living Catalog™ at these times, but not under the SPN or MSN listing. Just turn your dial at these times to find us. Also on San Francisco's Viacom Channel 6, Wednesdays at 7:30 PM and Saturdays at 7:00 PM."

Even with all this confusion, the 30-minute show, which reached 12 million viewers in 600 communities, produced 500–1,000 calls and 50–100 orders per segment and cost under $10,000 to produce, said Mr. Thalheimer in a speech in New York on Direct Marketing Day, in April 1984.

Now, however, The Sharper Image is moving away from cable, replacing it with 30-second spots on CBS and NBC morning news programs. The reason cited is not dissatisfaction with cable, but the limited audience. When Mr. Thalheimer approached cable networks with large audiences, such as ESPN, he was told that their specialized formats (all sports) were not right for his program.

"The new network spots are not as cost-effective, but do provide national exposure. They produce a high number of catalog requests, and occasionally sell a product," Mr. Thalheimer said. He firmly believes his cable show, which goes into detailed explanations of the newest products, many of which are electronics-oriented, would get enough interest for a half-hour show on network time. The show, as it appeared on cable, evolved from a simple multicommercial format to elaborate on-location coverage of products and how they work.

Other catalogers have not had as much success with cable. Williams-Sonoma, the upscale cookware catalog, tried a cooperative venture. A catalog request program that offered their catalog and two others was broadcast over cable TV. Pat Connolly, vice-president of Williams-Sonoma, says, "We pulled 37 cents per book on the test. It just barely paid the postage. And the average order was low, because you can't do a dollar select on cable. None of us repeated that test" (*Catalog Age,* Preview Issue [undated], p. 46).

Videotex

Videotex, on the other hand, seems to offer greater potential. A list of the players at the time of this writing follows.

1. Videotex America, called "Gateway," in its experimental program, allowed access via telephone and cable to 350 California homes. As developed by Times Mirror and Toronto-based Infomart, its participants were not charged a service fee; they used the system frequently for sending messages to each other, accessing news, and so on. (Gateway had a 20,000-plus page data base, a home shopping Comp-U-Star service, the Official Airlines Guide, and home banking.)

Tests indicate that 53 percent of the households in the initial experiment placed orders for merchandise; 33 percent found Gateway a more convenient method of shopping than ordinary catalogs.

Gateway charges advertisers $40 an hour for creation of the imagery for an electronic catalog. Additional charges are $4 a frame per month for storage and $15 a frame to code and link frames to the computer. There is a 1 percent transaction fee for orders placed over the system. Orders are received either via printouts, direct tie-in with the main computer, or electronic mail.

The Times Mirror has signed agreements with seven newspapers to explore videotex possibilities in the cities in which the newspapers are located. Pete Hoke, publisher of *Direct Marketing* and a strong believer in videotex, says that Times Mirror will again be up and running in southern California. This time there will be a rental fee of $30 per month for the service, but no charge for the terminal.

2. CBS/AT&T tested videotex in Ridgewood, New Jersey, using not only information, but graphics as well. Additionally, the actual accessing of information was exceptionally easy and programmable (allowing frequently sourced information to be retained and cutting down on search time). Reports indicate this test was most successful.

Again, Pete Hoke reports to us that Folio, Saks Fifth Avenue's catalog, received a 50 percent response to a catalog request page presented on videotex. No information is available on the conversion rate of requesters to customers.

3. The Viewtron system, launched in fall 1983, is backed by another publisher, Knight-Ridder, and is a reality in Miami, Florida. The number of home subscribers depends on which report you read–estimates range from 2,000 to 5,000. Viewtron charges the customer $600 for the terminal, plus a monthly usage fee. Viewtron will design and input frames for $45 each and charges 1 percent on transactions. Plans call for Viewtron, if successful, to expand into 13 more cities.

4. J. C. Penney and Keycom Electronics have plans for a Chicago launch.

5. IBM, CBS, and Sears plan future implementation of a joint effort.

International perspective

Videotex actually began in the late 1960s in England. Because the Post Telephone & Telegraph was concerned that the telephone equipment in which it had made an enormous investment was not being used to capacity (the English do not use the phone nearly so much as do Americans), it urged its engineers to design "something" that would encourage phone use. Thus, Prestel videotex was born. Little did the English realize that they had started a media revolution. Unfortunately, English consumers have not used Prestel to its fullest potential. Only 35,000 homes now subscribe to this service.

France, meanwhile, has Teletel in Versailles, going to 2,000 French families, and Minitel, a French quasi-videotex system, reaches 100,000 homes in the Brittany region.

In Canada, Grassroots offers standard videotex information, plus agribusiness data, to hundreds of farmers. This format will soon be introduced into California and there are plans to expand throughout the United States.

Germany's Bildschirmtext began with 2,000 terminals in Dusseldorf and 2,000 in Berlin. One smart marketer, Alfred Gerardi, has encouraged consumers to watch Bildschirmtext by offering them a numbered pin, which, if picked in a weekly drawing, awards the winner $150 worth of merchandise from one of the more than 30 catalog company advertisers. Through this method, an 80 percent viewership has been generated. Other systems with which Gerardi has successfully experimented are shows featuring the top ten records of the week and the top ten best-selling books of the week, which are available in 4,000 homes. Estimates are that 40 orders each of books and records are received every week.

Here in the United States, Viewtron advertiser Royal Silk not only offers customers the opportunity to purchase merchandise (see Figure 11-2) but also provides information on the proper care and cleaning of silk garments.

Videotex is growing on an international basis. Some responses, as in the German case, are outstanding, but the jury is still out on the long-term value of customers acquired through this method. Watch this industry closely. It's growing at a rate much faster than previously projected.

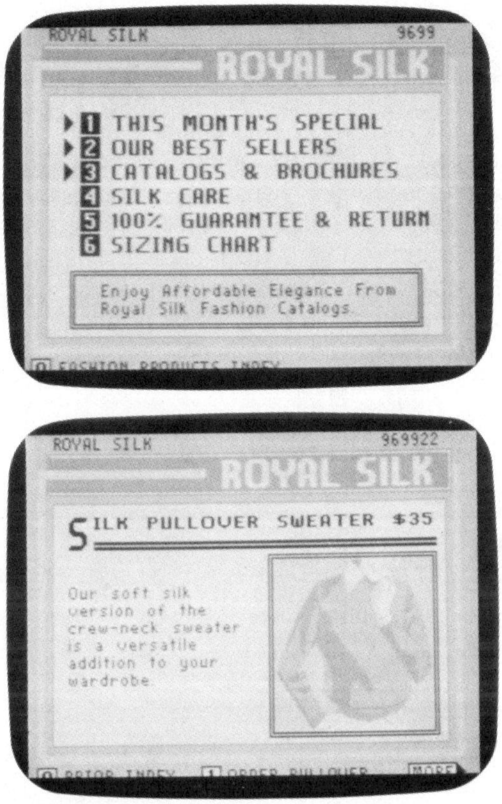

FIGURE 11-2
Two images from Viewtron's videotex "catalog" for Royal Silk. From: *Catalog Age,* March 1984, p. 129. ©1984 *Catalog Age* and used with permission.

Disadvantages

1 Videotex is a costly gamble in an unproven medium. Additionally, most data bases require a minimum order for a predetermined number of pages.

2 Graphics are primitive and "snowy." The picture is "printed" bit by bit and has a rough, computer-type finish. It can take up to 60 seconds for a full screen graphic. Since cost is partially based on time, this is both expensive and annoyingly slow. Consumers may lose interest.

3 There is little information on how best to use this new medium.

4 Videotex companies are presently unwilling to reveal specific information on the profile of the markets now being reached.

5 Limited space and time make it difficult to convey a sales story adequately.

6 Lack of audio limits effectiveness.

Advantages

1 Customers have easy access to product information.

2 Flexibility gives catalogers the capacity to quickly update just one page, or provide a daily special.

3 Subscribers with printers can produce their own instant record of transactions or specific pages of information.
4 Videotex reaches a potentially vast new audience.

In all likelihood, one of the most promising programs for catalogers will be a combination of mailings and videotex. As the subscriber base expands, videotex will become most cost-efficient. Full-motion graphics are expected to be in use by 1990, and audio is certainly one of the top priorities currently being addressed by videotex companies. Changes for the better can be expected, probably much sooner than most people think. So stay tuned to every development and don't let current technical problems blind you to the infinite possibilities of this new medium.

THE GRAPHIC ARTS

It is important to keep up to date on the dramatic new developments in prepress technology, where four-color imagery is the hot area right now. Current awareness here gives you a competitive edge. Graphic arts and trade industry publications and shows are hotlines to today's breakthroughs.

Color separations

One of the most exciting new developments is completely computerized image-processing systems (commonly known as separations, but in this case, much more detailed). Complete page makeups of color subjects can now be made without the intermediate steps previously necessary. These advanced systems can separate color, make corrections, move colored areas from place to place, contact, and screen almost anything you could ever want and probably more than you know what to do with. They then output the fully assembled film ready for platemaking. Several such systems are now available, the best known being the Sci-Tex Response 300. Others are about to make their debut.

On one system, the operator uses an electronic wand to move, delete, and rearrange images and elements almost limitlessly. The image is seen on a screen (like the one used with a computer). Background colors and image positions can be instantly changed, allowing the client to see exactly how the final product will look before it's made into film. This is at present an expensive process and the biggest complaint from operators is that no one yet knows how to put the sophisticated equipment to best use. It is, however, the "wave of the future," and as prices come down and experience is obtained on this equipment, its value will be immeasurable in terms of cost savings and error elimination.

Satellite transmission systems

R. R. Donnelley has gone to the heavens with satellite-transmitted four-color preliminary data, such as "digitized" separations. Even though Del Bishop, a spokesperson for Donnelley, is the first to admit that this technology does not have a great deal of immediate use for Donnelley customers, he says that Donnelley is betting on the future, installing and testing equipment now from which it could well derive immense benefit within the next five years. Right now, satellite transmissions are primarily being used for their speed; that last-minute correction can arrive even faster than the best overnight package service. Bishop told us, "One of the advantages of the satellite system now in place is its potential for archival images. For instance, you can put selected pages or selected images in an archive file and bring them up from catalog to catalog. Right now archiving is an expensive process, because the systems which do it don't do it as well as they should. If it's done on tape, the tape has to be searched sequentially to find the information wanted. If you put a page in archive, you are stuck with that page. In other words, the information has to be pulled out exactly as it was; the page can't be expanded or reduced. As new equipment comes on stream and processors and communicators between various computers are developed, it will become simpler to use our archives."

Gravure

A recent development in gravure allows both better color control and cost savings. Until recently, only continuous tone film was used to create the plate needed for printing gravure. Correcting on continuous tone film is time-consuming and requires highly skilled craftsmanship.

A new piece of equipment allows halftone screen films to be used. Because halftone film is divided into dots, which are easier to color correct, the film is less expensive to produce. Additionally, a chromalin, showing how the ultimate printed product will look, is available with halftones, but not with continuous tones. Now, gravure printers can supply halftone, or chromalin, proofs of a product before going on press.

The future holds many more uses for electronic prepress systems. Keep up with the exciting developments in the graphic arts industry and you'll be one of the first to reap the benefits.

Holography

Invented in 1948, holography has always mystified and tantalized. How can a flat image display what appears to be a three-dimensional image? Several years ago, a famous New York jewelry store stopped traffic with a window display that showed what looked like a hand, beautifully adorned with an exquisite, immense diamond ring, reaching out of the window toward the pedestrians. But producing a cost-efficient hologram, made by recording light waves on film, was expensive and impractical. The problems surrounding holograms were further complicated by the fact that a special light was needed to view the three-dimensional image. Then, in 1958 the laser was developed, which lent itself to more refined methods of hologram preparation, and in 1969, Steve Benton developed a hologram that could be seen using a normal light bulb.

Today, holograms can be produced almost as easily as any printed piece. Although quoted prices are from 1½ to 2 cents per square inch, this can be misleading, as quantity, quality, and preparation are big factors in the real cost. There are many different types of holograms, from those called two-dimensional, to classical, to achromatic (black and white). The possibilities for use in the catalog industry are limited only by current technology and creativity. Imagine, for instance, a cover that actually "reaches out and grabs" the customer's attention. *National Geographic* was one of the first to make dramatic use of this new technology by displaying a holographic eagle on the cover of its March 1984 issue. Chances are, catalogers won't be long in following suit.

Part 12
LEGALITIES

COMMON SENSE, LAWS AND REGULATIONS

Federal and state laws and regulations that affect the mail order business were not created to put direct marketers out of business nor to inhibit the responsible newcomer. Most of them are based on common sense, truth, and fairness in advertising.

This chapter is a light once-over. Get a copy of the actual regulations that seem to affect you and read them; this is as important as any of the merchandising or financial homework we have advised you to do. Then take any questions you have to your attorney.

Observation 1: sales taxes

Sales taxes are inescapable. Consumers are used to paying them when they make retail purchases and expect to pay them when they order via the mail. The bases on which they are collected in the mail order business are easily understood.

Observation 2: FTC regulations

The Federal Trade Commission (FTC) is a silent partner in your operation. It has a clear set of rules, which you must follow to the letter.

Observation 3: USPS regulations

The U.S. Postal Service (USPS) is very important to you. It has rules and requirements regarding package dimensions, mail classifications, rates, and so on. It also has rules designed to protect consumers, both you and your customers. Pay close attention to all the requirements for mail order marketers.

And don't forget that direct marketers are important to the U.S. Postal Service as well. They are regarded as a newly found "gold mine" by the postmaster general's office, because they basically "pay the freight" for third-class mail and contribute about $500 million annually toward the institutional costs of the postal system.

But individual marketers must follow the rules; the USPS will undoubtedly see that you do. The following publications will keep you up to date on what all USPS requirements are and any changes that are made.

Memo to Mailers—Public & Employee Communications Department, U.S. Postal Service, Washington, DC 20260-3100; monthly; free to firms generating large quantities of mail.

Postal Bulletin—Superintendent of Documents, U.S. Government Printing Office, Washington, DC 20036; weekly.

Postal World—JPL Publications, 128 C Street N.W., Washington, DC 20001; biweekly.

USPS Domestic Mail Manual—Superintendent of Documents, U.S. Government Printing Office, Washington, DC 20036.

Observation 4: industry self-regulation

Strong industry self-regulation has served the mail order trade well in the long run. The Direct Marketing Association has promulgated its *Guidelines for Ethical Business Practice,* consisting of 40 articles covering all aspects of the mail order business that interface with the consumer directly. You can easily live by them, and if you incorporate them into your company philosophy and operation, you will be covering two fronts: customer relations and regulatory reality.

Observation 5: privacy issue

The privacy issue looms large in the 1980s, as major strides are made in the computerization of society. The American public, Congress, and state legislatures are becoming increasingly conscious of the issue of guaranteeing or safeguarding the privacy of the individual. This preoccupation has extended its reach into the subject of mailing lists. Mistakenly, mailing lists have been viewed as a conduit through which personal information is transferred from one mailer to another.

As an outgrowth of the *Privacy Act of 1974,* the Privacy Protection Study Commission (PPSC) was created. One of its tasks was to determine whether mail order marketers should be required to remove from their mailing lists the names of any individual who specifically requested removal.

When the commission made its recommendations, it stopped short of advocating that the proposal be made law, only because it considered that adequate self-regulatory measures were in place within the direct marketing industry. DMA had already created the Mail Preference Service (MPS), designed to allow consumers' names to be deleted from or added to large numbers of mailing lists. By contacting the association, consumers can have their preference input on a computer tape that is then circulated among the major mailing list service bureaus to be used in merge/purge runs against companies' mailing lists.

An even better solution for both consumers and regulators is a practice begun at the time of the PPSC investigation. Many mail order companies offer their customers the option of having their names removed from the mailing lists they make available for rental or exchange. Some companies place the name removal option copy on the order form with other mailing and order instructions. Others insert a flier within the catalog or mailing piece. Still others insert the notice in the package containing the ordered product. Such company self-regulation preempts the need for federal legislation.

States are increasingly restricting the commercial availability of "public" mailing lists, such as those of utility customers and motor vehicle registrants. Be aware of these restrictions. (DMA and the industry press monitor developments at the state level and can keep you informed.) Current and future restrictions can be managed, if all do their share by allowing customers to delete their names from lists if that is their preference. In fact, the vast majority of companies that give their customers this option have found that only a small percentage of customers actually ask to have their names deleted.

Sales and use taxes

The basic premise of "nexus" is at the core of questions of liability of mail order companies to collect and remit sales and use taxes on a state-by-state basis. The questions are: Do you have a business presence in a given state beyond the use of a common carrier or the U.S. Postal Service to communicate and transact purchases? Does your company have a retail store, outlet, warehouse, sales office, redemption center, or similar continuous presence in a state, which, regardless of activities related to the mail order business, enjoys the advantages of municipal services?

If the answer to either of these is yes, your company is probably liable for collecting taxes and reporting to each state involved. This concept is defined as "sufficient nexus" by the U.S. Supreme Court, which has handed down several decisions as the arbiter of cases brought by varying state tax commissions against direct marketers and other businesses dealing with interstate commerce.

Many, if not all, states are now trying to impose jurisdictional nexus on direct mail marketers. One reason for their increased fervor is the need to meet budget demands by finding new sources of revenue. And some believe that they are trying to protect local merchants. Uniform national guidelines for state taxation of interstate commerce have been a long time coming and are still nowhere in sight.

If your catalog company has a presence in a state or customer contact beyond the mails, seek legal counsel on whether to register and collect sales and use taxes. If you don't collect taxes, states may later impose this obligation, and you may wind up with staggering penalties and past liability suits as well. The time to investigate this is now.

Practical tips on collecting and reporting

For the states in which you are liable for tax collection:

- Get a copy of each state's tax table from the state tax commission. The tables will state the tax rates for cities, counties, and so on.
- On the order form, ask your customers to remit the appropriate sales tax: for example, "New York Residents Add Applicable Sales Tax," or "Residents of Illinois and New York, Add Local Taxes," and provide a space on the form for them to write in the amount.
- Although it is bothersome, you must reimburse a resident of a county with a lesser tax rate for overpayment of taxes. It is illegal to collect the highest tax rate on all orders from a given state. Avoid the problem by charging the correct amount.
- File quarterly and yearly state sales tax reports for each applicable state. To avoid penalties, observe all state collection and reporting deadlines closely.
- Keep adequate records of collection and reporting for as long as each state requires. This can be quite a few years. Check with each state

tax commission to determine its requirements. Failure to do so opens the door for state auditors to construct their own estimate of your liability.

- Program your computer "flags" by zip code (county may not be sufficient) to indicate the appropriate sales tax due.
- Tax rates are subject to frequent change. Keep informed of changes in the states with which you are concerned. If you undercollect, you may have to pay the increase from profits.

THE FEDERAL TRADE COMMISSION

Significant trade regulation rules (TRR) as well as guidelines and advisory opinions that affect mail order operations have been issued by the Federal Trade Commission. The directives in the following list are particularly important to catalogers. You should be familiar with their contents from the moment of your operation's start-up.

- Mail Order Merchandise (30-Day) Rule
- Guides against Deceptive Advertising of Guarantees
- Magnuson-Moss Warranty Act
- Guides Concerning the Use of Endorsements and Testimonials in Advertising
- Guides against Deceptive Pricing
- Guides on the Use of the Words "Free" and "New"

Copies of these regulations can be obtained from the Federal Trade Commission, Office of Public Information, Sixth and Pennsylvania Avenues N.W., Washington, DC 20580 (202-523-3598—Public Reference Branch).

FTC regulations are included in *The U.S. Code of Federal Regulations, Title 16, Commercial Practices,* Chapters 1 and 2 (January 1979), published by the Office of the Federal Register, National Archives and Records Services, General Services Administration, and sold by the U.S. Government Printing Office, Washington, DC 20036.

Interpretations, summarizations, and in many instances, the full text of the regulations are found in *Do's & Don'ts in Advertising Copy,* available from the Council of Better Business Bureaus, 1150 17th Street N.W., Washington, DC 20036.

Be sure to get copies of the regulations and read them; better yet, read them with the assistance of an attorney. A summary of the regulations (minus as much "legalese" as possible) follows.

The Mail Order Merchandise Rule

The Mail Order Merchandise Rule, more commonly called the 30-Day Rule, was issued in 1976 to deal with the problem of late or undelivered mail order merchandise. The rule outlines specific time requirements and notification procedures for the fulfillment of mail orders.

In essence, the Mail Order Merchandise Rule states that unless there is a reasonable basis to believe that goods will be shipped within 30 days of receipt of a properly completed order, an advertiser must include a clear and conspicuous notice of the time in which shipment is expected to be made. In other words, if you know you won't be shipping until six or eight weeks after an order is received, say so somewhere in the catalog.

Option notices

If no statement is included in the catalog, the merchandise must be shipped within 30 days.

If there is a shipping delay, the 30-Day Rule requires that you notify your customers of the delay and inform them of their options. The first "option" notice must be sent before the promised shipping date or within 30 days after the order is received. It must plainly indicate the revised shipping date (of 30 days or less) and it must provide customers with the option to consent to the delay or to cancel the order and get a refund. The notice must also inform customers that nonresponse to this first notice is considered their consent to a delay of 30 days or less.

If you are unable to ship the merchandise on or before the revised shipping date, you must send a "renewed option" notice, which informs customers of their right to consent to a further delay, or to cancel the order and receive a prompt refund, and that if they do not agree to this delay in writing, their order will be canceled. Unless you receive your customer's express written consent to the second delay before the first delay period ends, you must cancel the order and provide a full refund.

You do not have to send a renewed option notice to customers who consent to an indefinite delay in response to the first notice. However, these customers retain their right to cancel the order any time before shipment.

Option notices can be included in form letters (see Figures 8-13 and 8-14 and "Inventory Control" in Part 8). They must be sent via first-class mail and should include a means for customers to respond with their preference, such as a prepaid business reply card or envelope. The FTC does allow for the use of an 800 number to cancel orders. However, if there is ever a significant problem or an FTC audit of your system of delay handling, your 800 number order canceling system must meet FTC's standards of adequacy: that the 800 number system could readily and consistently be used to cancel an order and that you provide adequate competent staff to take cancellations and the records to back them up. It is not advisable to rely solely on the 800 number system for order cancellations.

There have been a number of substantial FTC actions against direct marketers for violation of the 30-Day Rule. The most notable of these cases involved the JS&A Company based in Northbrook, Illinois, and headed by Joseph Sugarman, which markets consumer and business electronic products such as calculators, telephones, computers, and a host of the most advanced electronic products, via print space ads and catalogs. The company is noted for its lengthy selling copy and trend-setting advertising layouts. It is also well known for its rapid growth to multimillion-dollar sales status in a few short years.

But a series of concurrent problems starting with a computer breakdown in the winter of 1979 disabled the company, affecting order fulfillment and back-order computer records. Reports indicate that only a fraction of the several thousand orders that were being processed were affected, but the FTC made an investigation.

The pivotal problem in FTC's eyes is the wording of the delay notice, which was in the spirit of the regulation but was viewed by the FTC as a violation. After protracted court battles—which have received extraordinary industry-wide coverage—the case is still before the courts and, as of mid-1984, has cost over $500,000 in legal fees.

The JS&A case is a bellwether that the industry has taken very much to heart. JS&A is not a borderline or fraudulent operation; rather, it is an eminently respectable firm, with excellent intentions. Be sure to follow the 30-Day Rule to the letter.

Are you affected?

The 30-Day Rule probably affects your company. Its provisions affect all mail order firms, publishers, companies who offer premiums, and retail businesses that receive orders for merchandise to be shipped. It applies to orders generated through catalogs, direct mail packages, telephone marketing, space advertising in magazines and newspapers, and orders generated through TV and radio. If you are selling subscriptions, it applies to the fulfillment of the first issue. And if you are marketing a "continuity plan" product, you have your very own FTC-TRR on "negative option" programs. Only photo finishers and purveyors of seeds and growing plants are exempt.

When you analyze it, the rule is reasonable. Be sure to *monitor* your fulfillment operation carefully and systematically. The occasional mistake is not the problem; your day-to-day system of operation must be absolutely sound.

Guarantees and warranties

Mail order companies have not been singled out for specific FTC coaching on the subject of guarantees and warranties in advertising. We're lumped with all marketers and are subject to the FTC's Guides against Deceptive Advertising of Guarantees and to the FTC's enforcement power for the Magnuson-Moss Warranty Act.

The first point we'd like to make is that the actual number of customer returns of orders (that have been properly fulfilled) is very low. With women's ready-to-wear, the rate can reach 20 percent, but that is the highest category and is due to the fact that garment sizing varies significantly and "fit" is very often the issue. So, when you state a company policy of "Satisfaction Guaranteed, or Your Money Back," not very many people actually take you up on it. But for those who do, you must fulfill the promise.

Guarantees

From a regulatory point of view, there are seven FTC guides on the subject of the advertising guarantees and they cover the following:

1 Guarantees in General requires clear and conspicuous disclosure of the nature and extent of the guarantee, the manner in which the guarantor will perform, and the identity of the guarantor.

2 Prorata Adjustment of Guarantees covers where guarantees are used.

3 "Satisfaction or Your Money Back" Representations requires that any conditions or limitations on guarantees of refund be clearly stated. If a guarantee does not specify a time limit, the company must take back the merchandise no matter when. To avoid having to take back customer-damaged goods, the guarantor must specify "return in original

condition." But remember, customer service is important and returns are few, so make the guarantee as much to the customer's benefit as is economically possible.

4 Lifetime Guarantees defines "lifetime" as the customer's lifetime, unless clearly stated otherwise.

5 Savings Guarantees covers such statements as "Guaranteed lowest prices in town," or "Guaranteed to save you 50%." If you use or are considering using such claims or benefits, read the Guides against Deceptive Advertising of Guarantees.

6 Guarantees under Which the Guarantor Does Not or Cannot Perform treats the catchall category, which is exactly what it says it is.

7 Guarantee as a Misrepresentation specifies that a guarantee is not to be used or phrased to infer material facts. If it does, be prepared to assume legal responsibility for the truth of the representation.

These are short, to the point, and simple to understand. They should not present a compliance problem.

Warranties

The FTC issued a series of rules and interpretations to guide marketers, including mail order marketers, in the area of warranties. These rules apply only to written warranties covering consumer products. No one is required to give a written warranty nor is there a minimum requirement for the duration of a warranty.

However, if a product is warranted in writing by the manufacturer, then the mail order marketer must make this warranty available to the mail order customer before the sale. The marketer can print either the full text of the warranty *or* a notice that it may be obtained free on written request. The notice can be placed in one of three places in the catalog: on the same page with the merchandise copy; on the page facing the merchandise copy; or in a clearly referenced information section, such as the ordering information section of the catalog. Requests for warranty information (and these won't be many) should, of course, be filled promptly.

Endorsements and testimonials

Many direct marketers have found testimonials and endorsements to be valuable marketing tools. Often they add to the credibility of a marketer who is unfamiliar to a prospective customer. Endorsements by experts, celebrities, or organizations are common, as are testimonials of satisfied customers or users of a product.

According to FTC, endorsements encompass all advertising messages, whether verbal statements, demonstrations, pictures, signatures, seals, logos, and so on, whose message consumers are likely to believe reflects the opinions, beliefs, findings, or experience of a party other than the mail order company. An expert is someone who, as a result of a particular experience or education, has knowledge of the particular product or service superior to that generally acquired by ordinary individuals.

FTC has issued four Guides Concerning the Use of Endorsements and Testimonials in Advertising. They are straightforward and easy to understand and follow.

1 General Considerations covers three basic principles that are applicable to all endorsements and testimonials (which are considered identical to endorsements). They must be honest views of the endorser. They must not be distorted, reworded, or presented out of context. An endorser who is presented as a user of the product must be a bona fide user for as long as the message appears.
2 Consumer Endorsements specifies that if the consumer in the ad had *X* experience using a product, then all consumers should be able to get the same performance even under variable conditions. If the individual is presented as an actual consumer, then any photos must be of him or her, not of a model (or an actor) paid to represent the endorser (unless the ad so acknowledges). Avoid the problem by not using models in place of real spokespersons.
3 Expert Endorsements—Endorsements by Organizations handles much more detailed endorsements, involving testing procedures and collective judgment. Don't use either until you've thoroughly read the guide's requirements.
4 Disclosures of Material Connections. Generally, endorsers are neither offered nor ask for payment. If they are paid, then the ad must say so, unless they are celebrities or experts. An ad must also recognize any material connection between the endorser and the advertiser. However, the credibility of such ads is greatly reduced, so avoid them if possible.

Consult your attorney if you plan to use testimonials or endorsements. Contracts for testimonials are more or less "standard," but celebrity and expert endorsers often require negotiated contracts.

Deceptive pricing

The FTC has issued five Guides against Deceptive Pricing, intended to serve as "practical aids to the conduct of fair and legitimate merchandising." Although not aimed at direct marketers specifically, these guides cover offer structures often used by direct marketers, such as the "2-for-1 sale," "buy one, get one free," "1 cent sale," "limited offer," "wholesale price," "factory price," "list price," "manufacturers' suggested retail price," and "regularly, usually, formerly." Pricing in general is covered, so be sure to get a copy of the guides.

1 Former Price Comparisons covers the sale price compared with the former price of an item. You must have legitimately offered the product at the former price for the bargain offer to be valid. Increasing the original price with the express purpose of offering a large reduction

later is regarded as a deceptive practice. Even if there were no sales of an item at the former price, the bargain price is still valid. Beware of reducing an item's price insignificantly (for example from $10 to $9.99) so as to mislead the customer when the former price is not mentioned in the sale copy.

2 Retail Price Comparisons; Comparable Value. As the guide explains, if you claim to be selling at below retail prices in a certain geographic area, be reasonably certain that the higher price you quote is not appreciably more than the price at which the article is being sold in the area. Also, your merchandise must be of the same grade and quality as the merchandise with which you are comparing prices. If possible, clip and save the ad that shows the same or similar product offered at a higher price.

3 Advertising Prices That Have Been Established or Suggested by Manufacturers or Other Nonretail Distributors. Few products are sold at the manufacturers' suggested retail price. This guide states that only if a number of stores are carrying the product at the retail price can you represent a mail order price as significantly lower than the manufacturer's suggested price. Ask the product supplier whether there are such stores in your area and check local retailers yourself.

4 Bargain Offers Based upon the Purchase of Other Merchandise. "Buy one, get one free," "2-for-1 sale," and "50 percent off" are all legitimate offers that often perform well in mail order. However, you can't increase the price of the first item or decrease the quality or quantity of either item in order to make the offer profitable. It must be a legitimate saving to the customer, as this guide makes clear.

5 Miscellaneous Price Comparisons covers the catchall that states that variations from the price strategies mentioned in guides 1–4 are controlled by the same principles. For example, a "limited offer" must indeed be limited in time duration. A reduced price for seconds or irregulars cannot be compared with higher prices elsewhere for perfect merchandise.

These guides, as those mentioned earlier in the chapter, are easy to understand and follow. They ensure customers genuine and truthful sales.

"Free" and "new"

The FTC is unambiguous about the conditions under which direct mail marketing may use the terms *free* and *new* in describing merchandise.

"Free"

Offering an item free of charge with the purchase of another item is a powerful incentive to mail order customers. Customers assume that they are paying nothing for the free article and no more than the regular price for the other. FTC makes the same assumption.

All of the terms, conditions, and obligations on which the receipt and retention of the free item depend should appear in close proximity to the description of the offer of free merchandise or service. An asterisk near the word *free* is not regarded as sufficient. If, however, you don't want to give all of the information on the cover of your catalog (as one example), you can use the term "free offer" on the cover and direct the customer to the place inside the catalog where details can be found as long as you don't identify the item on the cover.

However, don't let these limitations stop you from making a free offer. Mail order customers are curious and adventurous by nature and can't resist turning "to page 10 for details." Once a prospect or customer gets inside the catalog, you are at least a third of the way to getting an order. This is one FTC requirement that can work directly in your favor.

Another reasonable FTC requirement concerns the use of the introductory offer that incorporates a free offer. In this case you must discontinue the offer after a limited time, then begin selling the product or service separately, at the same price at which it was promoted with the free offer. Free trial offers are acceptable if they clearly imply payment after the expiration period, and if all other terms are spelled out clearly within the promotion or catalog.

In addition, the order form of the mailing piece must contain all of the terms of the offer, since this is the advertiser's contract with the customer. However, if your ad is a space ad accompanied by a coupon, the coupon can refer to terms in the ad, but the terms must be in a prominent place in the ad, in easily readable type.

"New"

The FTC has issued several advisory opinions regarding the use of the word "new." Its position is that "it would be inclined to question use of any claim that a product is 'new' for a period of time longer than 6 months." Also, "A marketing program which lasts for more than 6 months and covers less than 15% of the population would not disqualify an eventually widely marketed product from being called 'new.' " According to FTC, new means "recently discovered, invented, or developed," not new to a marketing area. Bear this definition in mind when using the word "new," and be circumspect.

Dry testing

A practice very seldom used by catalogers, "dry testing," is the mail order method of promoting a product by mail before it has been manufactured or purchased as inventory. It sounds dangerous, and it is. Its only advantage is that it allows responses to the offer to dictate whether the proposed product should, in fact, be issued or made available. It is a legal practice, yet FTC is monitoring its use and has issued an advisory opinion, which includes the following requirements for a dry test.

- The promotion must clearly state that sale of the product is only planned.

- The copy must indicate that an expression of interest or the placement of an order does not necessarily mean that the consumer will get the item.
- If plans to sell the product are dropped, notice must be given to prospective customers within four months of the mailing of the first solicitation.
- Consumers must be given the opportunity to cancel, and no substitutions of other products can be made.

Credit regulations

The FTC administers the maze of consumer credit regulations for mail order marketers, including the Truth in Lending Act and Regulation Z issued under that act concerning consumer credit selling; the Fair Credit Billing Act; the Equal Credit Opportunity Act implemented by Regulation B and of direct application to most mail order marketers; the Fair Credit Reporting Act; and the Fair Debt Collection Practices Act. If you plan to offer your own house credit, consult your attorney first. All of these regulations are quite detailed and lengthy.

The Fair Credit Reporting Act deals with the use of books called "credit guides," which contain consumers' credit ratings, and the prescreening of prospective direct mail customers for credit worthiness. Get a copy of the regulation if you are contemplating the use of either of these services. The act also contains many specific requirements for extending house credit directly.

The Fair Debt Collection Practices Act applies only to debt collection agencies, which are retained by companies to collect their debts. Mail order firms employing such agencies should be familiar with the operating restrictions and guidelines imposed on the agencies.

Debt collectors may not (among other restrictions):

- use any false, deceptive, or misleading representation or means in connection with the collection of any debt.
- "engage in group conduct . . . which is to harass, oppress, or abuse any person."

However, collection agencies do not have an exclusive license to collect bad debts. Many direct marketers administer their collection efforts internally. It makes a great deal of sense to set up an in-house system for credit checking and preliminary dunning by letters and telephone. Bad debt is a bottom-line negative on all mail order promotions. It can range from as low as 1–2 percent to as high as 15–20 percent. A systematic approach to establishing internal control devices that keep the bad level to a manageable amount has been put together by Arthur Winston, an attorney active in the mail order industry. His article "Internal Credit and Collection Procedures for Direct Marketers" appears in the Direct Marketing Association's *Direct Mail Marketing Manual.* Contact DMA at 6 East 43rd Street, New York, NY 10017, to purchase a copy.

Sweepstakes

Many direct marketers have found that a sweepstakes can be effective in boosting mail order response (see under "Sales Facilitators and Incentives," Part 6). A close look will show that publishers use them extensively to solicit subscriptions and renewals. Fund raisers have also used them effectively, as have many catalogers.

Although the FTC has not issued a specific regulation or guide on conducting a sweepstakes, the subject is of ongoing interest to it. Many states have specific laws governing sweepstakes, ranging from complete bans to requirements for posting bonds. These laws are often complex. It is also important to know that the U.S. Postal Service prohibits lotteries by mail. A lottery consists of three elements: chance, consideration, and prize—with consideration usually meaning some form of payment. Filling out an order form, affixing a stamp, and rubbing "a magic spot" are not yet regarded as "consideration," but many states are adding restrictions.

Before deciding to run a sweepstakes, seek legal guidance, or contact one of the several "full-service" professional firms that administer sweepstakes. You can also consult the Promotion Marketing Association of America, in New York City, which systematically tracks state requirements on sweepstakes and contests. The Direct Marketing Association has issued a set of guidelines relative to sweepstakes promotion by direct marketers. Request a copy from its Government Affairs Office, 1730 K Street N.W., Suite 905, Washington, DC 20006.

LEGAL CHECKLIST

The following checklist may be helpful in determining whether you are "covered" under all of the major regulations for mail order marketers.

- ✔ Do you have copies of the USPS documents that state the physical-dimension requirements for third-class mail, as well as USPS prohibitions and definitions of mail fraud? Do you subscribe to postal publications so that you'll be up to date regarding changes?
- ✔ Are you collecting and remitting sales and use taxes for the appropriate states according to the "sufficient nexus" theory? Is your attorney informed regarding these procedures?
- ✔ Do you conform to the DMA's *Guidelines for Ethical Business Practice*?
- ✔ Are you familiar with the FTC Mail Order Merchandise Rule regarding delayed delivery? Do your option notices conform to the language requirements of the rule? Are you always within the "time" periods specified by the rule? Are your order fulfillment records updated accordingly?
- ✔ Do you offer any direct or implied guarantee? Are you in compliance with the FTC Guides against Deceptive Advertising of Guarantees?
- ✔ Are any products you sell covered under written warranty? Have you complied with FTC regulations regarding the presentation of such information?
- ✔ Do you have an ongoing system whereby any item you offer, if covered under written warranty, is presented as such in the copy?
- ✔ Are any testimonials or endorsements you run acquired and presented in accordance with FTC requirements?

- ✔ Are any pricing structures you offer in compliance with the FTC Guides against Deceptive Pricing? Have you reviewed these guides carefully?
- ✔ Are any free offers carefully reviewed?
- ✔ Are you careful with your use of the word "new"?
- ✔ Do you ever dry test? If so, are you within the FTC's suggested guidelines?
- ✔ Do you use credit guides or prescreening techniques that would fall under the Fair Credit Reporting Act?
- ✔ Are the practices of the agencies you retain for debt collection in agreement with the Fair Debt Collection Practices Act?
- ✔ Do you have your own internal system to initiate dunning for bad debts?
- ✔ Do you offer your customers the option of having their names removed from the lists you rent to other mail order marketers and from your own lists?
- ✔ Does your service bureau regularly use the DMA Mail Preference Service quarterly "delete" tapes in any merge/purge operation you run with rented files?
- ✔ Do you have on file within the company a copy of all FTC regulations affecting mail order practice? Have all your key executives read the regulations? Has your direct marketing agency?

GLOSSARY

The direct marketing industry is no different from others in that it has its own "lingo," much of which has been used and explained in this book. In addition to these terms, you also need an understanding of the language used in the advertising world. Thus, we've compiled a list of the terms that you will most often hear and use.

Action devices. Techniques used to encourage customer participation, such as sweepstakes offers, that require the removal and affixing of a "stamp," the rubbing off of a "mystery" number, etc.

Actives. Respondents on a particular list who have taken action through purchase of a product, subscription to a magazine, and so forth, in a recent time period.

Address correction requested. Printed in the mailing address area of a catalog, this message alerts the post office that the mailer wishes, for a fee, to receive an updated address for persons who have moved.

Assigned mailing date. The date on which a rented list must be mailed, per a prior agreement between the list owner and the user. No other date may be used without the list owner's approval.

Backbone. The back or spine of a book where the pages are connected.

Back end. A term often used for the latter part of a catalog operation, most often from order receipt/entry through fulfillment and customer service.

Bangtail envelope. A preformed envelope with a perforated flap designed for use as an order form; most often used for promotional purposes. Often provided as the payment vehicle for oil companies, department stores, and so forth.

Batch. A grouping of orders.

Bill enclosure. Promotions for products or services that are inserted into bills received from companies. Product offerings may or may not be related to the companies issuing the bills.

Bindery. An area where the final trimming, stitching/stapling, order form insertion, and any necessary off-press folding is done.

Binding. Perfect bound—usually used only for thick catalogs or books. The bindery trims and glues the catalog together to form a stiff backbone. Saddle-stitched—the bindery gathers the sheets and staples them at the spine, creating a backbone. Side-wire-stitched—the bindery gathers and staples sheets on the left-hand side to form a backbone.

Bingo card. A reply card, inserted into a publication, listing sales literature, catalogs, and so forth, which consumers may request simply by checking the appropriate box and mailing the card. Information requested may or may not have a charge associated with it. Products/catalogs are generally covered in greater detail by advertisements or editorial located within the publication or adjacent to the postcard.

Block. A census term for the smallest area for which census data are tabulated, each one defined by a street, road, railroad track, stream, or other ground feature.

Blow-up. An enlargement.

Blueprint. Sometimes called "blues," or "bluelines," a prior-to-printing proof made from a negative or positive, used for checking type/photo position.

Body type. The type/copy used as main descriptive copy, as opposed to the headlines.

Boldface type. Type that is heavier than standard text type. Often used for headlines or paragraph lead-ins.

Book. Another word for catalog.

Booklet. Usually, a small flyer-type promotional piece.

Bounceback. Promotional material inserted into packages being sent to customers.

Bringing up the color. Color correcting; intensifying color on press or in separations.

Broadside. A single sheet of paper used for promotional purposes in a variety of ways such as newspaper insertion, bouncebacks, and so forth.

Brochure. Loosely used term; often refers to a promotional piece larger than a broadside but smaller than a catalog.

Broker. *see* List broker.

Bulk. The thickness of paper.

Bulk rate mail. A category of third-class mail that requires outgoing mail to be specially formatted prior to receipt at the post office in order to obtain postal discounts.

Business list. A compilation of individuals or companies with common business-associated interests, memberships, and so forth.

Buyer. The person responsible for sourcing merchandise for a catalog. Also, person on a list who has responded to solicitations offering mail order merchandise.

Cash buyer. A person who has responded to a mail order solicitation and has enclosed a check or money order with the order.

Cash-with-order. A requirement made by some list owners for full payment at the time the order is placed for rental of the list.

Catalog. A promotional book offering a variety of merchandise; contains descriptive copy and prices.

Catalog buyer. Someone who has purchased merchandise from a catalog.

Catalog requester. A prospective catalog buyer who has requested a copy of a catalog, for which there may or may not have been a charge.

Census tract. A subdivision of a Metropolitan Statistical Area (MSA); a tract has an average population of 4,000.

CHADs. Change of address. Also called COA.

Charge buyer. A person who has charged merchandise ordered by mail. Some use this term for persons who have paid for merchandise only after it has been delivered.

Cheshire label. Label printed on specially prepared paper. List names are reproduced on the labels, then mechanically affixed to mailings.

Chromalins. One method of proofing a color separation. Four separate, extremely thin plastic sheets (one for each color) are overlaid, producing a color reproduction of the separations.

Chromes. An often misused term, it actually refers to color transparencies. Also used as the nickname for chromalins.

Circulars. General term for printed promotional materials.

Cleaning. The updating, through removal of inaccurate or unusable data, of mailing lists.

COA. Change of address. Also called CHADs.

Coding. Identifying alpha and/or numerical key used on reply devices, such as order forms, coupons, labels, and so forth. Codes are used to track rented list performance, publication results, and so forth.

Collation. The orderly assembly of sheets or signatures during the bindery process.

Color print. A printed reproduction of a transparency or negative. Inexpensive, but not of top quality. Also called a "C" print.

Commission. The percentage a broker, list manager, or advertising agency receives on lists ordered or work done. Agreed to prior to implementation of list ordering or agency work done.

Compiler. A company that gathers and records names and addresses of persons having common characteristics. These names, which are made available for rental, are compiled from directories, registrations, and so forth.

Comprehensive. A type of layout, finely detailed, showing a close facsimile of how the final printed piece will look. Also called "Comp."

Computer personalization. Computer-generated, personalized printing used to tailor a particular message or to code mailing segments.

Computer service bureau. A data processing facility that performs such functions as merge/purge, list maintenance, analysis, and so forth.

Consumer list. At-home names and addresses of persons with similar buying interests or activities.

Continuity programs. Products offered in a continuous series of mailings. They usually consist of a common theme (such as book series) and are shipped at regular intervals.

Contributer list. A list of persons who have financially contributed, via the mails, to a particular fund-raising activity.

Controlled circulation. Distribution of a publication at no charge.

Conversion. Reformatting a number of computer tapes into one common format.

Conversion rate. The percentage of potential customers who, through a direct mail solicitation, become buyers.

Co-op mailing. A "shared" mailing, in which different offers, often from different companies, are presented to the consumer in one envelope. Postage costs are divided among the participants and a rental fee may be charged by the co-op organizer.

Cost per inquiry. The cost of a mailing or advertisement divided by the number of inquiries received from that mailing or advertisement.

Cost per order. Similar to cost per inquiry, but based on all costs associated with the acquisition of a customer or order.

Creative. Used as a noun in the catalog business, it means preprinting aspects of catalog preparation: design, layout, copy writing, and photography.

Crop. To trim part of a photo or copy.

Cross-section. A group of names and addresses segmented from a list in such a manner as to be as representative as possible of the entire list.

Data capture/entry. Any method of collecting and recording information.

Deadbeat. Customer who orders merchandise, but doesn't pay for it.

Decoys. Uniquely identifiable names, often intentional misspellings of a preselected group of names, which are inserted into ordinary list rental names. Decoys serve two main purposes: to alert catalogers of the arrival of mailings and to prevent list renters from unauthorized list usage.

Delivery date. The date on which a specific list order is to be received from the list owner by the list user or designated representative of the list user.

Demographics. Social and economic characteristics of individuals and/or households within a particular set of geographic boundaries.

Direct mail. The use of the post office for delivery of promotional materials soliciting some form of action on the part of the recipient.

Direct marketing. Any method of promotion that prompts the consumer to respond in a way that results in sales dollars from that specific promotion.

Direct response. *see* Direct marketing.

DMA. Acronym for Direct Marketing Association, the industry's major association.

DMA Mail Order Action Line. A service provided by DMA that attempts to help consumers resolve problems they may have encountered when shopping by mail.

DMA Mail Preference Service. A service provided by DMA that allows consumers to request that their names be added to or deleted from mailing lists.

Donor list. List of persons who have given monetary contributions to one or more charitable organizations.

Drop out. A term used when type is deleted from all four colors, resulting in "white" type.

Drop ship. A fulfillment function whereby the manufacturer of the product does the actual shipping of the item to the customer.

Dummy. A mock-up showing the position of photos, type, and folding format. Shows size, shape, and general "feeling" of promotional piece prior to printing.

Duplicate. Two or more name and address records that are found to be equal under the list user's basis of comparison. Often referred to as a "dupe."

Duplication elimination. Most often shortened to "dupe elimination." Refers to the removal of various names, determined to be the same by a variety of methods, from different lists.

Dye transfer. A high-quality, four-color print made from a transparency; most often used when retouching is needed.

Enamel. Coated paper that has a glossy finish.

Envelope stuffer. Promotional material inserted into an envelope along with such other items as statements, invoices, and so forth.

Exchange. *see* List exchange.

Expire. A segment of a subscriber list that has allowed subscriptions to expire.

First-time buyer. A person who has purchased a product or service from a particular company for the first time.

Folio. The page number as it appears on a printed page.

Free lance. An independent artist, writer, or photographer who is not on staff, but works on a per-project or hourly rate as the need arises.

Free sheet. Paper without mechanical wood pulp.

Free-standing insert. A promotional piece loosely inserted into a magazine or newspaper.

Frequency. How often a buyer has purchased during a certain time period, or in total.

Friend-of-a-friend. *see* Tell-a-friend.

Front end. Usually refers to the part of a catalog operation that occurs prior to actual receipt of orders. Includes areas such as merchandising, creative, and catalog production.

Gathering. The assembly of folded signatures put into correct sequence.

Gift buyer. Someone who has purchased a product for another person.

Gimmick. A promotional device, such as a sticker or rub-off area, designed to get the consumers' attention and urge them to act.

Groundwood pulp. Paper that contains wood pulp.

Hit. A name showing up on two or more lists.

Hot-line list. The most recent buyer segment of a particular list. The actual time period within which these buyers have purchased may vary from list to list.

House list. The customer base of names owned by a particular company. Acquired through any number of methods, the list is used to sell that company's products or services.

Imposition. The way in which pages are positioned in order to print correctly and fold correctly on a press.

Ink-jet. Computer-generated ink droplets that apply ink through a small orifice to form characters; often used for personalization.

Inquiry. A person who has requested information about a particular product or service, but has not purchased. There may or may not be a charge for the information received.

Julian date. A serial number showing the number of days that have elapsed since the beginning of the calendar year, that is, January 31 would be 31, February 6 would be 37.

Key coding. *see* Coding.

Layout. A drawing that indicates position of copy and layout as they will appear in the printed promotion.

Lettershop. The area/service that sees that printed material is properly collated, addressed, prepared for mailing discounts, and mailed. Also called "bindery."

List broker. The person who makes list recommendations and coordinates the necessary details between the list owner/manager and the list renter.

List cleaning. The removal of undesirable names and addresses from a house list.

List exchange. An agreement between two list owners to exchange, without rental fee, portions of their lists.

List maintenance. The updating of names and addresses on a house list.

List manager. The person responsible for encouraging others to rent a specific mailing list or lists. Can be an employee of the list owner or a company specializing in list promotion.

List owner. One who, by promotional activity or compilation, has developed a list of names having something in common. Or one who has purchased (as opposed to rented, reproduced, or used on a one-time basis) such a list from the developer.

List rental. An arrangement in which a list owner furnishes names on his or her list to a mailer, together with the privilege of using the list on a one-time basis only (unless otherwise specified in advance). For this privilege, the mailer pays the list owner a rental fee.

List sample. A segment of a list used for testing the profitability of that list.

List source. The specific medium from which the list names were generated.

Magnetic tape. A storage device for electronically recording and reproducing, through the use of a computer, defined bits of data.

Mail order. A method of business that, through the use of the U.S. Postal Service, solicits sales of products or services.

Mail order buyer. A person who has purchased a product or service in response to an offer received through the mail.

Make-ready. The time it takes for a printing press to prepare plates, as well as properly adjust inks and registration.

Match code. An abbreviation of data extracted from name and address records attempting to simplify the sequencing of records in a list and/or the identification of duplicate records.

Matte finish. A dull paper finish that has no gloss.

Mechanical. Also called paste-ups, boards, or finished art, mechanicals are the final assembly of position art and typeset copy.

Merge/purge. The combining of two or more lists and the elimination of duplicate names and addresses.

Metropolitan Statistical Area (MSA). The new name, now used by the Census Bureau, for Standard Metropolitan Statistical Area (SMSA). A county or group of counties containing at least one city of 50,000 population or more. Surrounding counties may be part of an MSA if considered integrated with the city.

Monetary. One of the mail order quality designation triumvirate (recency/frequency/monetary) that relates to the amount of money spent by a customer either in a specific period of time or in total.

Multibuyer. Correctly used, the term refers to a person who has purchased two or more *times* from the same company—*not* one who has bought more than one item from the same company. This term is frequently erroneously used to denote both types of buyers.

Negative. Photographic image on film showing the reverse of what is seen by the naked eye; dark colors are light, light colors are dark.

Negative option. A buying plan in which the customer or club member agrees to accept and pay for products or services announced in advance at regular intervals unless the individual notifies the company within a reasonable time after each announcement not to ship.

Nesting. The placement of one enclosure within another prior to inserting them into a mailing envelope.

Net-name arrangement. An agreement between list owner and list user, at the time of ordering or before, in which the list owner agrees to accept adjusted payment for less than the total names shipped. Such arrangements can be for a percentage of names shipped or names actually mailed. They can provide for a running charge or not.

Nixie. A mailing returned to the sender by the post office because of undeliverability.

***N*th name selection.** A fractional unit used in selecting a portion of a mailing list (i.e., a 10,000 test from a universe or select of 200,000 would give an *n*th of every twentieth name).

OK'd sheet. The printed sheet supplied while overseeing a printing job. The cataloger's signature is required before the press can begin printing at top speed. This sheet is retained by the pressmen to check against as print run continues.

Overlay. A transparent sheet positioned over artwork, which indicates specifics about the art under it. Over layouts, it might indicate props for photography. Over paste-ups, it would show color breaks, instructions, and so forth.

Overlays. Demographic data added to an existing file allowing selections that can enhance response.

Package insert. A promotion designed for inclusion in outgoing mail order–generated packages.

Pallet. A platform, often made of wood, on which goods are stored or transported.

Peel-off labels. *see* Pressure sensitive labels.

Penetration. Relationship of the number of individuals (or families) on a particular list compared with the total number possible for a particular universe (in toto, by state, zip code, etc.).

Personalization. Unique, printed message directed to an individual; often used on catalog order forms and back covers.

Piggy-back. An offer that rides free with another offer.

Poly bag. A printed, clear plastic bag used instead of a paper envelope.

Pop-up. A three-dimensional paper construction that "pops up" as the mailing piece (of which it is a part) opens.

Positive. A photographic image on film that looks like the original; the opposite of a negative.

Positive option. A method of distribution of products and services incorporating the same advance notice techniques as negative option, but requiring a specific order each time on the part of the member or subscriber.

Premium. A "bonus" product offered at no charge or at a minimal cost to consumers as an incentive to purchase a product or service, or as an inducement to place an order totaling a set dollar amount.

Press proof. A printed proof pulled on the paper to be used for actual printing, submitted prior to "on press" for color OK.

Pressure sensitive labels. A peel-off label, initially attached to a backing sheet, that is used as an address label. The self-adhesive label, usually complete with list code, is peeled off by the customer and attached to the order form.

Progressive proofs. Also called "progs"; a printed proofing method that separates colors by sequence, showing each color density and, when combined, how color should look when actually printed on press.

Prospect. A name on a mailing list, considered a probable buyer for a product never before purchased by this person.

Psychographics. Characteristics or qualities used to denote the life-style(s) or attitude(s) of customers and prospective customers.

Purge. The process of eliminating duplicates and/or unwanted names and addresses from one or more lists.

Recency. The latest purchase or other activity recorded for an individual or company on a specific customer list.

Reformatting. Changing a magnetic tape format from one arrangement to another more usable one. Also referred to as list or tape conversion.

Register. The alignment of color images when printing.

Repeat buyer. Another term for multibuyer.

Response rate. Percentage of orders received from a particular mailing.

Retouching. A process that corrects or improves artwork.

ROI. Return on investment.

Rollout. A larger continuation of a test mailing that initially consisted of a smaller quantity of a certain list.

Running charge. The price charged by a list owner for names run (or passed), but not used by a specific mailer.

Salting. Deliberate placing of decoy or dummy names in a list to trace list usage and delivery.

Scanner. A computerized method of color separating.

SCF (sectional center facility). A USPS distribution unit covering different post offices whose zip codes start with the same first three digits.

Selects. Specific segments of a mailing list.

Self-cover. A term employed when the same paper is used for the cover as is used for the interior of the catalog.

SKU (stock keeping unit) number. The number assigned to a product. Used for data entry, order fulfillment, analysis, and so forth.

Space buyer. A person who has purchased a product via an advertisement that has appeared in a publication.

Split test. Two or more samples from the same list, each considered to be representative of the entire list, used to test variations of a particular promotion.

Standard Metropolitan Statistical Area (SMSA). *see* Metropolitan Statistical Area.

State count. The number of names and addresses in a given list for each state.

Statement stuffer. A promotion piece specifically designed for insertion into an envelope that contains a bill or statement of a customer's account.

Stripping. The positioning of film (negative or positive) for platemaking prior to printing.

Swatching. The enclosure of actual fabric samples in a mailing piece. Or the photographic reproduction of fabric swatches representing color alternatives or pattern details.

Tell-a-friend. A customer or name acquired through the recommendation of a friend. Also called friend-of-a-friend.

Test panel. A term used to identify each of the parts or samples in a split test. Can also be a preset test segment of a particular list.

Token. A gimmick designed to be removed by the customer from one place and attached to another.

Transparency. A transparent photographic reproduction, such as a 35mm slide.

Unit of sale. The average dollar amount spent by a customer.

Universe. The total number of names contained on a particular list.

White mail. Untrackable mail; orders that have been received but, for a variety of reasons, cannot be allocated to a specific source. Also refers to mail that does not include orders/payment.

Widow. In typesetting, this term applies to a word or very short sentence on a line by itself at the end of a paragraph, especially at the top of a page.

Zip code. A group of five digits used by the U.S. Postal Service to designate specific post offices, stations, or branches. Some large companies and buildings also have their own zip code.

Zip code sequence. Arranging names and addresses in a list according to the numeric progression of the zip code in each record.

USEFUL PUBLICATIONS FOR CATALOGERS

Advertising Age. Published by Crain Communications, 740 North Rush Street, Chicago, IL 60611. Weekly.

Adweek. Published by ASM Communications, 820 Second Avenue, New York, NY 10017. Published in five regional editions: East, Southeast, Midwest, Southwest, and West. Weekly.

Cable/Videotex: A Compendium for Direct Marketers. Published by Direct Marketing Association, 6 East 43rd Street, New York, NY 10017. Monograph.

Catalog Age. Published by Folio, 125 Elm Street, New Canaan, CT 06840-4006. Bimonthly.

The Catalog Marketer. Published by Maxwell Sroge Publishing Company, The Sroge Building, 731 North Cascade Avenue, Colorado Springs, CO 80903. Semimonthly.

DM News. Published by DM News Corporation, 19 West 21st Street, New York, NY 10010. Monthly.

DMA Fact Book on Direct Marketing, 1983 Statistical Update. Published by Direct Marketing Association, 6 East 43rd Street, New York, NY 10017.

DMA Fact Book on Direct Marketing, 1984 Edition. Published by Direct Marketing Association, 6 East 43rd Street, New York, NY 10017.

1984 DMA International Fact Book. Second edition. Published by Direct Marketing Association, 6 East 43rd Street, New York, NY 10017.

Direct Marketing Magazine. Published by Hoke Communications, Inc., 224 Seventh Avenue, Garden City, NY 11530. Monthly.

Direct Newsletter. Published by Direct Magazine Associates, 60 East 42nd Street, New York, NY 10165. Monthly.

Domestic Mail Manual. Published by the United States Postal Service. Available from Superintendent of Documents, U.S. Government Printing Office, Washington, DC 20036.

The Effectiveness of 800 Numbers in Direct Mail Catalogs, Volume 1. Published by Direct Marketing Association, 6 East 43rd Street, New York, NY 10017. Monograph.

Friday Report. Published by Hoke Communications, Inc., 224 Seventh Avenue, Garden City, NY 11530. Weekly.

Memo to Mailers. Published by the Public & Employee Communications Department, U.S. Postal Service, Washington, DC 20260-3100. 8-page monthly newsletter.

Non-Store Marketing (NSM) Report. Published by Maxwell Sroge Publishing Company, The Sroge Building, 731 North Cascade Avenue, Colorado Springs, CO 80903. Biweekly.

Postal Bulletin. Published by the United States Postal Service. Available from Superintendent of Documents, U.S. Government Printing Office, Washington, DC 20036. Weekly.

Postal World: The Washington Newsletter for Mail Users. Published by JPL Publications, Inc., 128 C Street N.W., Washington, DC 20001. Biweekly.

ZIP Magazine. Published by North American Publishing Company, 322 Eighth Avenue, New York, NY 10001. 9 issues/year.

INDEX